MICROSOFT® ACCESS 2002

MARQUEE SERIES

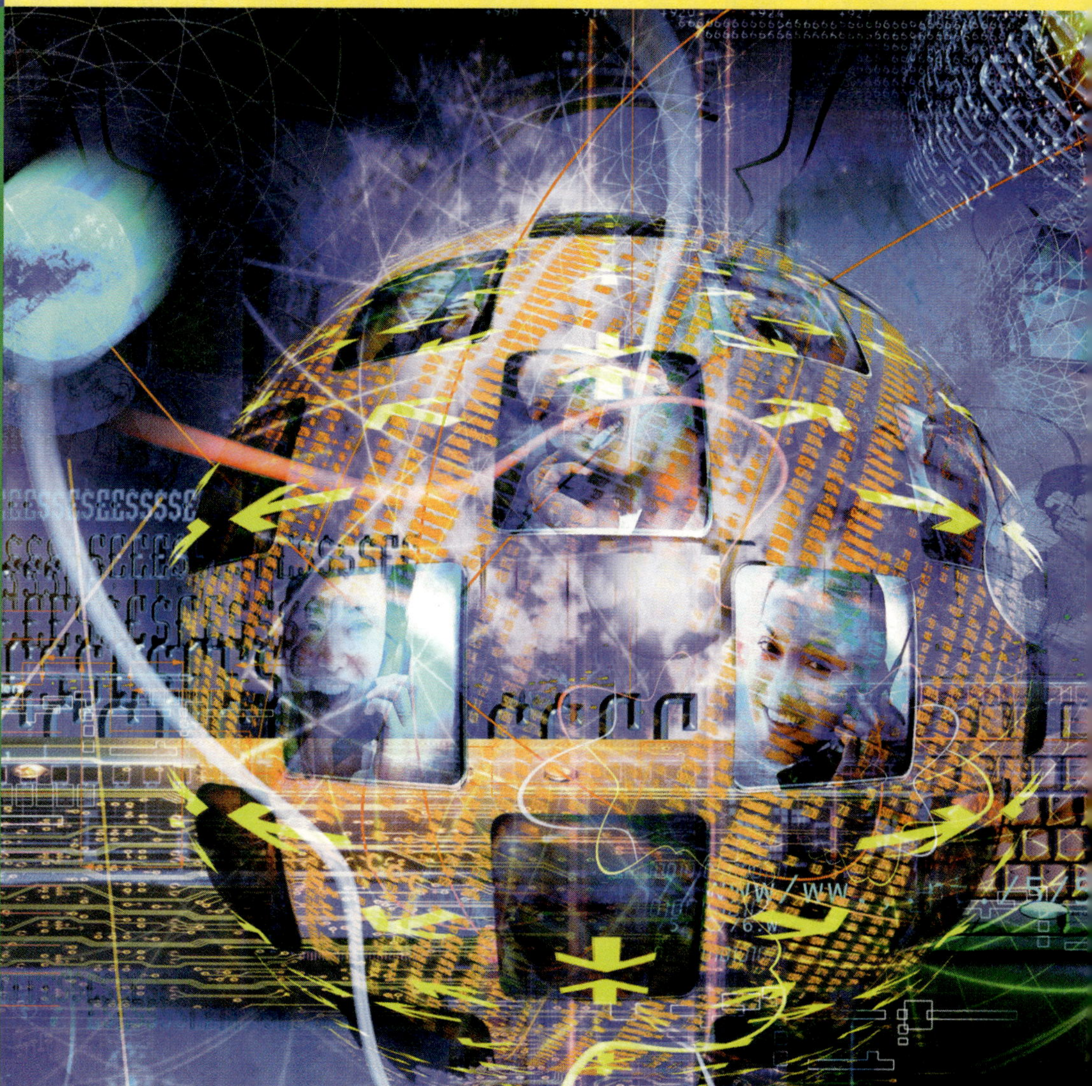

NITA RUTKOSKY Pierce College at Puyallup – Puyallup, Washington
DENISE SEGUIN Fanshawe College – London, Ontario

EMCParadigm

CONTENTS

Section 1: Maintaining Data in Access Tables — 3
- 1.1 Exploring Database Objects — 4
- 1.2 Adjusting Column Width; Navigating in Datasheet View — 8
- 1.3 Finding and Editing Records — 10
- 1.4 Adding Records in Datasheet View — 12
- 1.5 Adding Records in Form View — 14
- 1.6 Deleting Records in Datasheet View — 16
- 1.7 Sorting Records — 18
- 1.8 Previewing and Printing — 20
- 1.9 Formatting the Datasheet — 22
- 1.10 Using Help — 24
- 1.11 Compacting and Repairing a Database — 26
- *Features Summary — 28
- *Procedures Check — 28
- *Skills Review — 29
- *Performance Plus — 30

*These elements appear at the end of each section.

Section 2: Creating Tables and Relationships — 33
- 2.1 Creating a Table in Design View — 34
- 2.2 Using the Lookup Wizard — 38
- 2.3 Using the Input Mask Wizard — 40
- 2.4 Validating Field Entries — 44
- 2.5 Modifying Field Size and Default Value — 46
- 2.6 Creating a Table Using the Table Wizard — 48
- 2.7 Creating Relationships — 50
- 2.8 Creating a Form Using AutoForm — 52
- 2.9 Creating a New Database Using a Wizard — 54

Section 3: Creating Queries, Forms, and Reports — 65
- 3.1 Creating a Query in Design View — 66
- 3.2 Using the Simple Query Wizard — 68
- 3.3 Extracting Records Using Criteria Statements — 70
- 3.4 Performing Calculations in a Query — 72
- 3.5 Creating a Parameter Query — 74
- 3.6 Creating a Form Using the Form Wizard — 76
- 3.7 Modifying Controls in a Form — 80
- 3.8 Adding Controls to a Form — 82
- 3.9 Creating, Previewing, and Printing a Report — 84
- 3.10 Resizing Controls in a Report — 88

†Section 4: Modifying Tables and Reports, Performing Calculations, and Viewing Data — 97
- 4.1 Moving Fields — 98
- 4.2 Inserting and Deleting Fields — 100
- 4.3 Modifying Field Properties — 102
- 4.4 Adding a Calculated Control to a Form — 104
- 4.5 Modifying a Report; Creating a Calculated Control — 106
- 4.6 Using the Label Wizard — 110
- 4.7 Displaying Records in a Subdatasheet — 112
- 4.8 Applying and Removing Filters — 114
- 4.9 Creating Data Access Pages — 116
- 4.10 Inserting Hyperlinks — 120

†Integrated 2: Integrating Word, Excel, and Access — 129
- I-2.1 Exporting Access Data to Excel — 130
- I-2.2 Exporting Access Data to Word — 132
- I-2.3 Exporting an Access Report to Word — 134
- I-2.4 Importing Data to a New Table — 136
- I-2.5 Linking Data to a New Table and Editing Linked Data — 138
- Skills Review — 142

†Index — 144

†These sections are not included in *Office XP, Brief Edition*.

The Marquee Series Team: Michael Sander, Developmental Editor; Jennifer Wreisner, Senior Designer; Leslie Anderson, Michelle Lewis, and Desktop Solutions, Desktop Production; Desiree Faulkner, Tester; Sharon O'Donnell, Copyeditor; Lynn Reichel, Proofreader; and Nancy Fulton, Indexer.

Publishing Team: George Provol, Publisher; Janice Johnson, Director of Product Development; Tony Galvin, Acquisitions Editor; Lori Landwer, Marketing Manager; Shelley Clubb, Electronic Design and Production Manager.

Acknowledgment: The authors and publisher wish to thank the following reviewer for her technical and academic assistance in testing exercises and assessing instruction: Mary A. Walthall, Ph.D., St. Petersburg College, Clearwater Campus, Clearwater, FL

Library of Congress Cataloging-in-Publication Data
Rutkosky, Nita Hewitt.
  Microsoft Access 2002 / Nita Rutkosky, Denise Seguin.
    p.cm. – (Marquee series)
  Includes index.
  ISBN 0-7638-1465-2 (text) – ISBN 0-7638-1466-0 (text & CD)
  1. Microsoft Access. 2. Database management. I. Seguin, Denise. II. Title. III. Series

Trademarks: Some of the product names and company names included in this book have been used for identification purposes only and may be trademarks or registered trademarks of their respective manufacturers and sellers. The authors, editor, and publisher disclaim any affiliation, association, or connection with, or sponsorship or endorsement by, such owners.

Text + CD: 0-7638-1466-0
Order Number: 05554

© 2002 by Paradigm Publishing Inc.
  Published by EMCParadigm
  875 Montreal Way
  St. Paul, MN 55102

  (800) 535-6865
  E-mail: educate@emcp.com
  Web site: www.emcp.com

All rights reserved. No part of this book may be reproduced, stored in a retrieval system, or transmitted in any form or by any means, electronic, mechanical, photocopying, recording, or otherwise, without prior written permission of Paradigm Publishing Inc. Care has been taken to verify the accuracy of information presented in this book. However, the authors, editor, and publisher cannot accept any responsibility for Web, e-mail, newsgroup, or chat room subject matter or content, or for consequences from the application of information in this book, and make no warranty, expressed or implied, with respect to its content.

Printed in the United States of America   10 9 8 7 6 5 4 3 2

ACCESS SECTION 1
Maintaining Data in Access Tables

Managing business information effectively is a vital activity, since data forms the basis upon which transactions are conducted or strategic decisions are made. Microsoft Access is a database management system that is used to store, retrieve, and manage information. The type of information stored in an Access database can include such items as customer lists, inventory articles, human resources, and supplier lists. Activities that are routinely performed with a database include adding, editing, deleting, finding, sorting, querying, and reporting information. In this section you will learn the skills and complete the projects described here.

 *Note: The database files for this section are in the* Access S1 *subfolder in the* Access *folder on the CD that accompanies this textbook. Database files are large and will increase in size as you work with them, so do not copy the entire subfolder to a floppy disk. Copying files to a Zip disk, CD-RW, hard drive, or network folder is recommended. If a floppy disk must be used, copy each database to a separate disk as it is used in the text. When you have copied the database file, remove its read-only attribute so you can make changes to it. To remove the read-only attribute:*

1. Copy the database file from the CD (or the Internet Resource Center) to your storage medium.
2. In Access, display the Open dialog box with the drive active containing your storage medium.
3. Click once on the database file name.
4. Click To_o_ls on the Open dialog box toolbar and then click P_r_operties on the drop-down list.
5. At the Properties dialog box with the General tab selected, click R_ead-only in the Attributes section to remove the check mark.
6. Click OK to close the Properties dialog box.
7. Open the database file.

Skills
- Define *field, record, table, datasheet,* and *database*
- Start and exit Access
- Identify features in the Access window
- Open and close a database
- Open and close tables
- Adjust column widths
- Navigate in Datasheet view
- Find and edit records
- Add records
- Delete records
- Sort records
- Move columns in Datasheet view
- Preview and print a table
- Change the page orientation
- Change the background and gridline color of the datasheet
- Change the font
- Freeze columns
- Use the online help
- Compact and repair a database

Projects

 Add, delete, find, and sort records; format, preview, and print tables, and compact the Distributors database; find, edit, add, delete, and sort records, and format, preview, and print the Employees database.

 Maintain the Inventory database by adding and deleting records.

 Find student records and input grades into the Grades database; compact the Grades database.

 Delete records, sort, format the datasheet, and print two reports from the Costume Inventory database.

1.1 Exploring Database Objects

A *database* contains information logically organized into related units for easy retrieval. You access a database when you open a telephone book to look up a friend's telephone number, or browse the yellow pages looking for a restaurant. Microsoft Access is an application that is used to manage databases electronically. Information stored in an Access database is organized into *tables*. A table contains information for related items such as customers, suppliers, inventory, or human resources.

PROJECT: You will open and close two tables and a form in the Distributors database for Worldwide Enterprises to define and identify objects, fields, records, tables, datasheets, and forms.

STEPS

1. At the Windows desktop, click the Start button **Start** on the Taskbar.
   This causes a pop-up menu to display.

2. Point to *Programs*.
   Pointing to an option on the Start pop-up menu that displays with a right-pointing triangle after it causes a cascading side menu to appear.

3. Click *Microsoft Access*.

   PROBLEM: Depending on your system configuration, the steps you complete to open Access may vary. Check with your instructor if necessary.

4. Click the *Files* or the *More Files* link in the Open a file section of the New File Task Pane.
   Refer to the Section 1 opening page for instructions on copying a database file and removing the read-only attribute. These steps will have to be repeated for every database.

5. If necessary, change to the location where the student data files are located. To change to a different drive, click the down-pointing triangle to the right of the Look in text box and then select the correct drive from the drop-down list.

6. Double-click *WE Distributors1.mdb*.
   Access databases end with the file name extension *mdb*.

7. At the Access screen, identify the various features by comparing your screen with the one shown in Figure A1.1.
   Unlike other Microsoft Office applications, only one database can be open at a time. A database is comprised of a series of objects. Descriptions of the seven types of objects that can be stored in a database are presented in Table A1.1 on page 7. An open database file displays in a Database window that contains the names of the various objects.

ACCESS
4

SECTION 1: MAINTAINING DATA IN ACCESS TABLES

ACCESS

FIGURE A1.1 The Access Screen

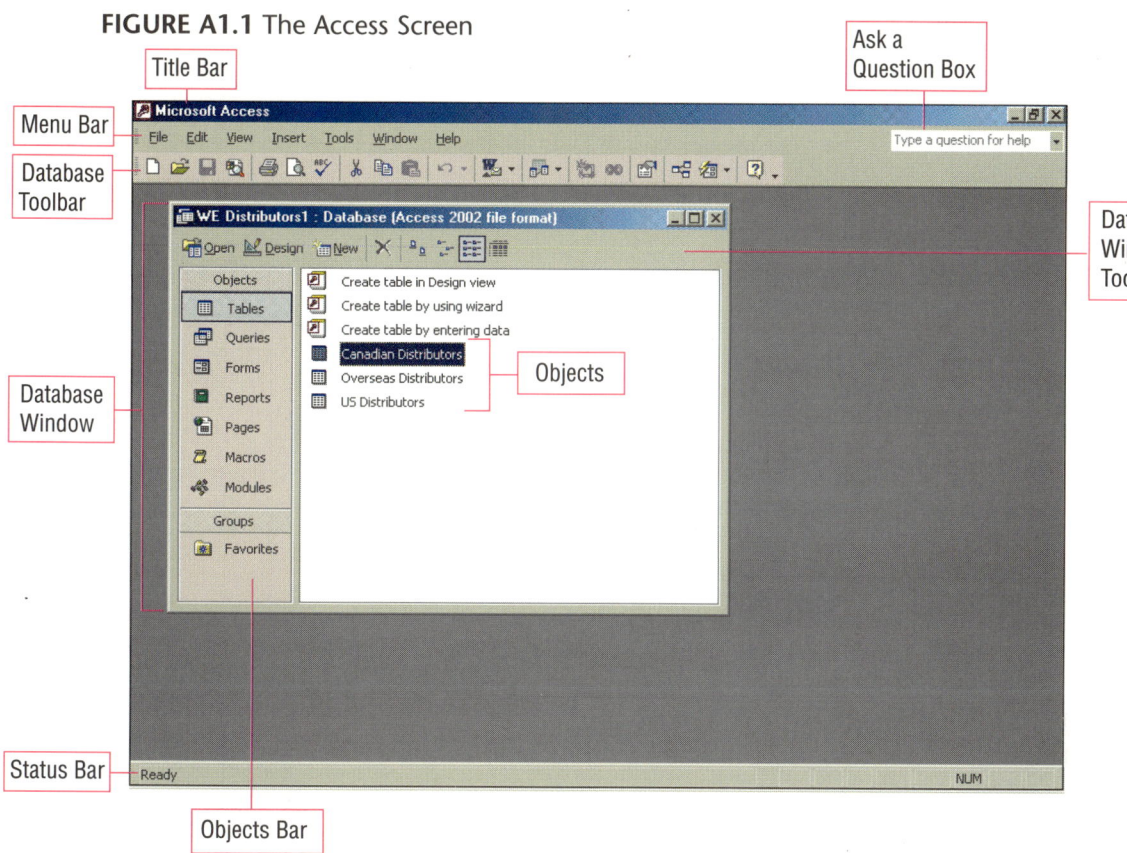

8. With Tables the default object selected on the Objects bar, double-click *Canadian Distributors*.

   Canadian Distributors is one of three tables stored within the database. Double-clicking the object named *Canadian Distributors* opens the table in Datasheet view. Datasheets display the contents of a table in a column/row format.

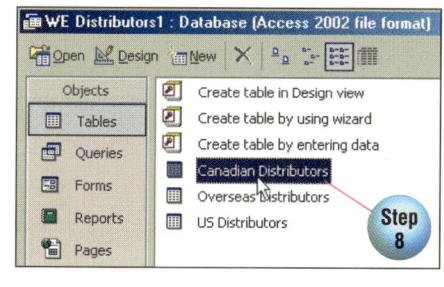

9. Compare your screen with the one shown in Figure A1.2 and examine the identified elements.

   The identified elements are further described in Table A1.2 on page 7.

FIGURE A1.2 Canadian Distributors Datasheet

(continued)

SECTION 1: MAINTAINING DATA IN ACCESS TABLES

ACCESS 5

10. Identify the fields and the field names in the Canadian Distributors table. Notice each field contains only one unit of information.

    The field names *Name, Street Address1, Street Address2,* and so on are displayed in the gray header row in Datasheet view.

11. Identify the records in the Canadian Distributors table. Each record is one row in the table.

    The right-pointing triangle to the left of *EastCoast Cinemas* in Figure A1.2 illustrates the active record.

12. Press the down arrow key four times to move the active record.

    The right-pointing triangle moves down as you move the insertion point and the Record number at the bottom of the window changes to indicate you are viewing record 5 of a total of 12 records.

13. Click the Close button ✕ at the right edge of the Canadian Distributors Table Title bar.

    The Canadian Distributors table closes and you are returned to the WE Distributors1 : Database window.

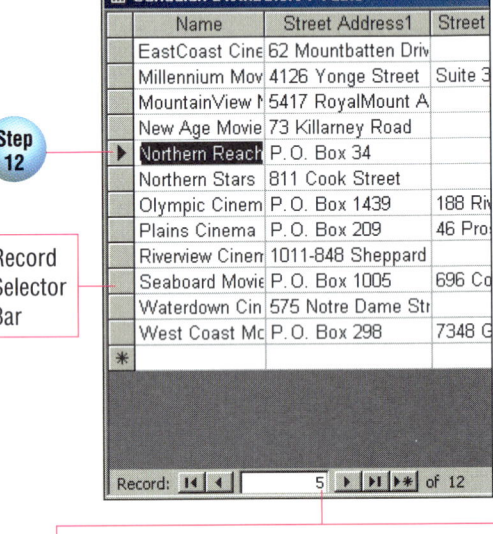

Record number changes as you move to a new record.

14. Move the mouse pointer over the table named US Distributors and then click the mouse to select the object.

15. Click Open on the Database window toolbar.

    The US Distributors table opens in Datasheet view.

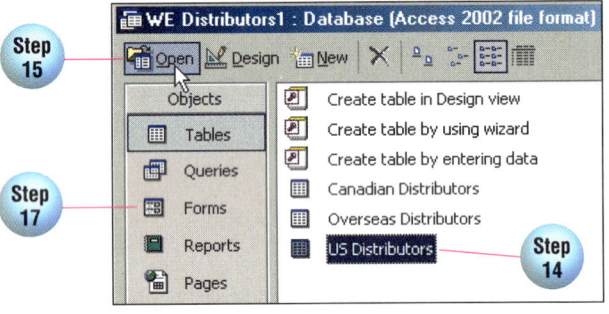

16. Click the Close button on the US Distributors Table Title bar.

17. Click the Forms button on the Objects bar.

18. Double-click *Overseas Distributors*.

    The Overseas Distributors form opens in Form view. A form is used to view and edit data one record at a time.

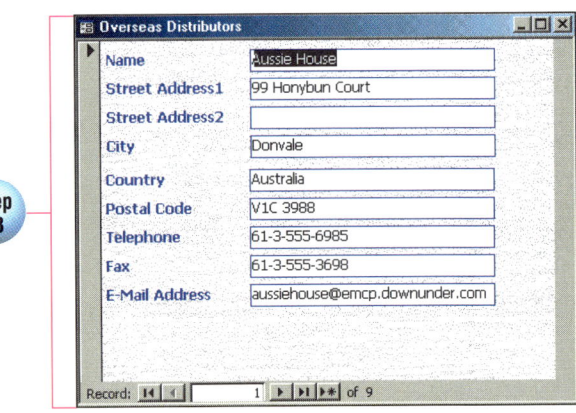

19. Click the Close button on the Overseas Distributors Title bar.

20. Click File and then Exit.

SECTION 1: MAINTAINING DATA IN ACCESS TABLES

ACCESS

TABLE A1.1 Database Objects

Object	Description
Tables	Organize data in fields (columns) and rows (records). A database must contain at least one table. The table is the base upon which other objects are created.
Queries	Used to display data from a table that meets a conditional statement and/or perform calculations. For example, display only those records in which the city is Toronto.
Forms	Allow fields and records to be presented in a different layout than the datasheet. Use to facilitate data entry and maintenance.
Reports	Print data from tables or queries. Calculations can be performed in a report.
Pages	Web pages designed for working with data from the Internet or an intranet.
Macros	Automate repetitive tasks.
Modules	Advanced automation through programming using Visual Basic for Applications.

TABLE A1.2 Elements of a Database

Element	Description
Field	A single component of information about a person, place, item, or object
Record	All of the fields for one unit such as a customer, supplier, or inventory item
Table	All of the records for one logical group
Datasheet view	Data for a table displayed in columns (fields) and rows (records)
Database	A file containing related tables

In Addition

Planning and Designing a Database

One of the first steps in designing a new database is to look at the format from which the input will originate. For example, look at an existing file card for a customer to see how the information is currently organized. Determine how you will break down all of the information into fields. Discuss with others what the future needs of the company will be for both input and output. Include extra fields for future use. For example, add a field for a Web site address even if you do not currently have URLs for your customers. Refer to Performance Plus Activity 5 at the end of this section for an exercise in the steps included in designing a new database.

In Brief

Start Access
1 Click Start.
2 Point to *Programs*.
3 Click *Microsoft Access*.

Open Objects
1 Open database file.
2 Select type of object from Objects bar.
3 Click object name.
4 Click *Open*.

SECTION 1: MAINTAINING DATA IN ACCESS TABLES

1.2 Adjusting Column Width; Navigating in Datasheet View

A table opened in Datasheet view displays data in a manner similar to a spreadsheet, with a grid of columns and rows. Columns contain the field values, with the field names in bold text in column headings. Records are represented in rows. A gray record selector bar is positioned at the left edge of the window. The Record Navigation bar displays along the bottom of the window with record selector buttons. Horizontal and/or vertical scroll bars appear if the entire table is not visible in the current window.

PROJECT: You will adjust column widths and practice scrolling and navigating through records using the US Distributors table.

STEPS

1. Start Access.

2. Click the WE Distributors1.mdb link in the Open a file section of the New File Task Pane.

    By default, the last four database files opened are displayed in the Open a file section of the New File Task Pane. The recently used file list option can be adjusted to include up to the last nine files opened.

3. With the WE Distributors1 database open, click Tables on the Objects bar and then double-click *US Distributors*.

    The US Distributors table opens in Datasheet view.

4. Click the Maximize button on the US Distributors Table Title bar.

    PROBLEM? If the table window is already maximized, the Maximize button is replaced with the Restore Window button. Skip step 4.

    Notice that some columns contain data that is not entirely visible. In steps 5–7, you will learn how to adjust the column widths using two methods.

5. With the active record the first row in the table and the insertion point positioned at the left edge of the text in the *Name* field, click Format and then Column Width.

6. Click the Best Fit button in the Column Width dialog box.

    The column is automatically widened to accommodate the width of the longest entry. In the next step you will widen a column using the mouse in the column headings row.

    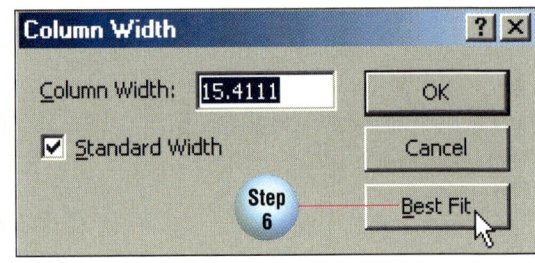

7. Position the mouse pointer on the right column boundary line in the Field Name headings row between columns two and three *(Street Address)* until the pointer changes to a vertical line with a left- and right-pointing arrow, and then double-click the left mouse button.

SECTION 1: MAINTAINING DATA IN ACCESS TABLES

ACCESS

Double-clicking the column boundary performs the Best Fit command.

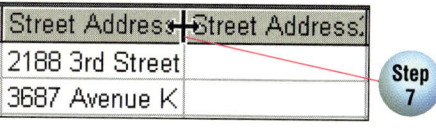

8. Click the right-pointing horizontal scroll arrow two or three times to scroll the datasheet to the right and view the remaining columns. (Scrolling can also be performed using keyboard commands, as shown in Table A1.3.)

9. Best Fit the *E-mail Address* column.

10. Drag the horizontal scroll box to the left edge of the horizontal scroll bar.

    This scrolls the screen to the left until the first column is visible.

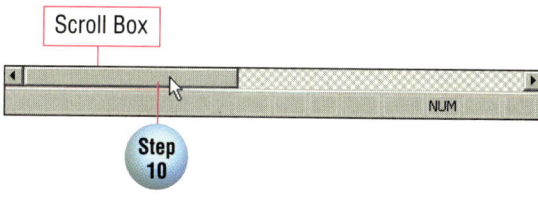

11. Best Fit the *Street Address2* column.

12. Click the Save button on the Database toolbar.

13. Click the Next Record button on the Record Navigation bar to move the active record down one row.

14. Click the Last Record button on the Record Navigation bar to move the active record to the last row in the table.

15. Click the Previous Record button on the Record Navigation bar to move the active record to the second last row in the table.

16. Click the First Record button on the Record Navigation bar to move the active record back to the first row in the table.

TABLE A1.3 Scrolling Techniques Using the Keyboard

Press	To Move to
Home	First field in the current record
End	Last field in the current record
Tab	Next field in the current record
Shift + Tab	Previous field in the current record
Ctrl + Home	First field in the first record
Ctrl + End	Last field in the last record

In Addition

Saving Data

Microsoft Access differs from other Office applications in that data is *automatically* saved as soon as you move to the next record or close the table. Database management systems are such a critical component of business activities that saving is not left to chance. The Save button was used in this topic to save the layout changes that were made when the column widths were enlarged.

In Brief

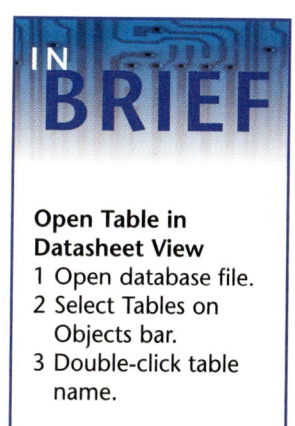

Open Table in Datasheet View
1 Open database file.
2 Select Tables on Objects bar.
3 Double-click table name.

SECTION 1: MAINTAINING DATA IN ACCESS TABLES

1.3 Finding and Editing Records

The Find command can be used to quickly move the insertion point to a specific record in a table. This is a time-saving feature when the table contains several records that are not all visible in one screen. Once a record has been located, click the insertion point within a field and insert or delete text as required to edit the record.

PROJECT: You have received a note from Sam Vestering that Waterfront Cinemas has changed its fax number and Eastown Movie House has a new P.O. Box number. You will use the Find feature to locate the records and make the changes.

STEPS

1. With the US Distributors table open and the insertion point positioned in the *Name* column, click the Find button on the Database toolbar.

   This displays the Find and Replace dialog box.

2. Key **Waterfront Cinemas** in the Find What text box and then click the Find Next button.

   The insertion point moves to record 17.

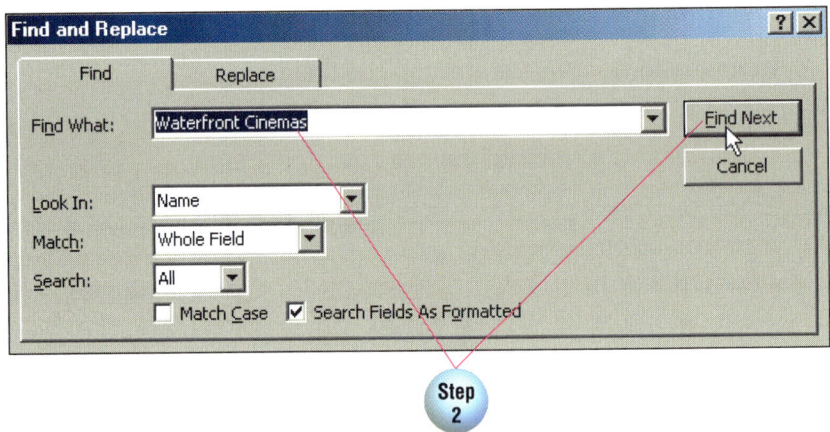

Step 2

3. Click the Close button on the Find and Replace dialog box Title bar.

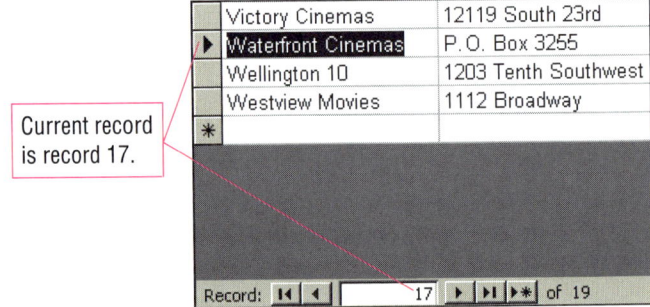

Current record is record 17.

4. Press Tab or Enter seven times to move to the *Fax* column.

   The entire field value is selected when you move from column to column using Tab or Enter. If you need to edit only a few characters within the field you will want to use *Edit* mode. As an alternative, you could scroll and click the insertion point within the field to avoid having to turn on *Edit* mode.

5. Press F2 to turn on *Edit* mode.

ACCESS
10

SECTION 1: MAINTAINING DATA IN ACCESS TABLES

ACCESS

6. Press the left arrow key four times, delete *3947*, and then key **4860**.

7. Look on the record selector bar for record 17 at the pencil icon that is displayed.

   The pencil icon indicates the current record is being edited and the changes have not yet been saved.

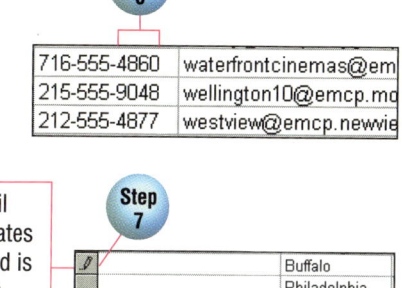

8. Press Enter twice to move to the next record in the table.

   The pencil icon disappears, indicating the changes have now been saved.

9. Click in any record in the *Street Address1* column and then click the Find button.

10. Key **P. O. Box 722** and then click the Find Next button.

    The insertion point moves to record 5.

PROBLEM? If no records are found, check your entry in the Find What text box—you may have missed keying a period or space, or keyed an incorrect letter or number.

11. Close the Find and Replace dialog box.
12. Press F2 to turn on *Edit* mode.
13. Press Backspace three times and then key **429**.
14. Click in any other record to save the changes to record 5.

In Addition

Using the Replace Command

Use the Replace tab in the Find and Replace dialog box to automatically change a field entry to something else. For example, in steps 9–12 you searched for P. O. Box 722 and then edited the field to change the box number to 429. The Replace command could have been used to change the text automatically. To do this, display the Find and Replace dialog box, click the Replace tab, key **P. O. Box 722** in the Find What text box, key **P. O. Box 429** in the Replace With text box, and then click the Find Next button. Click the Replace button when the record is found.

In Brief

Find a Record
1. Click in any row in the field by which you want to search.
2. Click Edit, Find or click the Find button.
3. Key the search text.
4. Click Find Next.

SECTION 1: MAINTAINING DATA IN ACCESS TABLES

1.4 Adding Records in Datasheet View

New records can be added to a table in either Datasheet view or Form view. To add a record in Datasheet view, open the table, click the New Record button on either the Table Datasheet toolbar or the Record Navigation bar, and then key the data. Press Tab or Enter to move from field to field. When you press Tab or Enter after keying the last field, the record is automatically saved. Initially, the new record will appear at the bottom of the datasheet until the table is closed. When the table is reopened, the records are rearranged to display alphabetically sorted by the field that has been defined as the primary key. In Addition on the next page describes a primary key field.

PROJECT: Worldwide Enterprises has signed two new distributors in the United States. You will add the information in the US Distributors table.

STEPS

1. With the US Distributors table open, click the New Record button on the Table Datasheet toolbar.

   The insertion point moves to the first column in the blank row at the bottom of the datasheet and the record navigation box indicates you are editing record 20.

2. Key **Dockside Movies** and then press Tab.

3. Key **P. O. Box 224** and then press Tab.

4. Key **155 S. Central Avenue** and then press Tab.

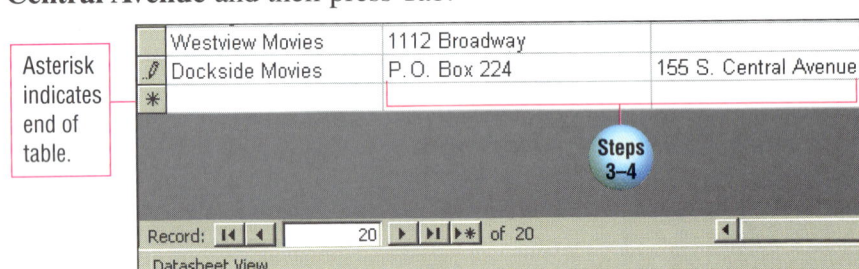

Asterisk indicates end of table.

5. Key **Baltimore** and then press Tab.

6. Key **MD** and then press Tab.

7. Key **21203** and then press Tab.

PROBLEM? Press Enter to move to the next field if you are using the numeric keypad to input numbers—it will be more comfortable.

8. Key **301-555-7732** and then press Tab.

9. Key **301-555-9836** and then press Tab.

10. Key **dockside@emcp.mdwt.net** and then press Tab.

    The insertion point moves to a new row when you press Tab or Enter after the last field in a new record to allow you to continue typing the next new record in the table. The record just entered is automatically saved.

ACCESS
12

SECTION 1: MAINTAINING DATA IN ACCESS TABLES

ACCESS

11. Key the following information in the next row:

    Renaissance Cinemas
    3599 Woodward Avenue
    Detroit, MI 48211
    313-555-1693
    313-555-1699
    renaissance-cinemas@
    emcp.worldnet.net

12. Increase the column width of the *E-Mail Address* column to view all of the data.

13. Close the US Distributors table. Click <u>Y</u>es when prompted to save changes to the layout of the table.

14. Reopen the US Distributors table to view where the new records are now positioned.

15. Close the US Distributors table.

New records initially appear at the bottom of the datasheet.

New records have now been rearranged alphabetically by name.

In Addition

Primary Key Field

When a table is created, one field is defined as the *primary key*. A primary key is the field by which the table is automatically sorted whenever the table is opened. The primary key field must contain unique data for each record. When a new record is being added to the table, Access checks to ensure there is no existing record with the same data in the primary key. If there is, Access will display an error message indicating there are duplicate values and will not allow the record to be saved. The primary key field cannot be left blank when a new record is being added, since it is the field that is used to sort and check for duplicates.

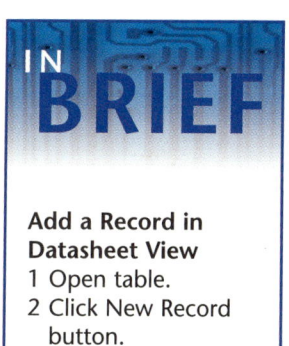

Add a Record in Datasheet View
1 Open table.
2 Click New Record button.
3 Key data in fields.

SECTION 1: MAINTAINING DATA IN ACCESS TABLES

1.5 Adding Records in Form View

Forms are used to enter, edit, view, and print data in tables. Forms are created to provide a user-friendly interface between the user and the underlying table of data. Adding records in a form is easier than using a datasheet since all of the fields in the table are presented in a different layout which usually allows all fields to be visible in the current window. Other records in the table do not distract the user since only one record displays at a time.

PROJECT: Worldwide Enterprises has just signed two new distributors in New York. You will add the information to the US Distributors table using a form.

STEPS

1. With the WE Distributors1 database open, click the Forms button on the Objects bar.

2. Double-click *US Distributors*.

   The US Distributors form opens with the first record in the US Distributors table displayed in the form. A Record Navigation bar appears at the bottom of the form.

3. Click the New Record button on the Record Navigation bar.

   A blank form appears in Form view and the Record Navigation bar indicates you are editing record number 22. Notice the New Record and Next Record buttons on the Record Navigation bar are dimmed.

4. Key **Movie Emporium** and then press Tab or Enter.

5. Key **203 West Houston Street** and then press Tab or Enter.

   Records are added to a form using the same navigation methods as those learned in the previous topic on adding records to a datasheet.

6. Key the remaining fields as shown below.

   When you press Tab or Enter after the *E-Mail Address* field, a new form will appear in the window.

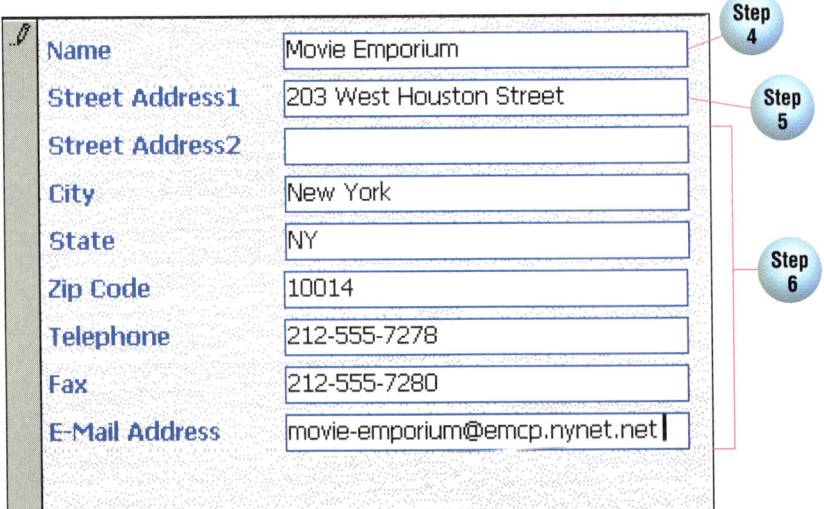

ACCESS

7. Key the following information in the new form for record 23:

   Cinema Festival
   318 East 11th Street
   New York, NY 10003
   212-555-9715
   212-555-9717
   cinemafestival@emcp.eastus.net

8. Click the First Record button on the Record Navigation bar.

   This displays the information for All Nite Cinemas in Form view.

9. Click the Last Record button on the Record Navigation bar.

   This displays the information for Cinema Festival in Form view.

10. Close the US Distributors form.

11. Reopen the US Distributors form.

12. Click the Last Record button on the Record Navigation bar.

    Notice the last record displayed is the information for Westview Movies, not Cinema Festival. Access displays forms in the same manner as a datasheet—sorted by the primary key.

13. Click the First Record button on the Record Navigation bar, and then click the Next Record button two times to view the information for Cinema Festival.

    Cinema Festival is record number 3 of 23 when it is sorted alphabetically on the *Name* field.

14. Scroll through the remaining records in Form view.

15. Close the US Distributors form.

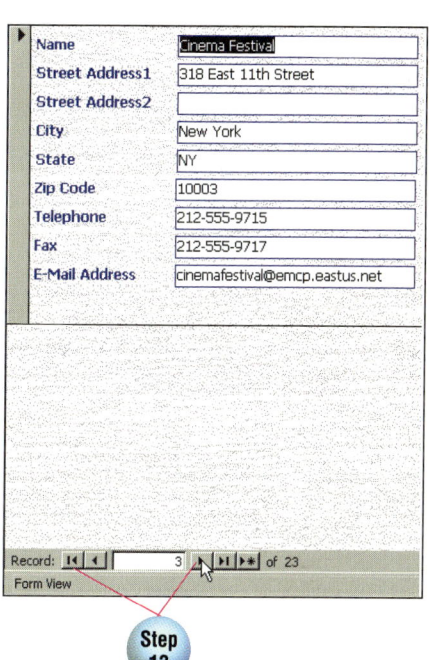

Step 13

In Addition

Scrolling in Form View Using the Keyboard

Records can be scrolled in Form view using the following keyboard techniques:
- Page Down displays the next record
- Page Up displays the previous record
- Ctrl + End moves to the last field in the last record
- Ctrl + Home moves to the first field in the first record
- Key a record value in the Specific Record box on the Record Navigation bar

In Brief

Add a Record in Form View
1. Open form.
2. Click New Record button.
3. Key data in fields.

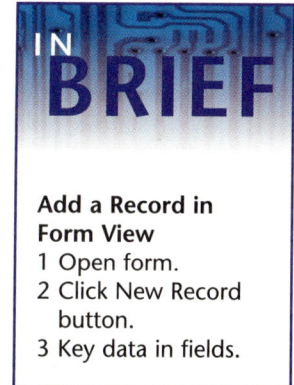

Key a record number in the Specific Record box in the Record Navigation bar to move directly to a particular record.

SECTION 1: MAINTAINING DATA IN ACCESS TABLES

ACCESS
15

1.6 Deleting Records in Datasheet View

Records can be deleted in either Datasheet view or Form view. To delete a record, open the table in Datasheet view or Form view, activate any field in the record to be deleted, and then click the Delete Record button on the Table Datasheet toolbar or the Form View toolbar. Access will display a message indicating the selected record will be permanently removed from the table. Click Yes to confirm the record deletion.

PROJECT: The Countryside Cinemas and Victory Cinemas distributor agreements have lapsed and you have just been informed that they have signed agreements with another movie distributing company. You will delete their records in the US Distributors table.

STEPS

1. With the WE Distributors1 database open, click Tables on the Objects bar.
2. Double-click *US Distributors*.
3. Click the insertion point in any field in the row for Countryside Cinemas.
   This selects record 4 as the active record.
4. Click the Delete Record button  on the Table Datasheet toolbar.

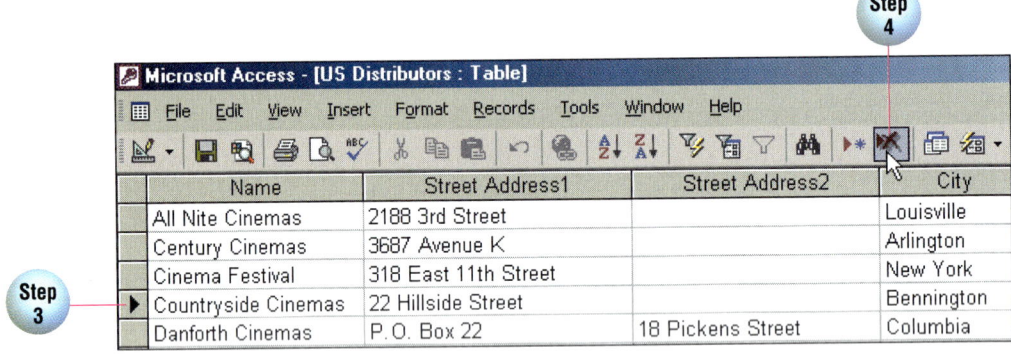

5. Access will display a message box indicating you are about to delete 1 record and that the undo operation is not available after this action. Click Yes to confirm the deletion.

PROBLEM? Check that you are deleting the correct record before clicking Yes. Click No if you selected the wrong record by mistake.

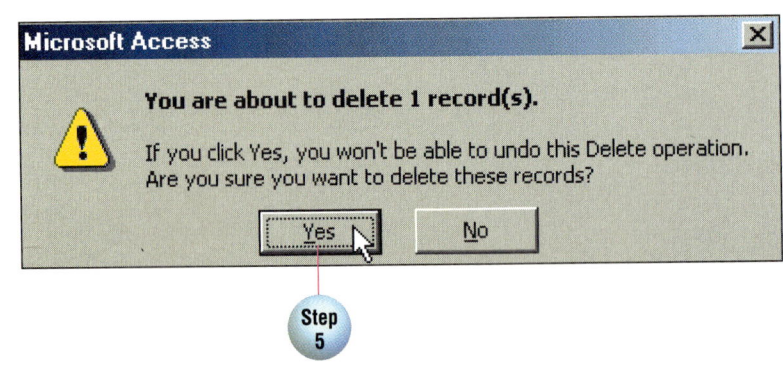

SECTION 1: MAINTAINING DATA IN ACCESS TABLES

ACCESS

6 Position the mouse pointer in the record selector bar for Victory Cinemas until the pointer changes to a black right-pointing arrow ➡ and then click the left mouse button.

This selects the entire row.

	Renaissance Cinemas	3599 Woodward Avenue
	Sunfest Cinemas	
Step 6 ➡	Victory Cinemas	12119 South 23rd
	Waterfront Cinemas	P.O. Box 3255
	Wellington 10	1203 Tenth Southwest
	Westview Movies	1112 Broadway

7 Click the Delete Record button on the Table Datasheet toolbar.

8 Click Yes to confirm the deletion.

9 Close the US Distributors table.

10 Click Forms on the Objects bar and then double-click *US Distributors*.

11 With the insertion point positioned in the *Name* field in the first record, click the Find button on the Form View toolbar.

12 Key **LaVista Cinemas** in the Find What text box and then click Find Next.

The active record moves to record 8.

13 Close the Find and Replace dialog box.

14 Click the Delete Record button on the Form View toolbar.

15 Click No when prompted to confirm the deletion.

The LaVista Cinemas record is restored in the table.

16 Close the US Distributors form.

In Addition

Backing up and Restoring Access Data

Deleting records is a procedure that should be performed only by authorized personnel; once the record is deleted, crucial data can be lost. Always back up the database file before deleting records. To do this, close the database. In a multi-user environment, ensure that all other users have closed the database. Launch Windows Explorer and use the Copy and Paste commands to copy the database to a secure area. If restoring a database becomes necessary, follow the same routine and copy the backup file from the secure area back to the folder in which the database normally resides. Any changes made to the database since the backup was performed will have to be redone.

IN BRIEF

Delete a Record
1. Open table in Datasheet view or Form view.
2. Click in any field in the record to be deleted.
3. Click Delete Record button.
4. Click Yes.

SECTION 1: MAINTAINING DATA IN ACCESS TABLES

1.7 Sorting Records

Records in a table are displayed alphabetically in ascending order by the primary key field. To rearrange the order of the records, click in any field in the column you want to sort by and then click the Sort Ascending or Sort Descending buttons on the Table Datasheet toolbar. To sort on more than one column, select the columns first and then click the Sort Ascending or Sort Descending button. Access will sort first by the leftmost column in the selection, then by the next column, and so on. Columns can be moved in the datasheet if necessary to facilitate a multiple-column sort. Access will save the sort order when the table is closed.

PROJECT: You will perform one sort routine using a single field and then perform a multiple-column sort. To do the multiple-column sort you will have to move columns in the datasheet.

STEPS

1. With the WE Distributors1 database open, click Tables on the Objects bar and then double-click *US Distributors*.

2. Click in any row in the *City* column.

3. Click the Sort Ascending button on the Table Datasheet toolbar.

    The records are rearranged to display the cities starting with A through Z.

4. Click the Sort Descending button on the Table Datasheet toolbar.

    The records are rearranged to display the cities starting with Z through A. In steps 5–7 you will move the *State* column to the left of the *Name* column to perform a multiple-column sort.

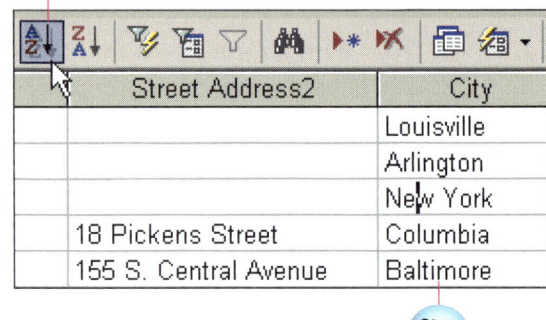

5. Position the mouse pointer in the *State* column heading until the pointer changes to a downward-pointing black arrow and then click the left mouse button.

    The *State* column is now selected and can be moved by dragging the heading to another position in the datasheet.

6. With the *State* column selected, move the pointer to the column heading *State* until the white arrow pointer appears.

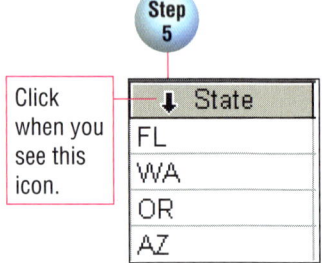

SECTION 1: MAINTAINING DATA IN ACCESS TABLES

⑦ Hold down the left mouse button, drag to the left of the *Name* column, and then release the left mouse button.

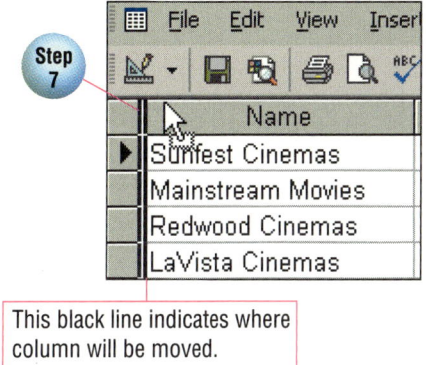

This black line indicates where column will be moved.

As you drag the mouse a thick black line will appear between columns, indicating the position to which the column will be moved when you release the mouse button. In addition, the mouse pointer displays with a gray box attached to it, indicating you are performing a move operation.

⑧ Click in any field in the table to deselect the *State* column.

⑨ Position the mouse pointer in the *State* column heading until the pointer changes to a downward-pointing black arrow, hold down the left mouse button, drag to the right until both the *State* and *Name* columns are selected, and then release the left mouse button.

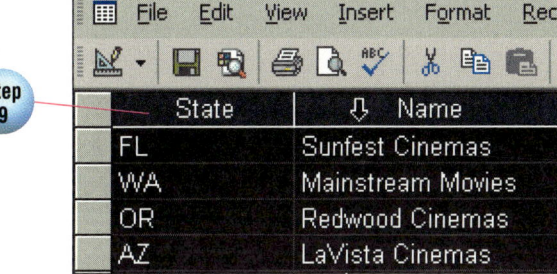

⑩ Click the Sort Ascending button.

The records are sorted first by State and then by Name.

⑪ Look at the four records for the state of New York. Notice the order of the records is Cinema Festival first, then Movie Emporium, then Waterfront Cinemas, and then finally Westview Movies.

⑫ Close the US Distributors table. Click Yes when prompted to save the design changes.

In Addition

More about Sorting

When you are ready to conduct a sort in a table, consider the following:
- records in which the selected field is empty are listed first.
- numbers are sorted before letters.
- numbers stored in fields that are not defined as numeric (i.e., Social Security Number or telephone number) are sorted as characters (not numeric values). To sort them as if they were numbers, all field values must be the same length.

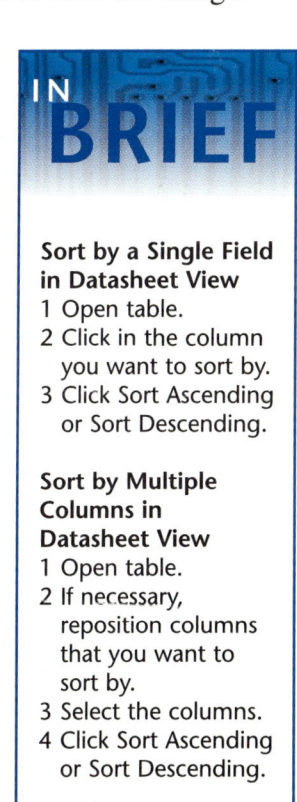

IN BRIEF

Sort by a Single Field in Datasheet View
1 Open table.
2 Click in the column you want to sort by.
3 Click Sort Ascending or Sort Descending.

Sort by Multiple Columns in Datasheet View
1 Open table.
2 If necessary, reposition columns that you want to sort by.
3 Select the columns.
4 Click Sort Ascending or Sort Descending.

SECTION 1: MAINTAINING DATA IN ACCESS TABLES

1.8 Previewing and Printing

Click the Print button on the Table Datasheet toolbar to print the table in Datasheet view. To avoid wasting paper, use Print Preview to view how the datasheet will appear on the page before you print a table. Change the margins or page orientation in the Page Setup dialog box.

PROJECT: Sam Vestering has requested a list of the US Distributors. You will open the table, preview the printout, change the page orientation, and then print the datasheet.

STEPS

1. With the WE Distributors1 database open, open the US Distributors table.

   Notice the datasheet is displayed sorted by the *State* column first and then by the *Name* column since the design changes were saved in the last topic.

2. Click the Print Preview button on the Table Datasheet toolbar.

   The table is displayed in the Print Preview window as shown in Figure A1.3.

FIGURE A1.3 Print Preview Window

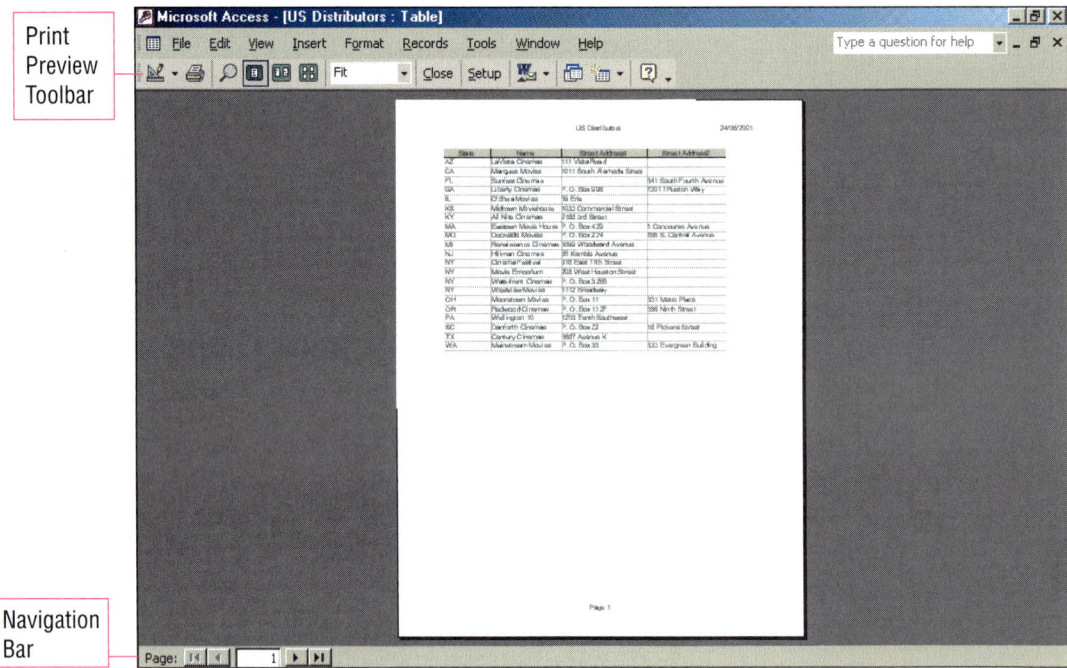

3. Move the mouse pointer (displays as a magnifying glass) over the body of the table and click the left mouse button.

   The zoom changes to 100% magnification.

4. Click the left mouse button again.

   The zoom changes back to *Fit*.

5. Click File and then Page Setup.

ACCESS

6 Click the Page tab in the Page Setup dialog box.

7 Click Landscape and then click OK.

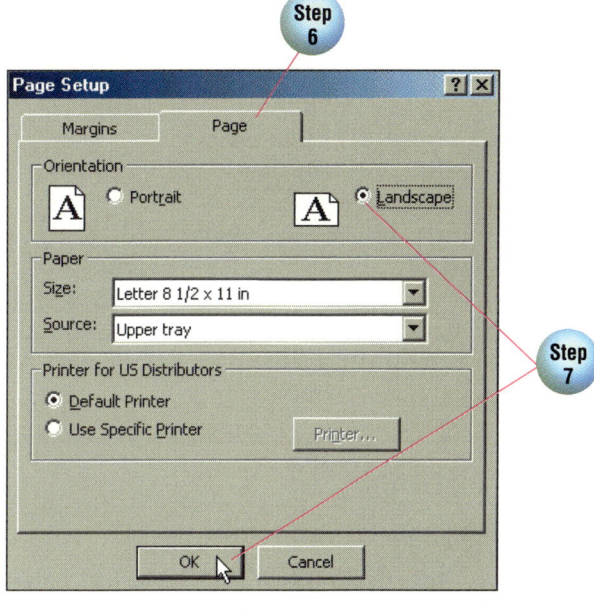

Landscape orientation rotates the printout to print wider than it is taller. Changing to landscape will allow more columns to fit on a page.

8 Click the Print button 🖨 on the Print Preview toolbar.

In a few seconds the table will print on the printer. The printout will require two pages, since there are too many columns to fit on one page even in landscape orientation. In the section titled Queries, Forms, and Reports you will learn how to create a report for a table that will give you more control over the layout of the page.

9 Click Close on the Print Preview toolbar.

10 Close the US Distributors table.

In Addition

Changing the Margins

The margins on the page are initially set to 1 inch at the top, bottom, left, and right. Display the Margins tab in the Page Setup dialog box to change the margins. Changing the left and right margins is another strategy that can be used to try to fit more columns on a page.

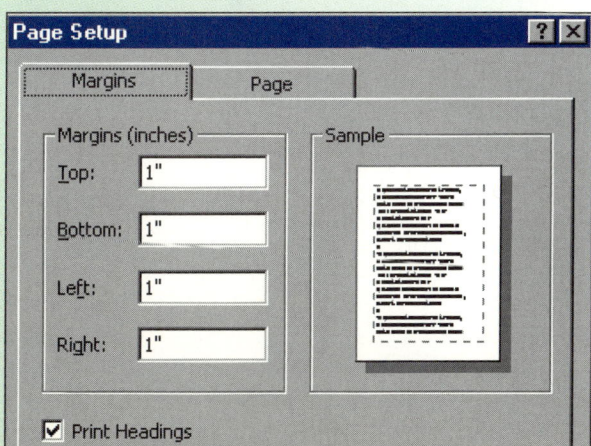

Change to Landscape Orientation
1 Click File, Page Setup.
2 Click Page tab.
3 Click Landscape.
4 Click OK.

SECTION 1: MAINTAINING DATA IN ACCESS TABLES

1.9 Formatting the Datasheet

The appearance of the datasheet can be changed using options on the Format menu. The default font and color of text in Access tables is 10-point Arial black. The Datasheet Formatting dialog box contains options to change the cell effect from the default flat appearance to raised or sunken appearance and alter the colors of the datasheet background and gridlines. Gridlines can be set to display horizontal lines only, vertical lines only, or both horizontal and vertical. The border and line styles of the datasheet, gridlines, and column headers can be changed from solid lines to a variety of other line styles.

PROJECT: You will change the appearance of the US Distributors datasheet by changing the background color, gridline color, font, and by freezing the first two columns so that scrolling right will not cause the *State* and *Name* columns to disappear.

STEPS

1. With the WE Distributors1 database open, open the US Distributors table.

2. Click F̲ormat and then Datash̲eet.

   The Datasheet Formatting dialog box opens. In this dialog box you can change the appearance of the datasheet by changing colors, choosing a cell effect, and choosing gridlines and border styles.

3. Click the down-pointing triangle to the right of the Background Color list box and then click *Aqua* in the drop-down list.

4. Click the down-pointing triangle to the right of the Gridline Color list box, scroll up the box, and then click *Dark Blue* in the drop-down list.

   The Sample section of the Datasheet Formatting dialog box displays the datasheet with the new settings.

5. Click OK to close the Datasheet Formatting dialog box.

6. Click F̲ormat and then F̲ont.

7. Scroll down the Font list box and then click *Times New Roman*.

8. Click *12* in the S̲ize list box and then click OK.

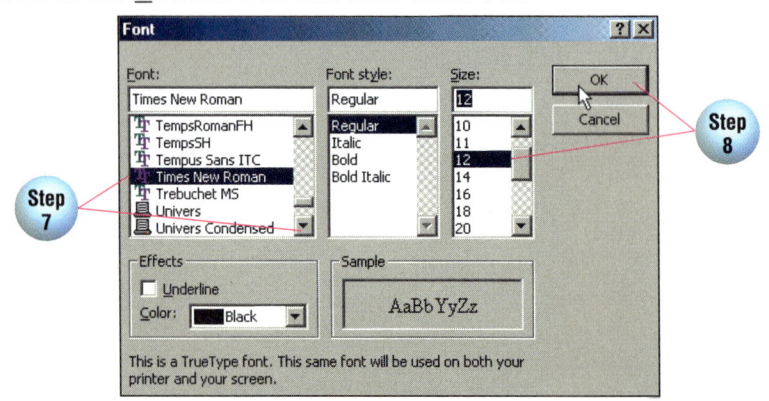

   Notice some columns have to be readjusted after increasing the font size to redisplay entire field values.

9. Adjust all of the column widths to Best Fit.

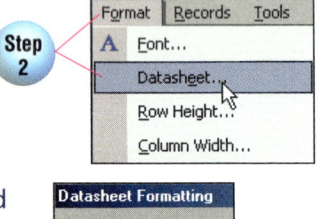

SECTION 1: MAINTAINING DATA IN ACCESS TABLES

⑩ Scroll right and down to view the datasheet with the new formats.

> As you scroll to the right, the *Name* column scrolls off the screen making it difficult to determine which US Distributor record you are viewing. In the next steps you will alleviate this problem by freezing the first two columns.

⑪ Scroll the datasheet left until you are viewing the first two columns.

⑫ Position the mouse pointer in the *State* column heading until the pointer changes to a downward-pointing black arrow, hold down the left mouse button, drag to the right until both the *State* and *Name* columns are selected, and then release the left mouse button.

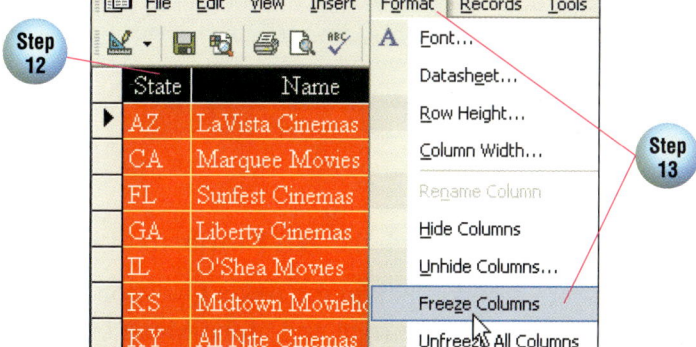

⑬ Click Format and then Freeze Columns.

⑭ Click in any field to deselect the first two columns.

⑮ Scroll right and up to view the datasheet. Notice the first two columns remain fixed and do not scroll off the screen.

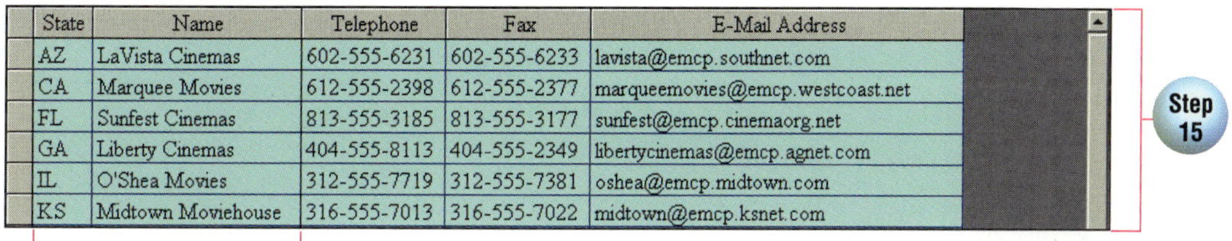

The first two columns remain fixed as you scroll right.

⑯ Click File, Page Setup, and then click the Page tab in the Page Setup dialog box.

> Access does not store page setup options with tables, therefore, these options must be set each time you print. In a later section you will learn how to create a report in which page setup options are stored.

⑰ Click Landscape and then click OK.

⑱ Click the Print button on the Table Datasheet toolbar.

> Notice on your printout that the frozen columns State and Name repeat at the left edge of each page.

⑲ Close the US Distributors table. Click Yes when prompted to save changes to the layout of the table.

IN BRIEF

Change Datasheet Formatting
1 Open table.
2 Click Format, Datasheet.
3 Change settings as desired.
4 Click OK.

Change Font
1 Open table.
2 Click Format, Font.
3 Change settings as desired.
4 Click OK.

Freeze Columns
1 Open table.
2 Select columns to remain fixed.
3 Click Format, Freeze Columns.

SECTION 1: MAINTAINING DATA IN ACCESS TABLES

1.10 Using Help

An extensive online help resource is available whenever you are working in Access by clicking in the Ask a Question box, keying a term, phrase, or question, and then pressing Enter. This invokes the online help facility from which you can locate information by clicking any of the topics displayed in the results list. If the topic you need assistance with is not displayed, try keying another term, or click the *None of the above, search for more on the Web* option at the bottom of the list. This will connect you with the Microsoft Office Web site where you can search for more information.

PROJECT: After printing the US Distributors table, you decide it would look better if the row heights were increased. You will use the online help to learn how to do this.

STEPS

1. With the WE Distributors1 database open, open the US Distributors table.

2. Click in the Ask a Question text box (currently reads *Type a question for help*) at the right end of the Menu bar.

    When you click in the Ask a Question box, an insertion point will appear and the text *Type a question for help* disappears. Once you have completed an initial search for help using the Ask a Question box, the drop-down list arrow will display a list of topics previously searched for in help.

3. Key **increase row height** and then press Enter.

    A list of help topics related to the term, phrase, or question appears below the Ask a Question box.

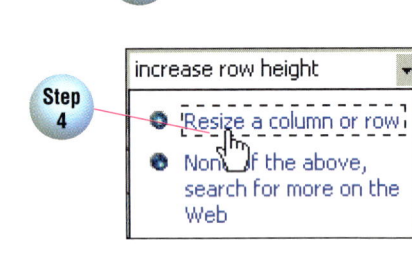

Step 3

4. Click *Resize a column or row*.

    As you move the mouse pointer over a help topic, the pointer changes to a hand with the index finger pointing upward. When you click a topic, the help information displays in a separate Microsoft Access Help window. You can continue clicking topics and reading the information in the Help window until you have found what you are looking for.

Step 4

5. Click *Resize rows* in the Microsoft Access Help window.

    The Help window expands below the selected topic to display information on the feature including the steps to complete the task. Blue underlined text is called a *hyperlink*, which means that further information can be displayed when the link is clicked.

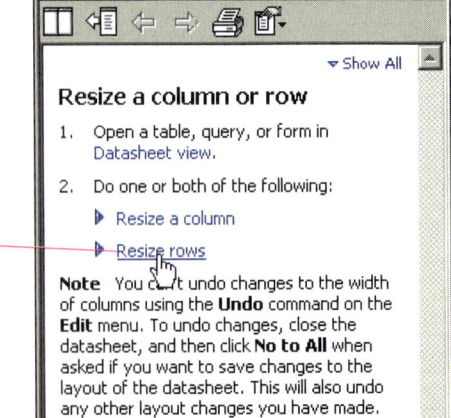

Step 5

6. Read the information below *Resize rows* in the Microsoft Access Help window. If you would like a hard copy of the information, click the Print button on the Microsoft Access Help toolbar.

SECTION 1: MAINTAINING DATA IN ACCESS TABLES

ACCESS

7 Click the Close button located on the Microsoft Access Help Title bar.

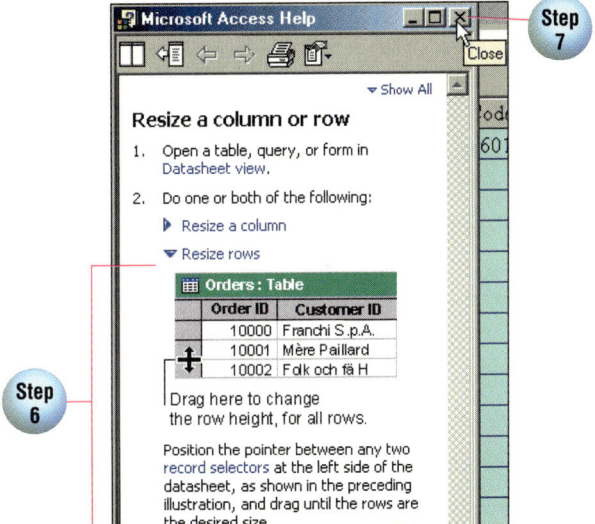

8 Position the mouse pointer on the bottom row boundary for record 1 in the US Distributors table until the pointer changes to a horizontal line with an up- and down-pointing arrow attached (as shown in the Help window).

9 Drag the pointer down until the row height is approximately doubled and then release the mouse button.

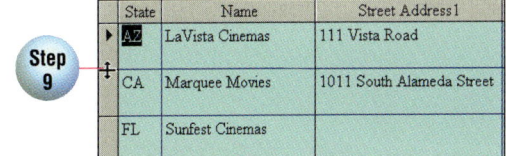

10 Preview the datasheet.

11 Change the Page Setup to print the datasheet in Landscape orientation.

12 Print the US Distributors table.

13 Close the US Distributors table. Click Yes when prompted to save the layout changes.

In Addition

The Office Assistant

Office XP includes an animated Office Assistant, shown at the right, that can be displayed while you are working. To turn on the Office Assistant, click Help and then Show the Office Assistant. The Office Assistant will provide information about specific topics, and sometimes will provide tips while you are working based on the actions you have just performed. Tips are indicated when the yellow light bulb appears over the animated assistant. Click the light bulb to read the tip and then click OK. To access online help from the assistant, click the Office Assistant, key a question, and then click Search.

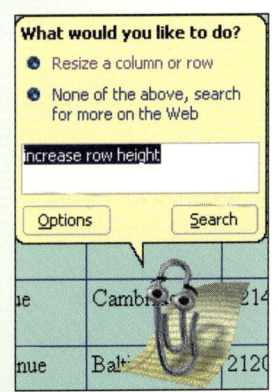

In Brief

Use Online Help
1. Click in the Ask a Question box.
2. Key a term, phrase, or question.
3. Press Enter.
4. Click a topic from the results list.
5. If necessary, continue selecting topics or hyperlinks.
6. Close the Microsoft Access Help window.

SECTION 1: MAINTAINING DATA IN ACCESS TABLES

ACCESS **25**

1.11 Compacting and Repairing a Database

Once you have been working with a database file for a period of time, the data can become fragmented because of records and objects that have been deleted. The disk space that the database uses may be larger than is necessary. Compacting the database defragments the file and reduces the required disk space. Compacting and repairing a database also ensures optimal performance while using the file.

PROJECT: You will run the compact and repair utility on the WE Distributors1 database.

STEPS

1. With the WE Distributors1 database open, click the Minimize button on the Microsoft Access Title bar.

2. Right-click the Start button on the Taskbar and then click Explore at the shortcut menu. If the Explorer window is not currently maximized, click the Maximize button on the Exploring Title bar.

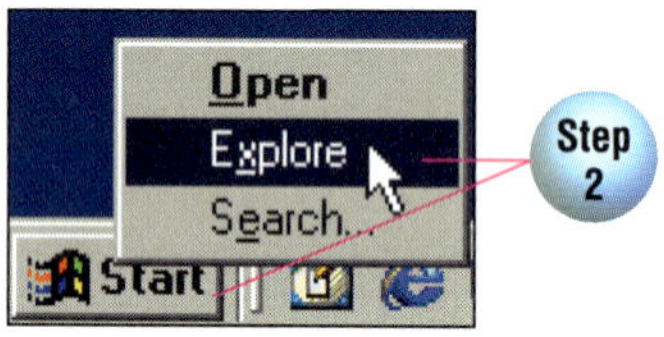

3. If necessary, scroll up the Folders pane and then click the drive and/or folder where the WE Distributors1.mdb file is stored.

   If your data files are stored in a subfolder, click the plus sign to the left of the folder name in the Folders list to expand the display.

4. Click View and then Details.

   This displays the file names with the file size, date, and time.

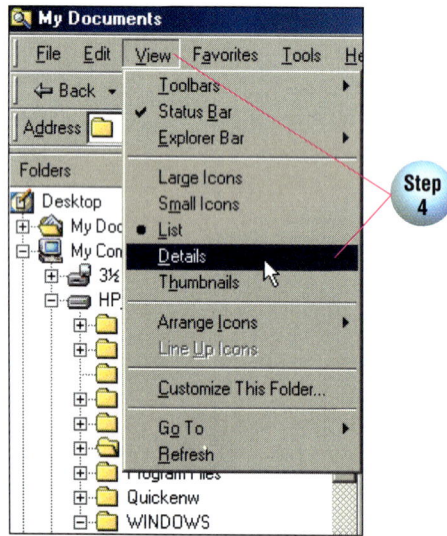

5. Locate the file WE Distributors1.mdb and then write down the file size of the database.

   File size = _____

PROBLEM? Two files will appear in the file list: WE Distributors1.ldb and WE Distributors1.mdb. The .ldb file is used to lock records so that two users cannot request the same record at the same time.

ACCESS
26   SECTION 1: MAINTAINING DATA IN ACCESS TABLES

ACCESS

6. Click the button on the Taskbar representing Access.

7. Click Tools, point to Database Utilities, and then click Compact and Repair Database.

   A message will display on the Status bar indicating the progress of the compact and repair process. In a multi-user environment, no other user can have the database open while the compact and repair procedure is running.

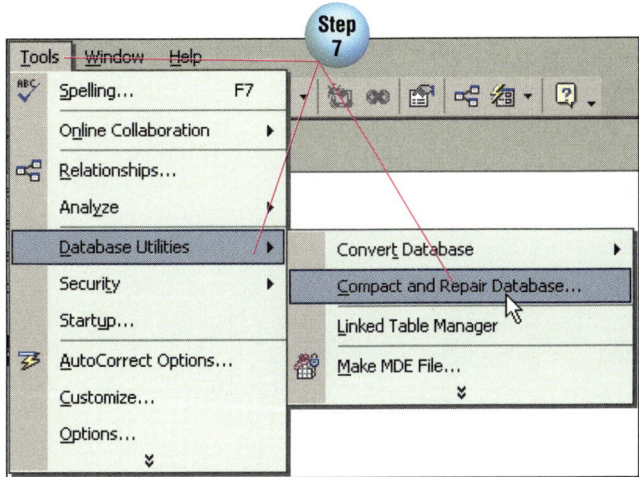

Step 7

8. Click File and then Close to close the WE Distributors1 database.

9. Click File and then Exit to exit Access.

10. Write down the new file size of the WE Distributors1.mdb file in the Windows Explorer window. Notice that the amount of disk space is lower.

    File size = _____

11. Click File and then Close to exit Windows Explorer.

In Addition

Automatic Compact and Repair

In the Options dialog box you can instruct Access to automatically compact a database every time you close it. To do this, open the database that you want Access to compact automatically. Click Tools and then Options. Select the General tab, click the Compact on Close check box, and then click OK.

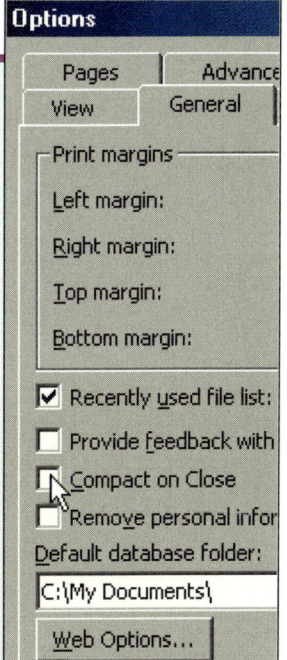

In Brief

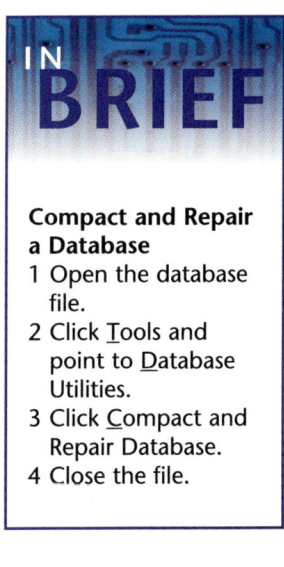

Compact and Repair a Database
1. Open the database file.
2. Click Tools and point to Database Utilities.
3. Click Compact and Repair Database.
4. Close the file.

SECTION 1: MAINTAINING DATA IN ACCESS TABLES

ACCESS 27

FEATURES SUMMARY

Feature	Button	Menu	Keyboard
Add record		Insert, New Record	Ctrl ++
Column width		Format, Column Width	
Compact and repair		Tools, Database Utilities, Compact and Repair Database	
Delete records		Edit, Delete Record	
Find		Edit, Find	Ctrl + F
Font		Format, Font	
Format a datasheet		Format, Datasheet	
Freeze columns		Format, Freeze Columns	
Help	Type a question for help	Help, Microsoft Access Help	F1
Page Setup		File, Page Setup	
Print Preview		File, Print Preview	
Print		File, Print	Ctrl + P
Sort Ascending		Records, Sort, Sort Ascending	
Sort Descending		Records, Sort, Sort Descending	

PROCEDURES CHECK

Matching: The Access screen in Figure A1.4 contains numbers pointing to elements of the datasheet window. Identify the element that corresponds with the number in the screen.

Horizontal scroll box   Office Assistant   Record selector bar
Maximize   Close   Table Title bar
Field names   Active Record   New Record
Record navigation bar   Scroll arrow   Minimize

1. _____
2. _____
3. _____
4. _____
5. _____
6. _____
7. _____
8. _____

FIGURE A1.4

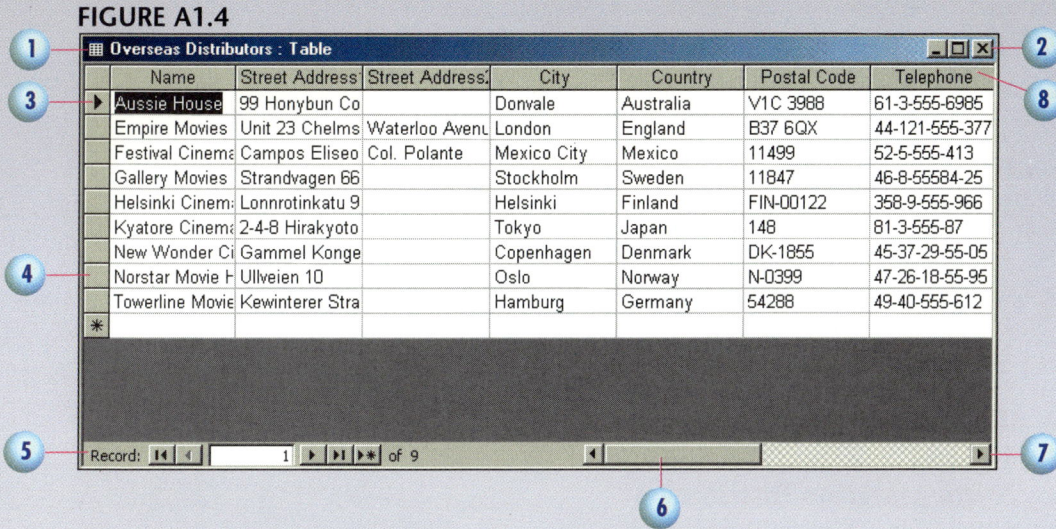

Identify the following buttons:

⋈ 9. _____

^A_Z↓ 10. _____

▶* 11. _____

🖨 12. _____

^Z_A↓ 13. _____

📄 14. _____

🔍 15. _____

SKILLS REVIEW

Activity 1: ADJUSTING COLUMN WIDTHS; FINDING AND EDITING RECORDS

1. Start Access and open the WE Employees1 database.
2. Open the Employee Dates and Salaries table.
3. Maximize the table.
4. Adjust all columns to Best Fit.
5. Find the record for Carl Zakowski and then change the birth date from *05/09/1967* to *12/12/1977.*
6. Find the record for Roman Deptulski and then change the salary from *$67,850.00* to *$71,320.00.* (Note: You do not need to key the dollar symbol, comma, and decimal.)
7. Find the record for Terry Yiu and then change the hire date from *04/12/1999* to *08/11/2001.*
8. Close the Employee Dates and Salaries table. Click Yes when prompted to save changes to the layout.

Activity 2: ADDING AND DELETING RECORDS

1. Open the Employee Dates and Salaries table.
2. Delete the record for Valerie Fistouris.
3. Delete the record for Edward Thurston.
4. Add the following employees to the table using Datasheet view:

SECTION 1: MAINTAINING DATA IN ACCESS TABLES

1085	**1090**
Yousef J El-Sayed	**Maria D Aquino**
12/22/68	**04/16/73**
03/14/01	**11/12/01**
European Distribution	**Overseas Distribution**
$38,467	**$38,467**

5 Close the table and then add the following record using the Employee Dates and Salaries form.

1095
Patrick J Kilarney
02/27/71
12/12/01
North American Distribution
$38,467

6 Close the Employee Dates and Salaries form.

Activity 3: SORTING RECORDS

1 Open the Employee Dates and Salaries table.
2 Sort the table in ascending order by *Last Name*.
3 Sort the table in descending order by *Annual Salary*.
4 Sort the table in ascending order first by *Department* and then by *Last Name*.
5 Close the Employee Dates and Salaries table without saving the changes to the design.

Activity 4: CHANGING THE FONT; CHANGING PAGE ORIENTATION; PRINTING A TABLE

1 Open the Employee Dates and Salaries table.
2 Change the font to 12-point Century Gothic.
3 Adjust all columns to Best Fit.
4 Change the page orientation to landscape.
5 Print and then close the Employee Dates and Salaries table. Click Yes when prompted to save changes.
6 Close the WE Employees1 database.

PERFORMANCE PLUS

Activity 1: Adjusting Column Width; Finding and Editing Records; Using Print Preview

1 Jai Prasad, instructor in the Theatre Arts Division of Niagara Peninsula College, has been called out of town to attend a family matter. The grades for SPE266 have to be entered into the database by the end of today. Jai has provided you with the following grades:

Student Number	Final Grade
138-456-749	A
111-785-156	C
378-159-746	B
348-876-486	A+
274-658-986	B
349-874-658	C

      255-158-498   C
      221-689-478   B
      314-745-856   B
      325-841-469   A
      321-487-659   D

2. Open the NPC Grades1 database.
3. Open the SPE266 Grades table.
4. Adjust column widths so that all data is entirely visible.
5. Enter the grades provided in step 1 in the related records.
6. Preview and then print the table.
7. Close the SPE266 Grades table. Click Yes when prompted to save changes.
8. Close the NPC Grades1 database.

Activity 2: FINDING, ADDING, AND DELETING RECORDS

1. Dana Hirsch, manager of The Waterfront Bistro, has ordered three new inventory items and decided to discontinue three others. Dana has asked you to update the inventory database.
2. Open the WB Inventory1 database.
3. Open the Inventory List table.
4. Locate and then delete the inventory items Pita Wraps; Tuna; and Lake Erie Perch.
5. Add the following new records to the Inventory List table.

    Item 051, Atlantic Scallops, case, Supplier Code 9
    Item 052, Lake Trout, case, Supplier Code 9
    Item 053, Panini Rolls, flat, Supplier Code 1

6. Adjust column widths so that all data is entirely visible.
7. Preview and then print the table.
8. Close the Inventory List table. Click Yes when prompted to save changes.
9. Close the WB Inventory1 database.

Activity 3: FINDING, SORTING, AND DELETING RECORDS; FORMATTING THE DATASHEET

1. You are the assistant to Bobbie Sinclair, business manager of Performance Threads. You have just been informed that several costumes in the rental inventory have been destroyed in a fire at a site location. These costumes will have to be written off since the insurance policy does not cover them when they are out on rental. After updating the costume inventory, you will print two reports.
2. Open the PT Costume Inventory1 database.
3. Open the Costume Inventory table.
4. Locate and then delete the records for the following costumes that were destroyed in a fire at a Shakespearean festival:
    Macbeth   Lady Macbeth   Hamlet   Othello   King Lear   Richard III
5. Sort the table in ascending order by *Character*.
6. Preview and then print the table.
7. Sort the table in ascending order first by *Date Out*, then by *Date In*, and then by *Character*.
8. Change the Background color of the datasheet to Silver and the Gridline color to Blue.
9. Save the changes to the design of the table.
10. Preview and then print the table.
11. Close the Costume Inventory table.
12. Close the PT Costume Inventory1 database.

SECTION 1: MAINTAINING DATA IN ACCESS TABLES

Activity 4: USING COMPACT AND REPAIR

1. You have been investigating buying larger hard drives for the computers in the Theatre Arts Division since the new software the college is using requires more disk space. Cal Rubine, chair of the Theatre Arts Division of Niagara Peninsula College, has advised you that the equipment budget for the current year is used up. You will have to try to find ways to use disk space more efficiently.
2. Open Windows Explorer.
3. Navigate to the folder where the student data files are stored.
4. Write down the disk space the NPC Grades1 database is currently using.
   File size = _____
5. Minimize the Windows Explorer window.
6. Open the NPC Grades1 database.
7. Compact the database.
8. Close the NPC Grades1 database.
9. Switch to the Windows Explorer window.
10. Write down the disk space the NPC Grades1 compacted database is now using.
    File size = _____
11. Exit Windows Explorer.

Activity 5: FINDING INFORMATION ON DESIGNING A DATABASE

1. Use Access's Help feature to find information on the steps involved in designing a database. *(Hint: Use the keyword "create" in your question.)*
2. The help window for About designing a database lists several basic steps that should be followed when designing a database. Read the information presented in the first four links.
3. Use Microsoft Word to create a memo to your instructor as follows:
   - use one of the memo templates.
   - include an opening paragraph describing the body of the memo.
   - list the basic steps to designing a database in a bulleted list.
   - briefly describe the first four steps.
4. Save the memo in Word and name it Access S1-P1 Memo.
5. Print and close Access S1-P1 Memo and then exit Word.

Activity 6: CREATING A JOB SEARCH COMPANY DATABASE

1. You are starting to plan ahead for your job search after graduation. You have decided to start maintaining a database of company information in Access.
2. Search the Internet for company names, addresses, telephone numbers, and fax numbers for at least eight companies in your field of study. Include at least four companies that are out of state or out of province.
3. Open the Job Search1 database.
4. Open the Company Information table.
5. Enter at least eight records for the companies you researched on the Internet.
6. Adjust column widths as necessary.
7. Preview and then print the table.
8. Close the Company Information table.
9. Close the Job Search1 database.

ACCESS SECTION 2
Creating Tables and Relationships

Tables in a database file are the basis upon which all other objects are built. A table can be created in three ways: using Design view, using the Table Wizard, or by entering data in a blank datasheet. When a common field exists in two or more tables, the tables can be joined to create a relationship. A relationship allows the user to extract data from multiple tables as if they were one. In this section you will learn the skills and complete the projects described here.

Note: Before beginning this section, delete from your disk any database files you created in Section 1. Next, copy to your disk as you need them the database files contained in the **Access S2** *subfolder in the* **Access** *folder on the CD that accompanies this textbook. Remove the read-only attribute from each database as you copy it.*

Skills
- Create a table in Design view
- Set the primary key for a table
- Confine data to a list of values using the Lookup Wizard
- Set a pattern for data using the Input Mask Wizard
- Verify data entry using a Validation Rule
- Limit the number of characters allowed in a field
- Enter a default value to display in a field
- Create a table using the Table Wizard
- Create a relationship between two tables
- Enforce referential integrity
- Create an AutoForm
- Create a database using the Database Wizard

Projects

 Create and modify tables to store employee benefit information, employee addresses, employee review and development activities, and expenses; create relationships between a Vendors and a Purchases table, and an Employees and an Expenses table; create an AutoForm to facilitate data entry; create a new database to store contact information.

 Create a table to store student grades for a course in the Theatre Arts Division.

 Modify and correct field properties in the Costume Inventory table to improve the design.

 Create a Suppliers table in the Inventory database and create a relationship between the Suppliers table and the Inventory List table.

 Create a new database to track employee expense claims.

2.1 Creating a Table in Design View

Creating a new table in Design view involves the following steps: entering field names, assigning a data type to each field, entering field descriptions, modifying properties for the field, designating the primary key, and naming the table object. All of the preceding steps are part of a process referred to as "defining the table *structure*." Fields comprise the structure of a table. Once the structure has been created, records can be entered into the table in Datasheet view.

PROJECT: Rhonda Trask, human resources manager for Worldwide Enterprises, has asked you to review the employee benefit plan files and enter the information in a new table in the WE Employees2 database.

STEPS

1. Open WE Employees2.

2. With Tables already selected on the Objects bar, double-click *Create table in Design view*.

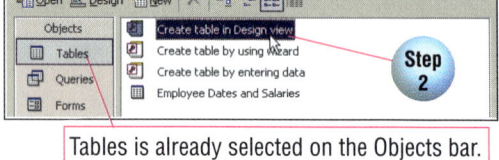

Tables is already selected on the Objects bar.

This opens the Table1 : Table window, where the structure of the table is defined. Each row in the top section represents one field in the table.

3. With the insertion point already positioned in the *Field Name* column in the first row, key **Emp No** and then press Enter or Tab to move to the next column.

The message at the right side of the Field Properties section changes at each column to provide information on the current option (see Figure A2.1).

PROBLEM? Do not key additional characters—field names can contain letters, numbers, and some symbols. Periods (.), commas (,), exclamation points (!), or square brackets ([]) are not accepted in a field name.

FIGURE A2.1 Field Properties Option Message

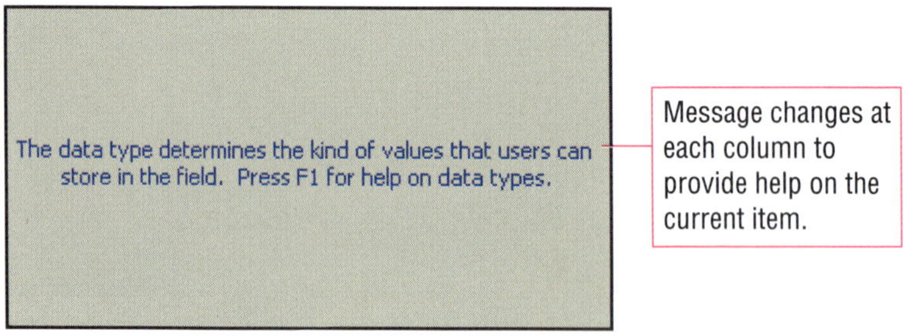

The data type determines the kind of values that users can store in the field. Press F1 for help on data types.

Message changes at each column to provide help on the current item.

4. With *Text* already entered in the *Data Type* column, press Enter or Tab to move to the next column.

Table A2.1 on page 37 provides a list and brief description of the available data types. The *Emp No* field will contain numbers; however, leave the data type defined as Text since no calculations will be performed with employee numbers.

ACCESS

5. Key **Enter the four-digit employee number** in the *Description* column and then press Enter to move to the second row.

   Entering information in the *Description* column is optional. The *Description* text appears in the Status bar when the user is adding records in Datasheet view.

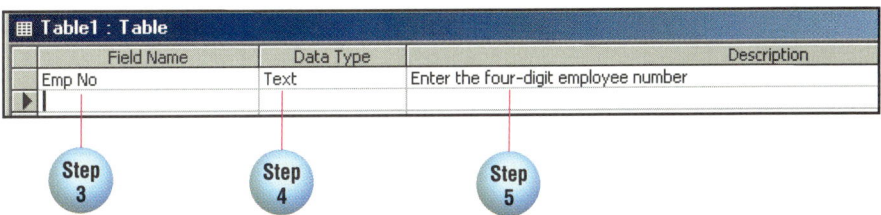

6. Key **Pension Plan** in the *Field Name* column in the second field row and then press Enter.

7. Click the down-pointing triangle in the *Data Type* column, click *Yes/No* in the drop-down list, and then press Enter.

   See Table A2.1 on page 37 for a description of the Yes/No data type.

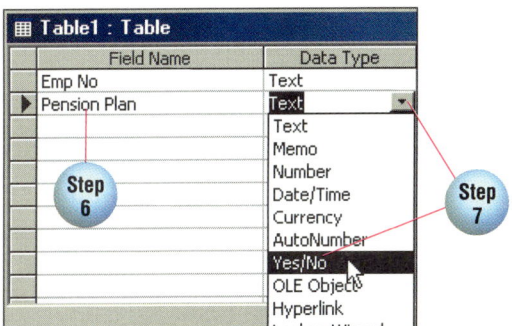

8. Key **Click or press the spacebar for Yes; leave empty for No** and then press Enter.

9. Enter the remaining field names, data types, and descriptions as shown in Figure A2.2. Click the down-pointing triangle in the *Data Type* column to select data types other than Text.

   FIGURE A2.2 Table Entries

Field Name	Data Type	Description
Emp No	Text	Enter the four-digit employee number
Pension Plan	Yes/No	Click or press the spacebar for Yes; leave empty for No
Dental Plan	Yes/No	Click or press the spacebar for Yes; leave empty for No
Premium Health	Yes/No	Click or press the spacebar for Yes; leave empty for No
Dependents	Number	Key the number of dependents
Life Insurance	Currency	Key the life insurance benefit

10. Click the insertion point in any character in the *Emp No* field row.

    This moves the field selector (right-pointing triangle) to the *Emp No* field. In the next step you will designate the *Emp No* field as the primary key for the table.

11. Click the Primary Key button on the Table Design toolbar.

    A key icon will appear in the field selector bar to the left of *Emp No*, indicating the field is the primary key for the table. The primary key is the field that will contain unique data for each record in the table. In addition, Access automatically sorts the table data by the primary key field when the table is opened.

(continued)

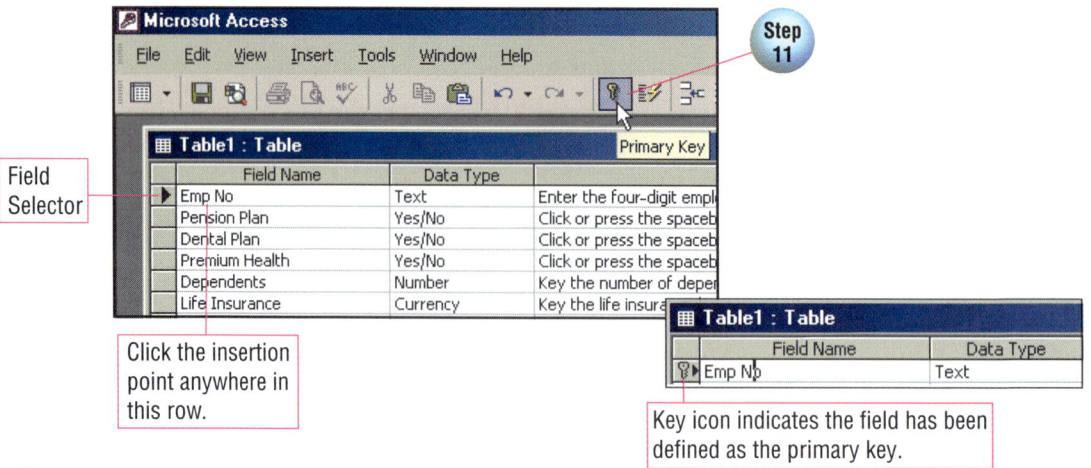

12. Click the Save button on the Table Design toolbar.

    The Save As dialog box opens.

13. Key **Employee Benefits** in the Table Name text box and then press Enter or click OK.

    Once the table is saved, the table name appears in the Title bar.

14. Click the View button 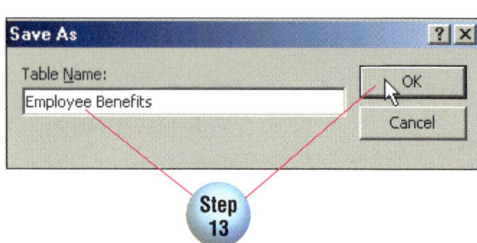 on the Table Design toolbar.

    The View button switches to Datasheet view, where you can enter records into the new table. The insertion point is automatically positioned in the first field for the first record. Notice the description *Enter the four-digit employee number* displays in the Status bar.

15. Key **1001** and then press Enter.

16. Press the spacebar or click the box in the *Pension Plan* column and then press Enter.

    A check mark in the box indicates Yes, True, or On in a *Yes/No* field.

17. Press Enter to leave the *Dental Plan* box empty and move to the next column.

    An empty box indicates No, False, or Off in a *Yes/No* field.

18. Press the spacebar or click the box in the *Premium Health* column and then press Enter.

19. Key **2** in the *Dependents* column and then press Enter.

20. Key **150000** in the *Life Insurance* column and then press Enter.

    The dollar symbol, comma in the thousands, decimal point, and two zeros are automatically inserted in the field since the data type was defined as Currency.

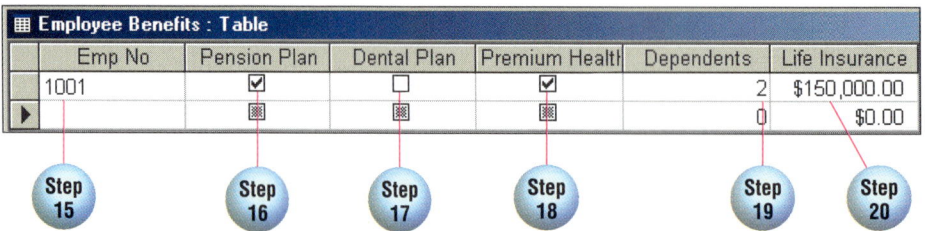

ACCESS

SECTION 2: CREATING TABLES AND RELATIONSHIPS

21. Key the following two records in the datasheet:

Emp No	**1005**	*Emp No*	**1010**
Pension Plan	**Yes**	*Pension Plan*	**Yes**
Dental Plan	**Yes**	*Dental Plan*	**No**
Premium Health	**Yes**	*Premium Health*	**No**
Dependents	**3**	*Dependents*	**0**
Life Insurance	**175000**	*Life Insurance*	**100000**

22. Close the Employee Benefits table.

TABLE A2.1 Data Types

Data Type	Description
Text	Alphanumeric data up to 255 characters in length, such as a name or address. Fields that will contain numbers that will not be used in calculations, such as a student number or telephone number, should be defined as Text.
Memo	Alphanumeric data up to 64,000 characters in length.
Number	Positive and/or negative values that can be used in mathematical operations. Do not use for values that will calculate monetary amounts (see Currency).
Date/Time	Stores dates and times. Use this format to ensure dates and times are sorted properly. Access displays an error message if an invalid date is entered in a Date/Time data field.
Currency	Values that involve money. Access will not round off during calculations.
AutoNumber	Access will automatically number each record sequentially (incrementing by 1) when you begin keying a new record. If you do not define a primary key and you respond Yes for Access to define one for you when you save the table, Access creates an AutoNumber data field.
Yes/No	Data in the field will be either Yes or No, True or False, On or Off.
OLE Object	Used to embed or link objects created in other Office applications (such as Microsoft Word or Microsoft Excel) to an Access table.
Hyperlink	Field that will store a hyperlink such as a URL.
Lookup Wizard	Starts the Lookup Wizard, which creates a data type based on the values selected during the wizard steps. The Lookup Wizard can be used to enter data in the field from another existing table or display a list of values in a drop-down list for the user to choose from.

In Addition

Creating a Table by Adding Records

A new table can be created by keying data directly into a blank datasheet. Double-click *Create table by entering data* in the Database window. Fields are initially named *Field1*, *Field2*, and so on, as shown below. When you save the datasheet, Access assigns data types and formats for each field based on the entry in each column. A field can be renamed in the datasheet by double-clicking the column header, keying a new name, and then pressing Enter. Once the table has been created it can be edited by opening the table in Design View.

In Brief

Create a Table in Design View
1. Open database or create a new database.
2. Click Tables on the Objects bar.
3. Double-click *Create table in Design view*.
4. Key field names, descriptions, and assign data types in the Table dialog box.
5. Assign the primary key field.
6. Click Save button.
7. Key a name for the table and press Enter.

SECTION 2: CREATING TABLES AND RELATIONSHIPS

2.2 Using the Lookup Wizard

Create a *Lookup* field when you want to restrict the data entered into the field to a list of values from an existing table, or a list of values that you enter in the wizard dialog box. The Lookup tab in the Field Properties section in Table Design view contains the options used to create a *Lookup* field. Access includes the Lookup Wizard, which facilitates entering the option settings.

PROJECT: You will use the Lookup Wizard to create a new field in the Employee Benefits table that will display a drop-down list of vacation entitlements in Datasheet view.

STEPS

1. With WE Employees2 open, *right*-click the Employee Benefits table name in the WE Employees2 : Database window and then click Design View at the shortcut menu.

2. Click in the *Field Name* column in the blank row below *Life Insurance*, key **Vacation**, and then press Enter.

3. Click the down-pointing triangle in the *Data Type* column and then click *Lookup Wizard* from the drop-down list.

4. Click *I will type in the values that I want* and then click Next.

PROBLEM? If you press Enter by mistake and find yourself at the next step in the Lookup Wizard, click Back to return to the previous dialog box.

5. Click in the blank row below *Col1*, key **1 week**, and then press Tab.

6. Key **2 weeks** and then press Tab.

7. Key **3 weeks** and then press Tab.

8. Key **4 weeks** and then click Next.

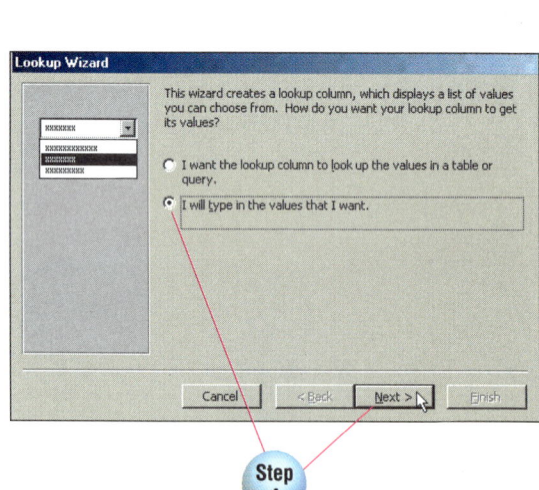

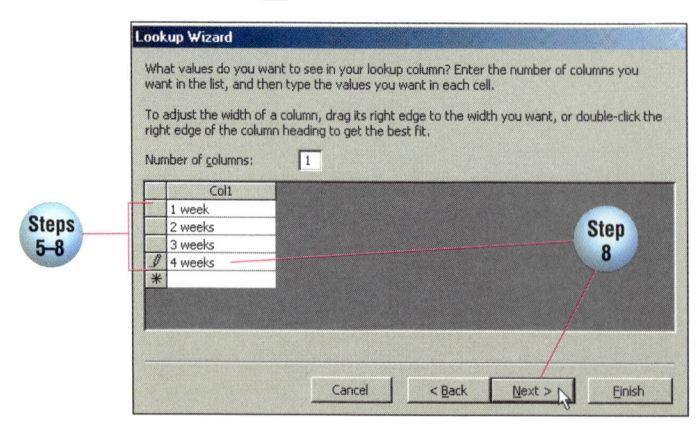

SECTION 2: CREATING TABLES AND RELATIONSHIPS

ACCESS

9. Click Finish in the last Lookup Wizard dialog box to accept the default label *Vacation*. No entry is required in the *Description* column.

10. Click the Lookup tab in the Field Properties section and view the entries made to each setting by the Lookup Wizard.

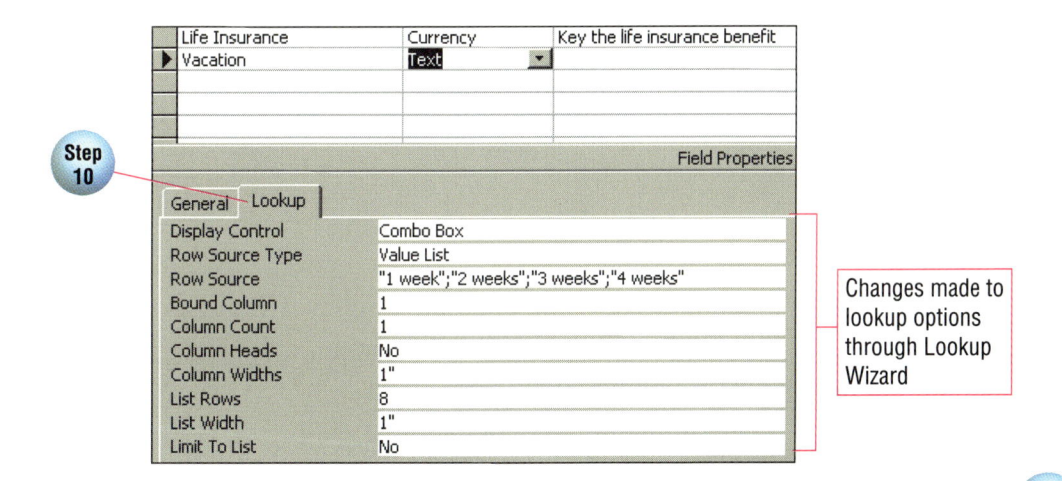

Step 10

Changes made to lookup options through Lookup Wizard

11. Click the Save button.

12. Click View to switch to Datasheet view.

13. Click in the *Vacation* column in the first row in the datasheet, click the down-pointing triangle that appears, and then click *4 weeks* from the drop-down list.

Step 13

14. Press the down arrow key to move to the *Vacation* column in the second row.

15. Click the down-pointing triangle and then click *3 weeks*.

16. Press the down arrow key, click the down-pointing triangle, and then click *3 weeks*.

17. Close the Employee Benefits table.

In Addition

Looking Up Data from Another Table

In this topic the items in the drop-down list were created by keying them in rows at the second Lookup Wizard dialog box. Items in the drop-down list can also be generated by specifying an existing field in another table or query. To do this, click Next at the first Lookup Wizard dialog box to accept the default setting *I want the lookup column to look up values in a table or query*. At the second Lookup Wizard dialog box, select the table or query name that contains the field you want to use. Specify the field to be used to generate the list in the third dialog box, and then set the column width at the preview of the list in the fourth dialog box. Creating field entries using this method ensures that data is consistent between tables and eliminates duplicate keying of information, which can lead to data errors.

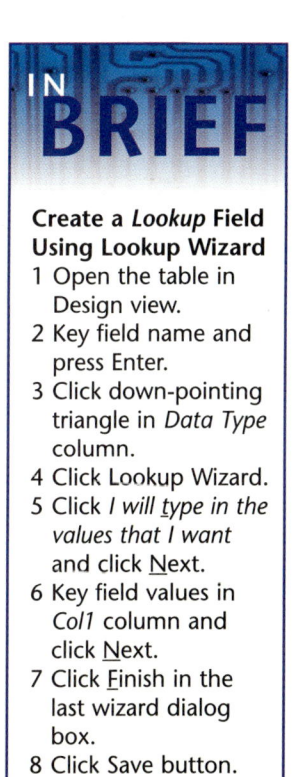

IN BRIEF

Create a *Lookup* Field Using Lookup Wizard
1. Open the table in Design view.
2. Key field name and press Enter.
3. Click down-pointing triangle in *Data Type* column.
4. Click Lookup Wizard.
5. Click *I will type in the values that I want* and click Next.
6. Key field values in *Col1* column and click Next.
7. Click Finish in the last wizard dialog box.
8. Click Save button.

SECTION 2: CREATING TABLES AND RELATIONSHIPS

2.3 Using the Input Mask Wizard

An *input mask* displays a pattern specifying how data is to be entered into a field. For example, an input mask could be defined in a telephone number field to display (___)___-____. This input mask indicates to the user that the three-digit area code is required for all telephone numbers. Input masks ensure that data is entered consistently in tables. The Input Mask Wizard is used to help create the entry in the Input Mask property box in the Field Properties section for the field.

PROJECT: You will create a new field in the Employee Benefits table for Pension Plan eligibility dates and include an input mask in the field indicating dates should be entered in the format *dd-mmm-yy*.

STEPS

1. With WE Employees2 open, open the Employee Benefits table in Design view.
2. Click in the *Field Name* column in the blank row below *Vacation*, key **RPP Eligibility Date**, and then press Enter.
3. Change the data type to *Date/Time* and then press Enter.
4. Key **Enter date as dd-mmm-yy (example: 12-Dec-02)**.
5. Click Save. 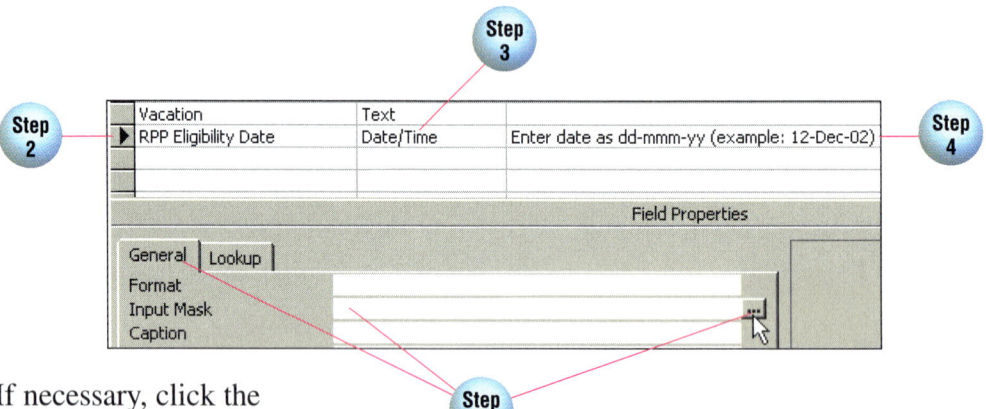
6. If necessary, click the General tab in the Field Properties section, click in the Input Mask property box and then click the Build button.

PROBLEM? If the Input Mask Wizard has not been installed, a message will appear asking if you want to install it now. Check with your instructor.

7. Click *Medium Date* in the first Input Mask Wizard dialog box and then click Next.

   The available input masks that display in the list box are dependent on the data type for the field for which you are creating an input mask.

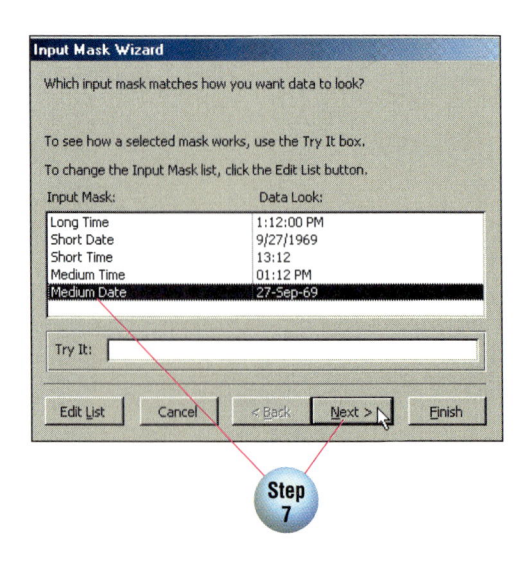

ACCESS
40

SECTION 2: CREATING TABLES AND RELATIONSHIPS

8 Click Next in the second Input Mask Wizard dialog box.

This dialog box displays the input mask code in the Input Mask text box and sets the Placeholder character that will display in the field. The default Placeholder is the underscore character. Other available Placeholder characters are #, @, and !.

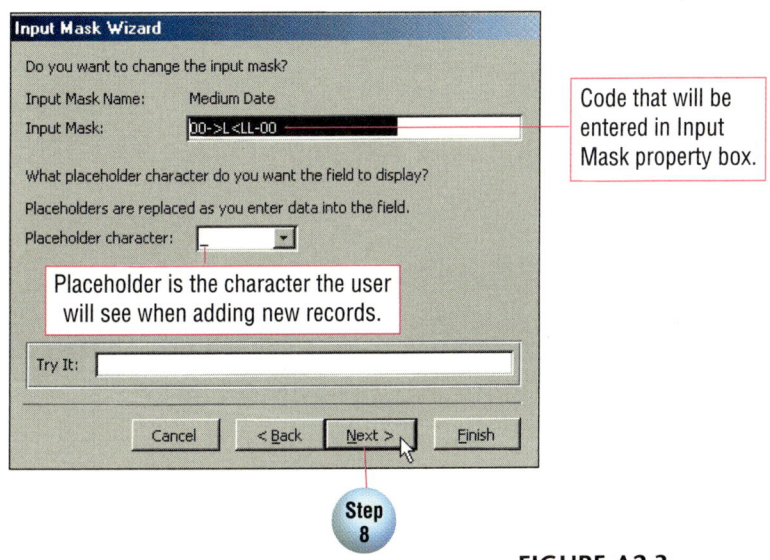

Code that will be entered in Input Mask property box.

Placeholder is the character the user will see when adding new records.

Step 8

FIGURE A2.3

Input mask field property created by the Input Mask Wizard.

9 Click Finish at the last Input Mask Wizard dialog box.

The input mask 00->L<LL-00;0;_ is entered in the Input Mask property box for the *RPP Eligibility Date* field, as shown in Figure A2.3.

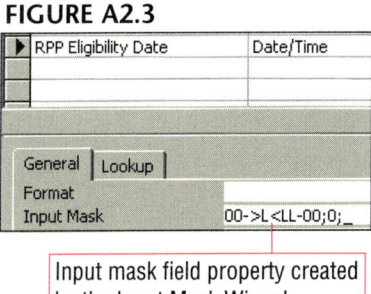

10 Click the Save button and then click the View button to switch to Datasheet view.

11 Maximize the Employee Benefits table if it is not already maximized.

12 Click in the *RPP Eligibility Date* column for the first row in the datasheet.

The input mask __-___-__ appears in the field.

PROBLEM? If the input mask does not appear right away, start to key the date in step 13. As soon as you key the first character in the field, the mask will appear.

13 Key **22-Jan-98** and then press the down arrow key.

Access displays *1/22/1998* in the field. By default, dates are displayed in the datasheet as *m/dd/yyyy*. In steps 14–17 you will format the field to display the date in the same format as the input mask.

14 Click the View button to switch to Design view.

The View button toggles between Datasheet view and Design view depending on which view is active.

(continued)

SECTION 2: CREATING TABLES AND RELATIONSHIPS

ACCESS **41**

15. With *RPP Eligibility Date* as the selected field, click in the Format field property box, click the down-pointing triangle that appears, and then click *Medium Date* in the drop-down list.

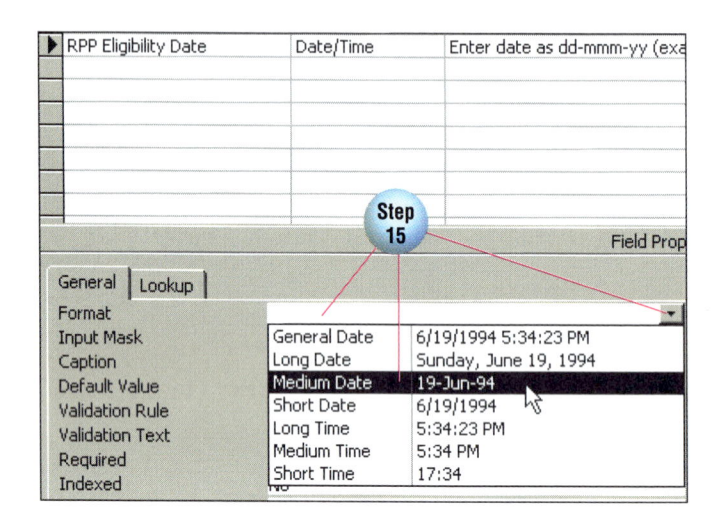

16. Click Save and then click View to switch to Datasheet view.

17. Click in the *RPP Eligibility Date* column in the second row in the datasheet and then key **15-Feb-99**.

    In the next step you try to enter a date using the format *mm/dd/yy* to see how the input mask restricts this entry.

18. Click in the *RPP Eligibility Date* column in the third row in the datasheet and then key **07/09/99**.

    A beep will sound when you key / and 09/. The only part of the entry that will be accepted is *07*. The insertion point remains in the month section of the date.

19. Press Backspace twice to delete *07*, key **30-Jul-99**, and then press Enter.

    The difference between the input mask and the format property is that the input mask *restricts* the data that is entered into the field, while the format property controls the *display* of the data that is accepted into the field.

20. Best Fit the column width of the *RPP Eligibility Date* column.

ACCESS

42

SECTION 2: CREATING TABLES AND RELATIONSHIPS

21. Close the Employee Benefits table. Click Yes when prompted to save changes to the table layout.

In Addition

Editing Input Masks

The Input Mask Wizard dialog box shown below displays the available input masks for a field that is defined as Text. The Input Mask Wizard only works with Text or Date/Time data field types. Click in the Input Mask property box and insert or delete characters as needed to edit an input mask created by the wizard. For example, the social security input mask does not accommodate similar number formats for countries other than the United States.

To create an input mask for Canadian social insurance numbers, use the wizard to create the social security input mask. After the entry has been created, click in the Input Mask property box and modify the entry as shown below. Other input masks such as a telephone number can be edited to include an extension number.

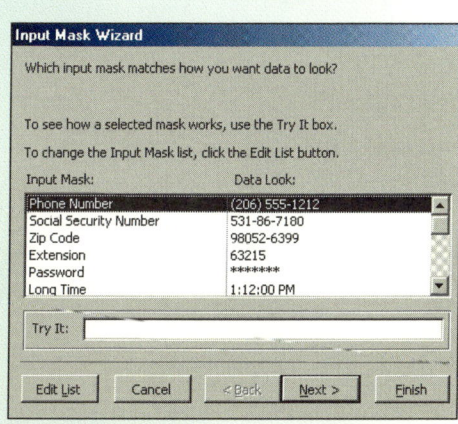

IN BRIEF

Create an Input Mask for a Field
1. Open the table in Design view.
2. Key field name, assign data type, and key description.
3. Click Save button.
4. Click in the Input Mask property box.
5. Click the Build button.
6. Click the input mask you want to create.
7. Click Next.
8. Select Placeholder character.
9. Click Next.
10. Click Next to store data without symbols.
11. Click Finish at the last wizard dialog box.
12. Click Save button.

Input Mask created for Social Security Number: 000\-00\-0000;;_
Edited entry for Canadian Social Insurance Number: 000\-000\-000;;_

SECTION 2: CREATING TABLES AND RELATIONSHIPS

2.4 Validating Field Entries

The *Validation Rule* property can be used to enter a conditional statement that is checked when data is entered into a field. Access displays an error message to the user if the data being entered does not meet the conditional test. For example, a validation rule for a customer number field could be that the customer number must be within a certain range of values. The *Validation Text* property is used to enter the content of the error message that you want the user to see. The Validation Rule and Validation Text properties are important data entry error-checking tools.

PROJECT: Worldwide Enterprises offers life insurance benefits up to a maximum of $199,999. You will add a validation rule and enter an error message in the validation text for the *Life Insurance* field in the Employee Benefits table to ensure no benefit exceeds this maximum.

STEPS

1. With WE Employees2 open, open the Employee Benefits table in Design view.

2. Click in the *Life Insurance* field row.

    This selects the *Life Insurance* field and displays the field properties.

3. Click in the Validation Rule property box, key **<200000**, and then press Enter.

    Pressing Enter after keying the validation rule moves the insertion point to the Validation Text property box.

4. Key **Enter a value that is less than $200,000**.

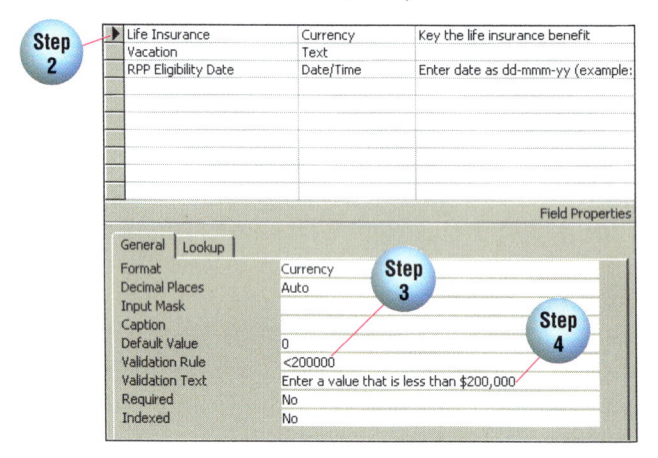

5. Click the Save button.

    Since a validation rule has been created *after* data has been entered into the table, Access displays a warning message.

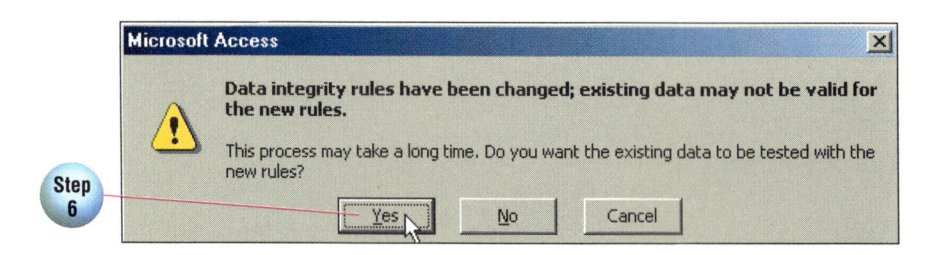

6. Click Yes to instruct Access to test the data with the new rules.

SECTION 2: CREATING TABLES AND RELATIONSHIPS

7 Click the View button to switch to Datasheet view.

8 Add the following record to the table:

Emp No	**1015**
Pension Plan	**Yes**
Dental Plan	**Yes**
Premium Health	**Yes**
Dependents	**2**
Life Insurance	**210000**

When you enter *210000* into the *Life Insurance* field and press Enter or Tab, Access will display an error message. The text in the error message is the text you entered in the Validation Text property box.

9 Click OK at the Microsoft Access error message.

10 Backspace to delete *210000*, key **199999**, and then press Enter.

11 Enter the following data in the two remaining fields:

Vacation	**4 weeks**
RPP Eligibility Date	**17-Nov-00**

Emp No	Pension Plan	Dental Plan	Premium Health	Dependents	Life Insurance	Vacation	RPP Eligibility Date
1001	✓	☐	✓	2	$150,000.00	4 weeks	22-Jan-98
1005	✓	✓	✓	3	$175,000.00	3 weeks	15-Feb-99
1010	✓	☐	☐	0	$100,000.00	3 weeks	30-Jul-99
1015	✓	✓	✓	2	$199,999.00	4 weeks	17-Nov-00
				0	$0.00		

12 Close the Employee Benefits table.

In Addition

Other Validation Rule Examples

Validation rules should be created whenever possible to avoid data entry errors. The examples below illustrate various ways to use the validation rule to verify data.

Field Name	Validation Rule	Data Check
Customer No	>1000 And <1100	Limits customer numbers to 1001 through 1099
Credit Limit	<=5000	Restricts credit limits to values of 5000 or less
State	"CA"	Only the state of California is accepted
Order Qty	>=25	Quantity ordered must be a minimum of 25

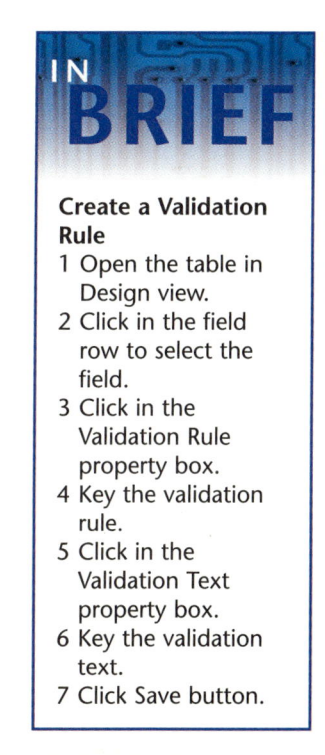

In Brief

Create a Validation Rule
1. Open the table in Design view.
2. Click in the field row to select the field.
3. Click in the Validation Rule property box.
4. Key the validation rule.
5. Click in the Validation Text property box.
6. Key the validation text.
7. Click Save button.

SECTION 2: CREATING TABLES AND RELATIONSHIPS

2.5 Modifying Field Size and Default Value

The *Field Size* property can be used to limit the number of characters that are allowed in a field entry. For example, a field size of 6 for a customer number field would prevent customer numbers greater than 6 digits from being stored in a record. The *Default Value* property is useful if most records will contain the same value. The value will appear in the field automatically when a new record is added to the table. The user will have the option of accepting the default value by pressing Enter or Tab at the field, or of overwriting the default by keying a different value.

PROJECT: Worldwide Enterprises uses a four-digit employee number. You will modify the Field Size property for the *Emp No* field to set the maximum number of characters to 4. Since most employees opt into the Pension Plan, you will set the default value for the *Pension Plan* field to Yes.

S T E P S

1. With WE Employees2 open, open the Employee Benefits table in Design view.

2. With the *Emp No* field already selected, drag the pointer over the value *50* that appears in the Field Size property box to select it.

   Alternatively, click in the Field Size property box to activate the insertion point and then delete *50*.

3. Key **4**.

4. Click in the *Pension Plan* field row to display the *Pension Plan* field properties.

5. Click in the Default Value field property box.

6. Key **Yes**.

7. Click the Save button.

   Since the field size for a field was changed *after* data has been entered into the table, Access displays a warning message that some data may be lost.

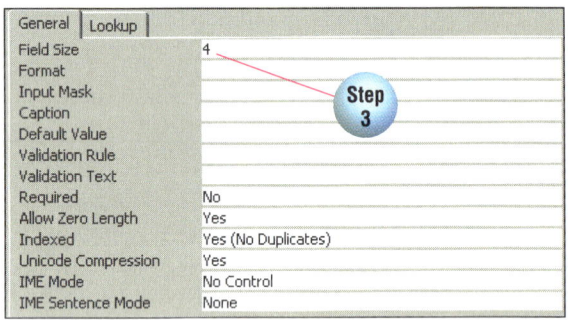

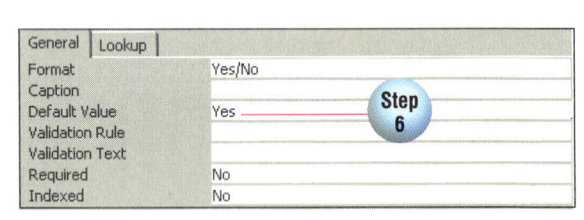

8. Click Yes to instruct Access to continue.

   If a large amount of data was entered into a table before the field size was changed, always make a backup of the file before changing the Field Size property. To check for errors, compare the old data in the field with the new data after Access saves the table.

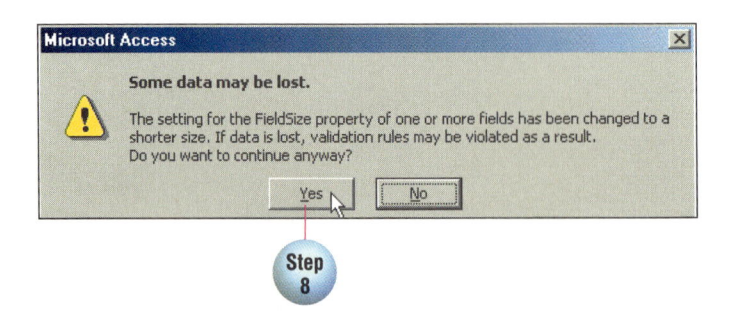

9. Click the View button to switch to Datasheet view.

   Notice the *Pension Plan* column in the blank row at the bottom of the datasheet contains a check mark since the default value is now Yes.

10. Key **10201** in the *Emp No* field in the blank row at the bottom of the datasheet and then press Enter.

    A beep will sound when you key **1** at the end of the field. Access did not accept any characters after the fourth character that was typed.

11. Press Enter at the *Pension Plan* field to accept the default value of Yes.

12. Enter the following data in the remaining fields:

Dental Plan	**No**
Premium Health	**No**
Dependents	**0**
Life Insurance	**100000**
Vacation	**4 weeks**
RPP Eligibility Date	**05-Feb-01**

Emp No	Pension Plan	Dental Plan	Premium Health	Dependents	Life Insurance	Vacation	RPP Eligibility Date
1001	✓	☐	✓	2	$150,000.00	4 weeks	22-Jan-98
1005	✓	✓	✓	3	$175,000.00	3 weeks	15-Feb-99
1010	✓	☐	☐	0	$100,000.00	3 weeks	30-Jul-99
1015	✓	✓	✓	2	$199,999.00	4 weeks	17-Nov-00
1020	✓	☐	☐	0	$100,000.00	4 weeks	05-Feb-01

13. Best Fit all columns in the datasheet, change the page orientation to landscape, and then print the Employee Benefits table.

14. Close the Employee Benefits table. Click <u>Y</u>es to save layout changes.

In Brief

Set the Field Size
1. Open the table in Design view.
2. Click in the field row to select the field.
3. Click in the Field Size property box.
4. Key the maximum number of characters for the field.
5. Click Save button.

Set the Default Value
1. Open the table in Design view.
2. Click in the field row to select the field.
3. Click in the Default Value property box.
4. Key the default value to appear in the field.
5. Click Save button.

In Addition

Default Field Size

The default field size property will vary depending on the data type. The default value for a text field is 50. If the data type is Numeric, the default field size is *Long Integer*. Long Integer will store *whole numbers* from −2,147,483,648 to 2,147,483,648 (negative to positive). Press F1 while the insertion point is positioned in the Field Size property box to display in the Help window the various field size settings for a numeric field.

SECTION 2: CREATING TABLES AND RELATIONSHIPS

2.6 Creating a Table Using the Table Wizard

Creating a table using the Table Wizard involves choosing the type of table from a list of sample tables and then selecting fields from the sample field list. Access creates the field names and assigns data types based on the samples. Once created, the fields in the table can be edited in Design view.

PROJECT: You will use the Table Wizard to create a new table that will store employee addresses.

STEPS

1. With WE Employees2 open, double-click *Create table by using wizard*.

2. Click *Employees* in the Sample Tables list box.

3. Click *EmployeeNumber* in the Sample Fields list box and then click the Add Field button `>` to the right of the Sample Fields list box.

   This inserts the *EmployeeNumber* field in the Fields in my new table list box and moves the selected field in the Sample Fields list box to the next field after *EmployeeNumber*, which is *NationalEmplNumber*.

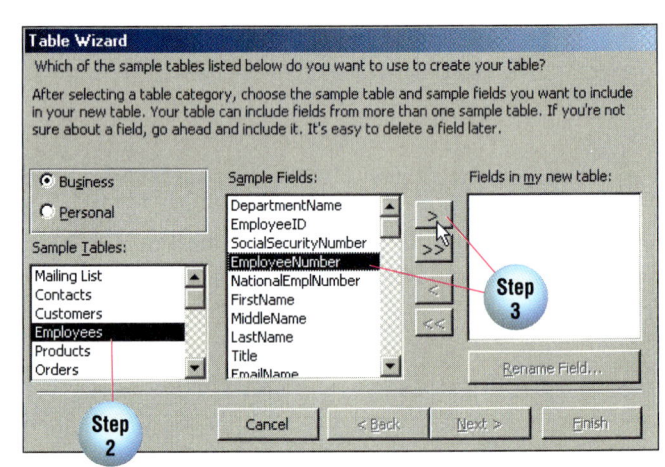

4. Double-click *FirstName* in the Sample Fields list box.

   Double-clicking a field name in the Sample Fields list box is another method of adding the field in the Fields in my new table list box.

5. Double-click the following field names in the Sample Fields list box.

   MiddleName
   LastName
   Address
   City
   StateOrProvince
   PostalCode

   PROBLEM? Can't locate some of the field names? You will need to scroll down the Sample Fields list box.

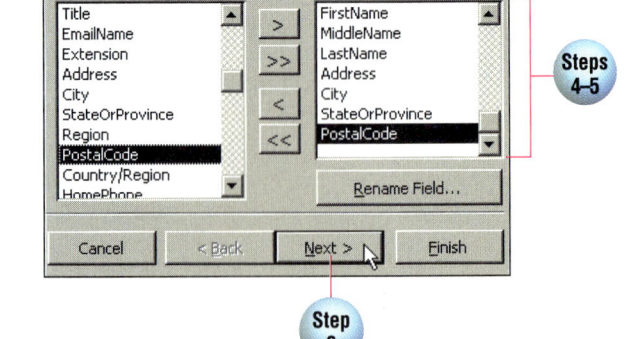

6. Click Next.

7. Click Next at the second Table Wizard dialog box to accept the table name *Employees* and *Yes, set a primary key for me*.

⑧ Click Next at the third Table Wizard dialog box to accept *not related to 'Employee Benefits'* in the My new 'Employees' table is list box, since the new table is not related to either of the two existing tables in the database.

⑨ Click *Modify the table design* at the fourth Table Wizard dialog box, and then click Finish.

> The new Employees table appears in the Design view window. When you elected to let Access set the primary key field, Access added the field *EmployeesID* to the table with the data type of AutoNumber. In steps 10–13 you will modify the primary key by deleting the *EmployeesID* field and modifying *EmployeeNumber*.

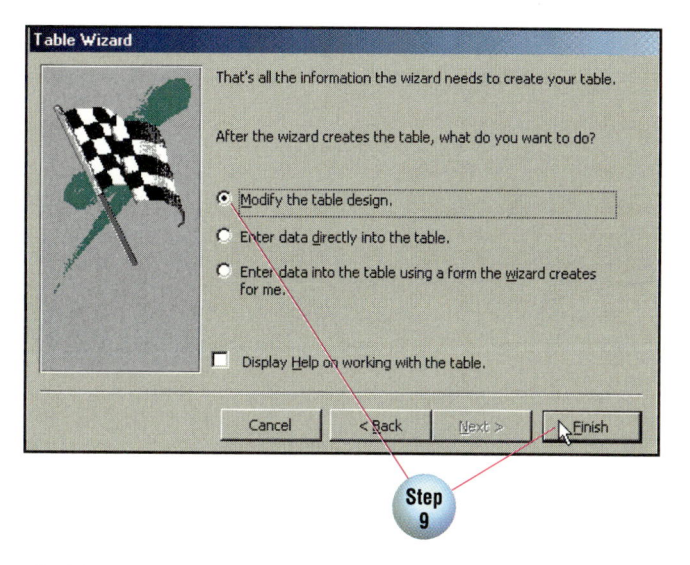

Step 9

⑩ Click in the field selector bar next to *EmployeesID* and then click the Delete Rows button on the Table Design toolbar.

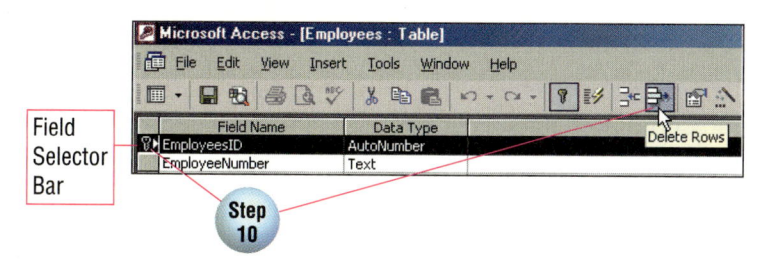

Step 10

⑪ Click Yes to confirm the deletion.

⑫ Make the following changes to the *EmployeeNumber* field:

Field Name	**Emp No**
Field Size	**4**

⑬ Make *Emp No* the primary key field.

⑭ Click the Save button.

⑮ Close the Employees table.

⑯ Close the WE Employees2 database.

IN BRIEF

Create a Table Using Wizard
1. Open the database file.
2. Double-click *Create table by using wizard*.
3. Click type of table in Sample Tables list box.
4. Add fields from Sample Fields list box to Fields in my new table list box.
5. Click Next.
6. Choose table name and primary key and click Next.
7. Choose to enter data directly in the table or edit the table in Design view.
8. Click Finish.

SECTION 2: CREATING TABLES AND RELATIONSHIPS

2.7 Creating Relationships

Access is sometimes referred to as a relational database management system. A relational database is one in which relationships exist between tables, allowing two or more tables to be treated as if they were one when generating reports or looking up data. Joining one table to another using a field common to both tables creates a relationship. Access allows for three types of relationships: one-to-many, one-to-one, and many-to-many. In a relationship, one table is called the *primary* table and the other table is called the *related* table. In a one-to-many relationship, the common field value in the primary table is often the primary key field since only one record can exist for each unique entity. The related table can have more than one record for the same field value in the primary table.

PROJECT: You will create a one-to-many relationship between the Vendors table and the Purchases table in a database that is used to record purchase information.

STEPS

1. Open WE Purchases2.

2. Open the Vendors table, look at the field names and data in the datasheet, and then close Vendors.

3. Open the Purchases table, look at the field names and data in the datasheet, and then close Purchases.

   Notice that the Purchases table has more than one record for the same vendor number since buying goods and services from the same vendor several times within a year is possible. You will create a one-to-many relationship between the Vendors table and the Purchases table. Vendors is the primary table in this relationship since only one record for each vendor will exist. Purchases is the related table—many records for the same vendor can exist.

4. Click the Relationships button on the Database toolbar.

5. With *Purchases* already selected in the Show Table dialog box, click Add.

PROBLEM: Show Table dialog box does not appear? Right-click in Relationships window and then click Show Table at the shortcut menu.

6. Click *Vendors* and then click Add.

7. Click Close to close the Show Table dialog box.

   A common field in two tables is the basis upon which the tables are joined. In the next step, you will drag the common field *Vendor_No* from the primary table (Vendors) to the related table (Purchases).

   Purchases table field list box added to Relationships window in step 5.

8. Position the mouse pointer over the Vendor_No field name in the Vendors field list box, hold down the left mouse button, drag the pointer left to the Vendor_No field name in the Purchases field list box, and then release the mouse button.

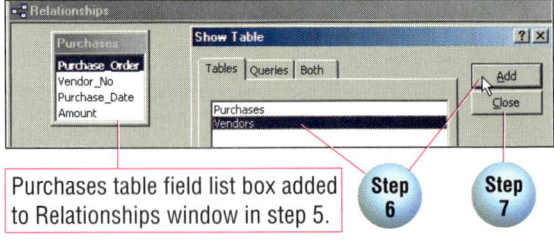

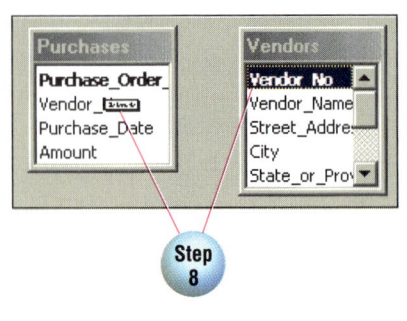

   The Edit Relationships dialog box appears when you release the mouse button.

9. Click the Enforce Referential Integrity check box in the Edit Relationships dialog box and then click Create.

   Referential integrity means that Access will ensure that a record with the same vendor number already exists in the primary table (Vendors) when a new record is being added to the related table (Purchases). If no matching record exists, Access will display an error message.

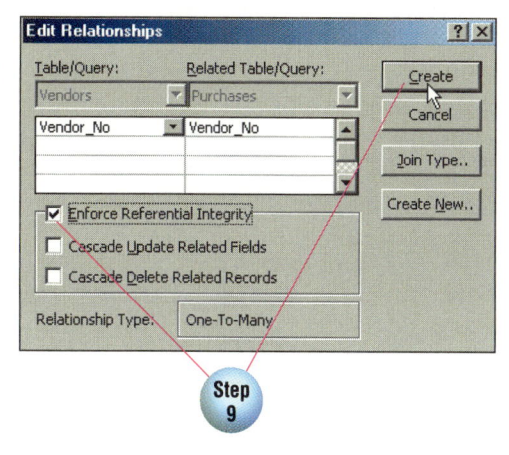

10. Click the Save button.

    A black line (referred to as a *join line*) joins the two tables in the Relationships window. A *1* appears next to the primary table, Vendors, indicating the *one* side of the relationship and the infinity symbol ( ) appears next to the related table, Purchases, indicating the *many* side of the relationship.

11. Click the Close button on the Relationships window Title bar.

12. Open the Purchases table.

    In steps 13–15 you will test the referential integrity by attempting to add a record for a vendor that does not exist in the primary table.

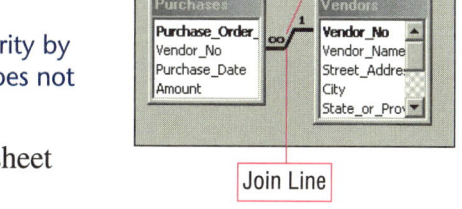

13. Click the New Record button on the Table Datasheet toolbar.

14. Key **6549** in the *Purchase_Order_No* column and then press Enter.

15. Key **150** in the *Vendor_No* column and then press Enter.

16. Press Enter through the *Purchase_Date* and *Amount* fields to move to the next row.

    Access displays an error message indicating you cannot add or change a record because a related record is required in the Vendors table.

17. Click OK to close the message window.

18. Close the Purchases table. Click OK at the error message that appears for the second time. Click Yes at the second error message box to close the object and confirm that the data changes will be lost.

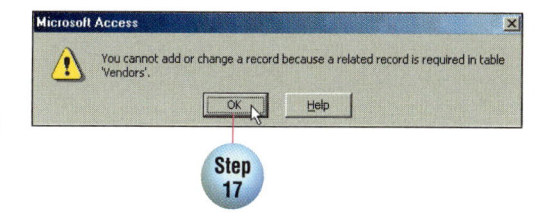

In Addition

One-to-One Relationships

A one-to-one relationship exists when both the primary table and the related table will contain only one record for the common field. For example, in the WE Employees2 database that has been used throughout this section, the Employees table would contain only one record for each employee. The Employee Benefits table would also contain only one record for each employee. If the tables were joined on the common *Emp No* field, a one-to-one relationship would be created.

SECTION 2: CREATING TABLES AND RELATIONSHIPS

2.8 Creating a Form Using AutoForm

As previously seen, a form provides a better alternative than a datasheet to view, enter, and edit records. With a form, only one record is displayed at a time. The fields can be arranged so that all fields are visible on one screen. If tables are related in the database, the related tables can be displayed in subforms in the primary form so that all the tables can be updated at the same time. This alleviates the need to open each table individually and enter records. A form created with AutoForm inserts all of the fields in the specified table in columnar, table, or datasheet format.

PROJECT: You will use AutoForm to create a columnar form that will display the vendor information from the Vendors table on one screen.

STEPS

1. With the WE Purchases2 database open, click Forms on the Objects bar.

2. Click the New button on the Database window toolbar.

3. Click *AutoForm: Columnar* in the New Form list box.

4. Click the down-pointing triangle next to the Choose the table or query where the object's data comes from text box, click *Vendors* in the drop-down list, and then click OK.

In a few seconds the Vendors form appears, with the data from the first record in the table displayed in the form as shown in Figure A2.4.

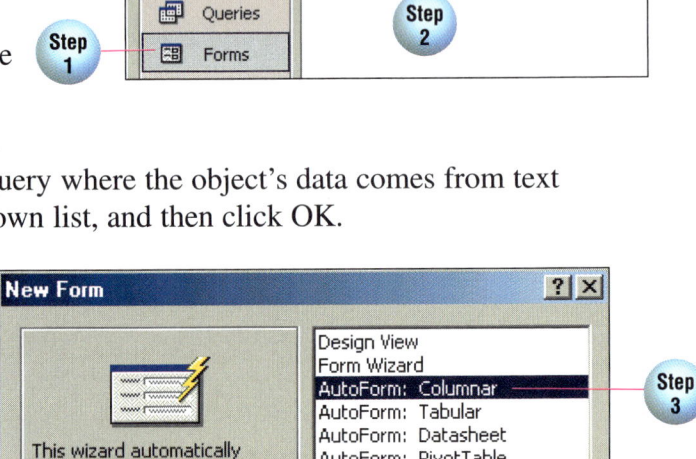

FIGURE A2.4 Vendors Form

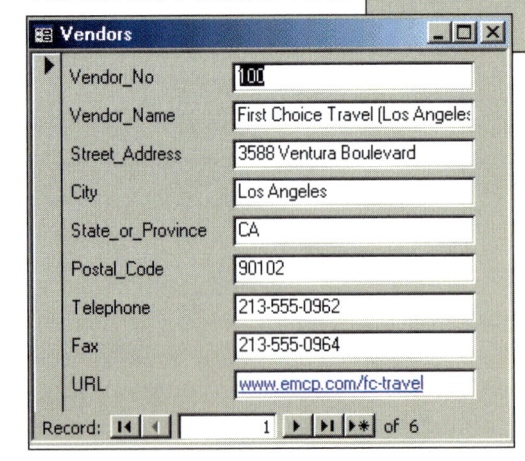

SECTION 2: CREATING TABLES AND RELATIONSHIPS

ACCESS

5. Click the Next Record button on the Record Navigation bar to display record 2 in the form.

6. Click the Last Record button on the Record Navigation bar to display record 6 in the form.

7. Click the First Record button on the Record Navigation bar to display record 1 in the form.

8. Print only the first record of the form. To do this, click File and then Print. Click Selected Record(s) in the Print Range section of the Print dialog box and then click OK.

9. Click the Close button on the Vendors form Title bar.

10. Click Yes to save changes to the design of the form.

11. Click OK in the Save As dialog box to accept the default form name *Vendors*.

12. Close the WE Purchases2 database.

In Addition

Tabular AutoForm

A tabular form displays one record below the other in a manner similar to a datasheet. The form displayed at the right was created by selecting *AutoForm: Tabular* and *Purchases* in the New Form dialog box.

In Brief

Create a Form Using AutoForm
1. Click Forms on the Objects bar.
2. Click New.
3. Click *AutoForm: Columnar, AutoForm: Tabular,* or *AutoForm: Datasheet*.
4. Choose table to create the form.
5. Click OK.

SECTION 2: CREATING TABLES AND RELATIONSHIPS

2.9 Creating a New Database Using a Wizard

Access provides database wizards that can be used to create new database files. The wizards include a series of dialog boxes that guide you through the steps of creating the database by selecting from predefined tables, fields, screen layouts, and report layouts. When the database is created, a Main Switchboard window displays on the Access screen in place of the Database window. The Main Switchboard is a special type of form that contains options used to access the various objects generated by Access. The Main Switchboard form is automatically displayed each time the database is opened.

PROJECT: You will create a new database to store contact information for Worldwide Enterprises using the Contact Management Wizard.

STEPS

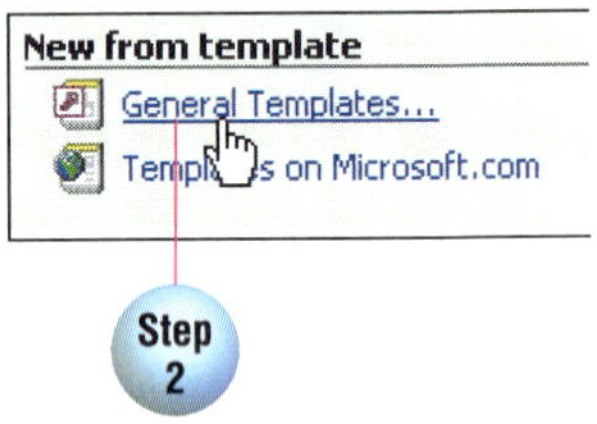

1. Click the New button on the Database toolbar.

2. Click the *General Templates* link in the New from template section of the New File Task Pane.

3. Click the Databases tab in the Templates dialog box and then double-click *Contact Management* in the Databases list box.

4. Key **WE Contacts** in the File name text box in the File New Database dialog box and then click Create.

5. Click Next at the first Database Wizard dialog box.

   This first dialog box contains information about the type of data the database will store.

6. Click Next at the second Database Wizard dialog box to accept the default fields in the tables.

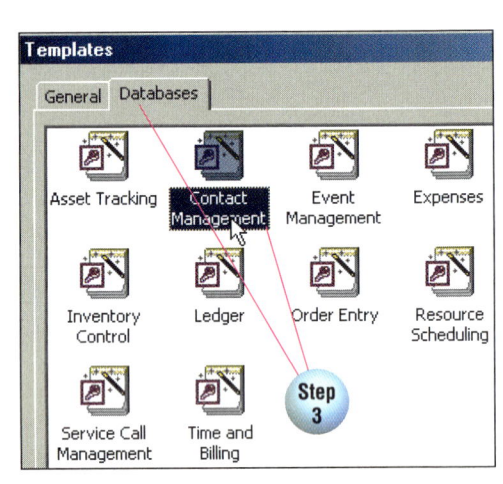

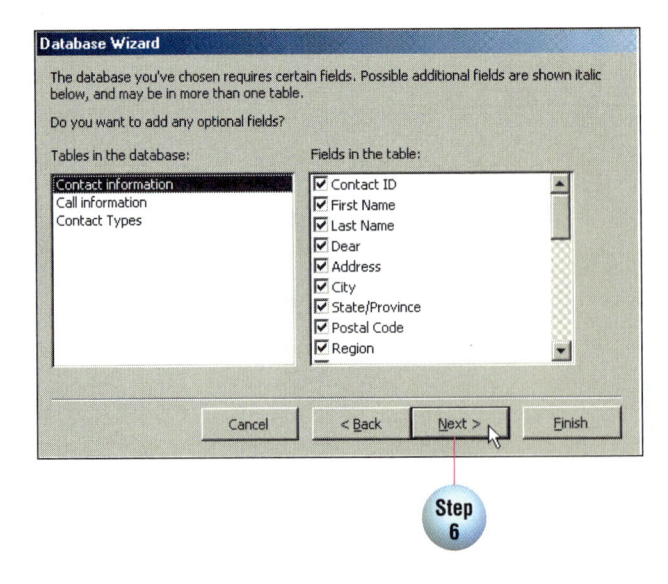

SECTION 2: CREATING TABLES AND RELATIONSHIPS

7 Click *International* as the screen display style in the third Database Wizard dialog box, and then click **N**ext.

> The preview box at the left of the Database Wizard dialog box changes to display the selected screen display style.

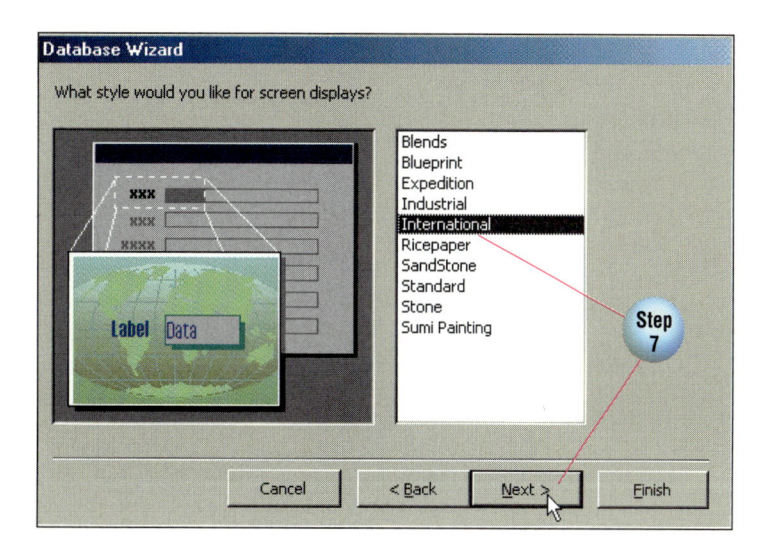

8 Click *Bold* for the report style in the fourth Database Wizard dialog box, and then click **N**ext.

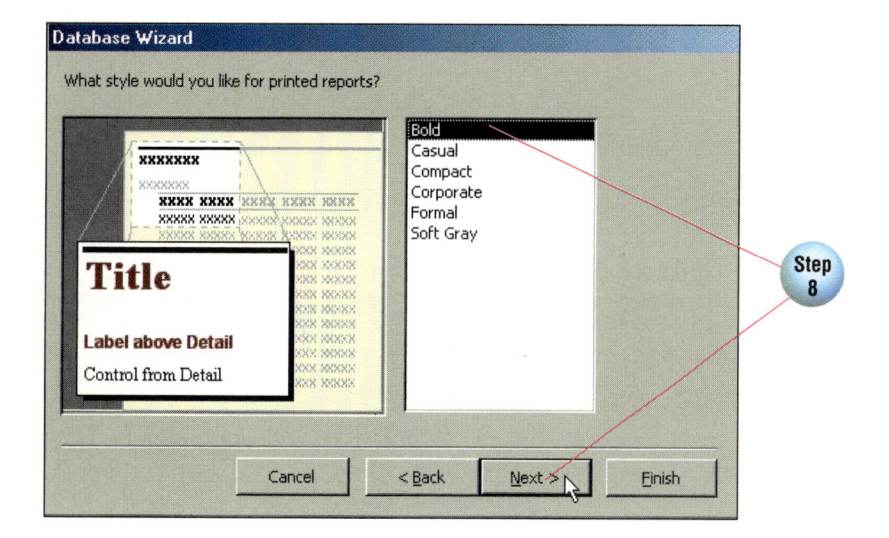

(continued)

SECTION 2: CREATING TABLES AND RELATIONSHIPS

9. Click Finish at the last Database Wizard dialog box to accept the default title of *Contact Management* for the database.

The Database Wizard will take a moment or two to create the tables, forms, and reports for the new database. A progress box will display indicating the tasks Access is completing. When the database is complete, Access will display the Main Switchboard window that is used to access the various components of the new database.

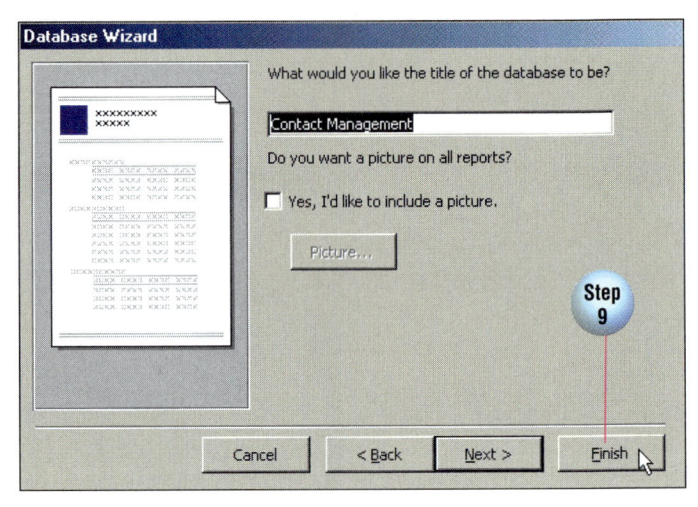

10. Click Enter/View Contacts in the Main Switchboard window.

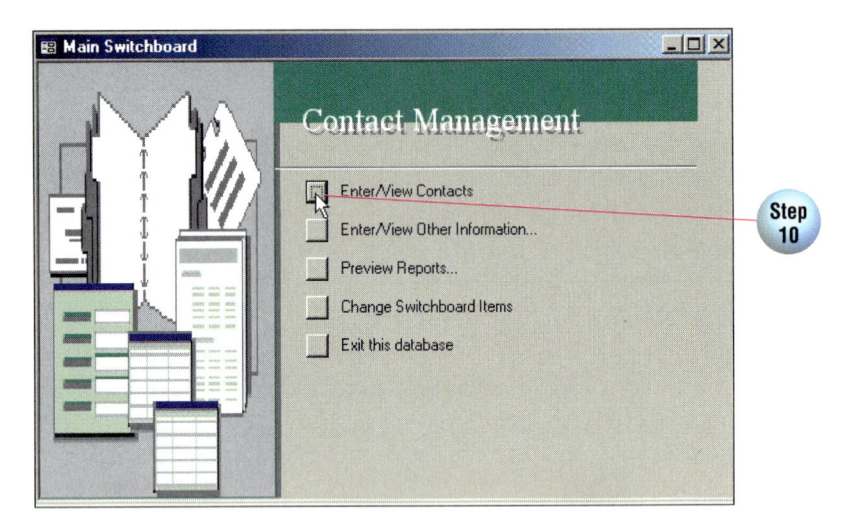

11. Key the data in the first record as shown in Figure A2.5.

FIGURE A2.5 Data for First Record

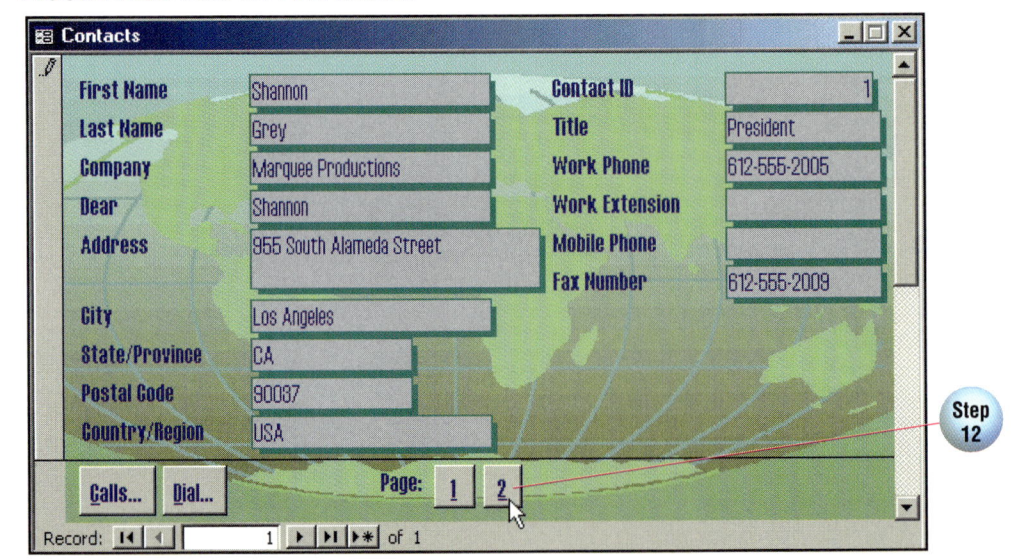

⑫ Click the button for Page 2 at the bottom of the record.

⑬ Key **sgrey@emcp.marquee.com** in the *Email Name* field.

⑭ Close the Contacts form.

⑮ Click Preview Reports in the Main Switchboard window.

⑯ Click Preview the Alphabetical Contact Listing Report.

⑰ Click the Print button on the Print Preview toolbar.

⑱ Click Close on the Print Preview toolbar.

⑲ Click Return to Main Switchboard in the Reports Switchboard window.

⑳ Click Exit this database in the Main Switchboard window.

In Addition

Closing the Main Switchboard

The Main Switchboard window can be closed if you prefer to work with the objects in the Database window. Click the Close button on the Main Switchboard Title bar. A minimized title bar with the name of the database will be positioned just above the Status bar. Click the Maximize or Restore button on the Database Title bar to restore the Database window. Tables or other objects can be customized by opening them in Design view and making the required changes. To return to the Main Switchboard after closing it, double-click *Switchboard* in the Forms list as shown at the right.

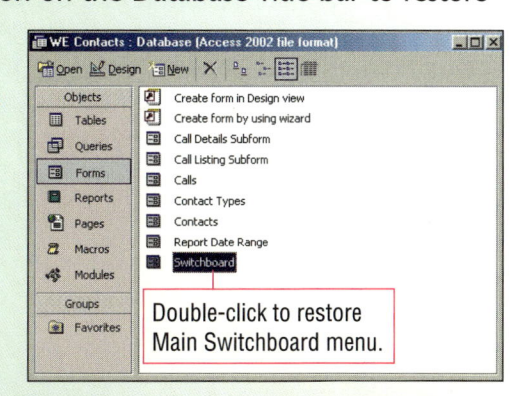

In Brief

Create a New Database Using a Wizard
1. Click New button.
2. Click *General Templates* link in New File Task Pane.
3. Click Databases tab in Templates dialog box and then double-click desired database wizard.
4. Key database file name and click Create.
5. Click Next.
6. Select tables and fields to include and click Next.
7. Select screen layout and click Next.
8. Select report style and click Next.
9. Key title for database and click Next.
10. Click Finish.

SECTION 2: CREATING TABLES AND RELATIONSHIPS

FEATURES SUMMARY

Feature	Button	Menu	Keyboard
AutoForm		Insert, Form	
Database Wizard	🗋	File, New	Ctrl + N
Datasheet view		View, Datasheet View	
Design view		View, Design View	
Lookup Wizard		Insert, Lookup Field	
Primary Key	🔑	Edit, Primary Key	
Relationships		Tools, Relationships	
Save table	💾	File, Save	Ctrl + S
Table Wizard		Insert, Table, Table Wizard	

PROCEDURES CHECK

Completion: In the space provided at the right, indicate the correct term or command.

1. A new table can be created in a database using Table Design view, or by selecting from predefined tables using this feature. _____
2. Assign a field this data type if the field will contain dollar values that you do not want rounded off in calculations. _____
3. This is the term for the field in a table that must contain unique information for each record. _____
4. This is the name of the wizard used to create a drop-down list of entries that will appear when the user clicks in the field. _____
5. This is the name of the wizard that is used to create a pattern in a field that indicates the format in which the data is to be entered. _____
6. Enter a conditional statement in this field property to prevent data that does not meet the criteria from being entered into the field. _____
7. This wizard automatically creates a form that includes all of the fields in the specified table with the fields arranged vertically. _____
8. Enter a value in this field property if you want the value to appear automatically in the field whenever a new record is created. _____
9. One table in a relationship is referred to as the primary table and the other table is referred to as this. _____
10. Click this button on the Database toolbar to select a Database Wizard. _____

SKILLS REVIEW

Activity 1: CREATING A TABLE IN DESIGN VIEW

1. Open the WE Employees2 database.
2. Create a table in Design view using the following field names and data types. You determine an appropriate description.

Field Name	Data Type
Emp No	Text
Supervisor	Text
Perf Review Date	Date/Time
Salary Increment Date	Date/Time
Training Days	Number

3. Define the *Emp No* field as the primary key.
4. Save the table and name it Review and Development.
5. Switch to Datasheet view and then enter the following two records:

Emp No	**1015**	*Emp No*	**1030**
Supervisor	**Sam Vestering**	*Supervisor*	**Roman Deptulski**
Perf Review Date	**5/20/03**	*Perf Review Date*	**1/24/03**
Salary Increment Date	**7/01/03**	*Salary Increment Date*	**3/03/03**
Training Days	**5**	*Training Days*	**10**

6. Best Fit the column widths.
7. Close the Review and Development table. Click Yes when prompted to save layout changes.

Activity 2: CHANGING FIELD SIZE; VALIDATING ENTRIES; CREATING AN INPUT MASK

1. Open the Review and Development table in Design view.
2. Change the field size for the *Emp No* field to *4*.
3. Create a validation rule for the *Training Days* field to ensure that no number greater than 10 is entered into the field. Enter an appropriate validation text error message.
4. Save the table. Click Yes to test the data with the new rules.
5. Use the Input Mask Wizard in each date field to set the pattern for entering dates to *Medium Date*.
6. Change the format property for the two date fields to display the date in the Medium Date format.
7. Save the table.
8. Switch to Datasheet view and add the following two records:

Emp No	**1035**	*Emp No*	**1040**
Supervisor	**Hanh Postma**	*Supervisor*	**Roman Deptulski**
Perf Review Date	**14-Mar-03**	*Perf Review Date*	**10-Mar-03**
Salary Increment Date	**01-May-03**	*Salary Increment Date*	**01-May-03**
Training Days	**8**	*Training Days*	**6**

9   Preview and then print the Review and Development table.
10 Close the Review and Development table.

Activity 3: CREATING A TABLE USING THE TABLE WIZARD; CREATING AN AUTOFORM

1   Double-click *Create table by using wizard*.
2   Scroll down the Sample Tables list box and then click *Expenses*.
3   Add the following fields from the Sample Fields list box to the Fields in my new table list box and then click Finish:

    EmployeeID
    ExpenseType
    AmountSpent
    DateSubmitted

4   Click the Design View button on the Table Datasheet toolbar to edit the table structure.
5   With *EmployeeID* selected in the *Field Name* column, key **Emp No**, change the Data Type to *Text*, change the Field Size property to *4*, and then delete the entry in the Caption field property box.
6   Save and then close the Expenses table.
7   Click Forms on the Objects bar and then create a new form using the AutoForm: Columnar wizard based on the Expenses table.
8   Using the Expenses form, add the following record to the Expenses table:

Emp No	**1001**
ExpenseType	**Sales**
AmountSpent	**$1,543.10**
DateSubmitted	**03/14/03**

9   Print the Expenses form.
10 Close the Expenses form. Click Yes to save changes and then click OK in the Save As dialog box to accept the default Form Name of *Expenses*.

Activity 4: CREATING A ONE-TO-MANY RELATIONSHIP

1   Open the Employees table in Datasheet view.
2   Add the following record to the table:

Emp No	**1001**
First Name	**Sam**
Middle Name	**Lawrence**
Last Name	**Vestering**
Address	**287-1501 Broadway**
City	**New York**
State/Province	**NY**
Postal Code	**10110**

3   Best Fit the column widths.
4   Change the page orientation to landscape.
5   Print and then close the Employees table. Click Yes when prompted to save layout changes.

6. Open the Expenses table in Design view.
7. With the *Emp No* field selected, click the Primary Key button to remove the *Emp No* field as a primary key. *(Note: You are removing the primary key in the Expenses table so that the relationship that will be created in steps 9–12 will be a one-to-many relationship. If* Emp No *remained as a primary key, Access would create a one-to-one relationship.)*
8. Click the Save button and then close the Expenses table.
9. Click the Relationships button on the Database toolbar.
10. Add the Employees and the Expenses tables to the Relationships window and then close the Show Table dialog box.
11. Create a one-to-many relationship by dragging the *Emp No* field name in the Employees field list box to the *Emp No* field name in the Employee Expenses field list box.
12. Click Enforce Referential Integrity and then click Create in the Edit Relationships dialog box.
13. With the Relationships window open, click File and then Print Relationships.
14. Click the Print button on the Print Preview toolbar, and then click the Close button on the Relationships for WE Employees2 Title bar.
15. Click Yes to save changes to the report design and then click OK in the Save As dialog box to accept the default Report Name of *Relationships for WE Employees2*.
16. Close the Relationships window.
17. Close the WE Employees2 database.

PERFORMANCE PLUS

Activity 1: CREATING A TABLE IN DESIGN VIEW; CREATING A LOOKUP FIELD

1. Gina Simmons, instructor in the Theatre Arts Division of Niagara Peninsula College, has asked you to create a new table to store the grades for the MKP245 course she teaches. Gina would like to be able to select the student grade from a drop-down list rather than key it in.
2. Open the NPC Grades2 database.
3. Create a new table in Design view using the following field names: *Student No*; *Last Name*; *First Name*; *Grade*. You determine the appropriate data type and descriptions for each field with the exception of the *Grade* field.
4. Use the Lookup Wizard in the *Grade* field to create a drop-down list with the following grades: A+, A, B, C, D, F.
5. Define the *Student No* field as the primary key.
6. Save the table and name it MKP245.
7. Enter the following four records in Datasheet view:

Student No	**111-785-156**	*Student No*	**118-487-578**
Last Name	**Bastow**	*Last Name*	**Andre**
First Name	**Maren**	*First Name*	**Ian**
Grade	**A+**	*Grade*	**C**
Student No	**137-845-746**	*Student No*	**138-456-749**
Last Name	**Knowlton**	*Last Name*	**Yiu**
First Name	**Sherri**	*First Name*	**Terry**
Grade	**B**	*Grade*	**D**

SECTION 1: CREATING TABLES AND RELATIONSHIPS

8 Best Fit the column widths.
9 Preview, print, and then close the MKP245 table.
10 Close the NPC Grades2 database.

Activity 2: CHANGING FIELD SIZE; VALIDATING ENTRIES; CREATING AN INPUT MASK

1 Bobbie Sinclair, business manager of Performance Threads, has asked you to look at the design of the Costume Inventory table and try to improve it with data restrictions and validation rules. While looking at the design, you discover an error was made in assigning the data type for the *Date In* field.
2 Open the PT Costume Inventory2 database.
3 Open the Costume Inventory table in Design view.
4 Change the *Date In* field to a Date/Time data field.
5 Change the field size for the *Costume No* field to *5*.
6 Performance Threads has a minimum daily rental fee of $80.00. Create a validation rule and validation text property that will ensure no one enters a value less than $80.00 in the *Daily Rental Fee* field.
7 To ensure no one mixes the order of the month and day when entering the *Date Out* and *Date In* fields, create an input mask for these two fields to require that the date be entered in the Medium Date format.
8 Since Performance Threads is open seven days a week, format the *Date Out* and *Date In* fields to display the dates in the Long Date format. This will add the day of the week to the entry and spell the month in full.
9 Save the table and then switch to Datasheet view.
10 Best Fit the columns.
11 Preview, print, and then close the Costume Inventory table.
12 Close the PT Costume Inventory2 database.

Activity 3: CREATING A TABLE USING THE TABLE WIZARD; ESTABLISHING RELATIONSHIPS

1 Dana Hirsch, manager of The Waterfront Bistro, has asked you to create a new table in the Inventory database that will store the supplier information. Since the Table Wizard provides a sample Suppliers table, you decide the wizard would be the most expedient method to use.
2 Open WB Inventory2.
3 Create a new table using the Table Wizard. Use the Suppliers sample table and add the following fields to the new table: *SupplierID*; *SupplierName*; *Address*; *City*; *StateOrProvince*; *PostalCode*; *PhoneNumber*; *FaxNumber*.
4 Choose the option to set the primary key yourself, select the *SupplierID* field as the primary key field, and set the type of data to *Numbers and/or letters I enter when I add new records*.
5 Accept all other default settings in the wizard dialog boxes.
6 Switch to Design view for the new table.
7 Change the field name for *SupplierID* to *Supplier Code*, change the field size to *50*, and delete the entry in the Caption field property box.
8 Enter the following record in the new table:

    Supplier Code   **1**
    SupplierName   **Danby's Bakery**
    Address   **3168 Rivermist Drive**

City	**Buffalo**
StateOrProvince	**NY**
PostalCode	**14280**
PhoneNumber	**(716) 555-4987**
FaxNumber	**(716) 555-5101**

9. Best Fit the column widths.
10. Change the page orientation to landscape, print, and then close the Suppliers table.
11. Display the Relationships window.
12. Create a one-to-many relationship based on the *Supplier Code* field with the Suppliers table as the primary table and the Inventory List table as the related table. Enforce referential integrity when you create the relationship.
13. Print the relationships. *(Refer to Skills Review Activity 4, steps 13–15 if you need help with this step.)*
14. Close the WB Inventory2 database.

Activity 4: CREATING A NEW DATABASE

1. Alex Torres, manager of the Toronto office of First Choice Travel, has asked you to help the accounting staff by creating a database to track employee expense claims information. You recall that Access includes a Database Wizard that will create the database tables, forms, and reports. The Database Wizard also creates the Main Switchboard form, which you feel the accounting staff would find easier to use.
2. Create a new database file named FCT Expenses using the Expenses Database Wizard. Use all of the default fields. Select a screen display and report style that the accounting staff would like. Accept all other default settings in the Database Wizard.
3. Enter the following record in the Expense Reports by Employee form. Leave any other fields blank.

Terry Blessing
3341 Ventura Boulevard
Los Angeles, CA 90102
President

Employee #	**LA-104**
Social Security #	**345-99-1234**
Work Phone	**(213) 555-0962**

4. Click the Expense Report Form button at the bottom of the record for Terry Blessing and then enter the following expense report data. Leave any other fields blank.

Exp Rpt Name	**Head Office**
Exp Rpt Descr	**Meeting in Toronto Office**
Dept Charged	**Executive Administration**
Advance	**675.00**
Paid	(click the check box)

5. Close the Expense Reports form.
6. With the Expense Reports by Employee form in the current window, click File and then Print. Click Selected Record(s) in the Print dialog box and then click OK.
7. Close the Expense Reports by Employee form.
8. Click Exit this database in the Main Switchboard window.

Activity 5: FINDING INFORMATION ON DELETING RELATIONSHIPS

1. Use Access's Help feature to find information on how to delete a relationship.
2. Print the Help topic that you find.
3. Open the WE Employees2 database.
4. Display the Relationships window and then delete the one-to-many relationship between the Employees and the Expenses tables.
5. Click Yes to confirm that you want to delete the selected relationship.
6. Save and then close the Relationships window.
7. Close the WE Employees2 database.

Activity 6: FINDING INFORMATION ON REQUIRED ENTRIES

1. Use Help to find information on requiring that data be entered into a field. For example, you want to specify that a field cannot be left blank. *(Hint: Key **blank fields** in the Ask a Question box.)*
2. Print the Help topic you find.
3. Open the WE Employees2 database.
4. Open the Employees table in Design view.
5. You want to make sure that all records in the table have an entry in the *PostalCode* field, since you will be using this table to print mailing labels. Using the information you learned in the online help, change the field property for the *PostalCode* field to ensure that the field will have data entered in it.
6. Save the table and switch to Datasheet view.
7. Add a new record to the table. Use your name and address as the *Employee* information. When you reach the *PostalCode* field, try to press Enter to move past the field without entering any data. When Access displays the error message, click OK. Enter your postal code in the *PostalCode* field.
8. Change the page orientation to landscape and then print the Employees table.
9. Close the Employees table and then close the WE Employees2 database.

Activity 7: CAR SHOPPING ON THE INTERNET

1. After graduation, you plan to reward yourself by buying a new car. Identify at least three different makes and models of cars that you like.
2. Search the Internet for the manufacturer's suggested retail price (MSRP) for the cars you would like to own, including whatever options you would order with the vehicle. *(Hint: Try searching by the manufacturers' names to locate their Web sites.)*
3. Create a new database in Access to store the information you find.
    - Click the New button on the Database toolbar, and then click the <u>Blank Database</u> link in the New section of the New File Task Pane.
    - Key **New Cars** in the File <u>n</u>ame text box in the File New Database dialog box and then click <u>C</u>reate.
4. Create a table named New Car Pricing using Design view. Include the manufacturer's name, brand, model of the car, options, and MSRP. Include other fields that you might want to track, such as color choice.
5. Best Fit the column widths.
6. Preview and then print the New Car Pricing table.
7. Close the New Car Pricing table and then close the New Cars database.

ACCESS SECTION 3
Creating Queries, Forms, and Reports

The ability to extract specific information from a table that can contain hundreds or thousands of records is an important feature in Access. Data is extracted from a table by performing a *query*. Creating a query is analogous to asking Access a question, such as *How many distributors are located in New York?* Forms are used to view, enter, and edit data. Generally, only one record at a time is displayed in a form. Forms can be designed to resemble existing forms used by the business, making the transition to an electronic database easier for employees. Reports are created to print the information in tables or queries in a variety of formats or styles. In this section you will learn the skills and complete the projects described here.

Note: Before beginning this section, delete from your disk any database files you created in Section 2. Next, copy to your disk as you need them the database files contained in the Access S3 *subfolder in the* Access *folder on the CD that accompanies this textbook. Remove the read-only attribute from each database as you copy it.*

Skills
- Create, run, and print a select query in Design view
- Add multiple tables to a query
- Create and run a query using the Simple Query Wizard
- Sort the query results
- Add criteria statements to a query
- Perform calculations in a query
- Create a parameter query
- Create a form using the Form Wizard
- Create a form with a subform
- Move and resize control objects
- Modify properties of controls
- Add objects using the Control Toolbox
- Create and print a report using the Report Wizard
- Resize controls in a report

Projects

Create queries to extract fields from tables to print custom employee lists, add criteria, and calculate pension contributions and monthly salaries; create and modify forms to facilitate data entry and viewing in the employees database; create and modify reports to produce custom printouts of employee and distributor data.

Create and print a query that will extract the records of students who achieved A+ in all of their courses.

Create a query, and create and print a report that lists all costumes rented in the month of August 2003; create and modify a form for browsing the costume inventory.

Create a query that prompts the user for a supplier code and then generates a list of inventory items for the specified supplier.

3.1 Creating a Query in Design View

A *query* is an Access object that is designed to extract specific data from a table. Queries can be created to serve a variety of purposes, from very simple field selection to complex conditional statements or calculations. When a table is viewed or printed in Datasheet view, all of the fields in the table are included. In its simplest form, a query selects only some of the fields from the table(s) to display or print. A criteria statement can be added to a query to display or print only certain records from the table(s). Queries can be saved for future use.

PROJECT: Rhonda Trask, human resources manager of Worldwide Enterprises, has asked for a list that includes employee number, employee name, date hired, department, and salary. This data is stored in two different tables. You will create a query to obtain the required fields from each table to generate the list.

STEPS

1. Open WE Employees3.
2. Click the Queries button on the Objects bar.
3. Double-click *Create query in Design view*.
4. Double-click *Employees* in the Show Table dialog box with the Tables tab selected.

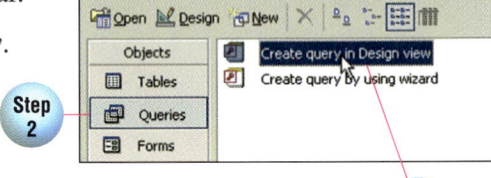

   A field list box for the Employees table is added to the top of the Query1 : Select Query window.

5. Double-click *Employee Dates and Salaries* in the Show Table dialog box.

   A black join line between the Employees and the Employee Dates and Salaries tables appears indicating a one-to-one relationship has been defined between the two tables.

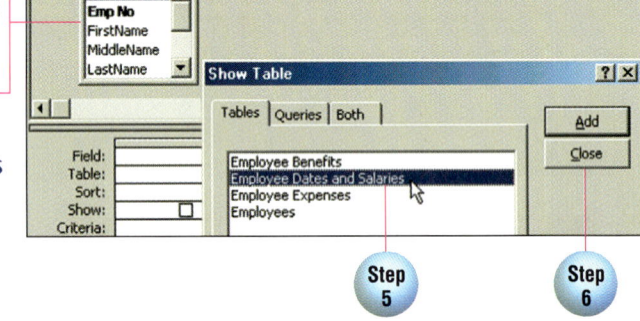

6. Click **C**lose to close the Show Table dialog box.

7. Double-click *Emp No* in the Employees field list box.

   Emp No is added to the Field row in the first column of the design grid. In steps 8 and 9 you will practice two other methods of adding fields to the design grid.

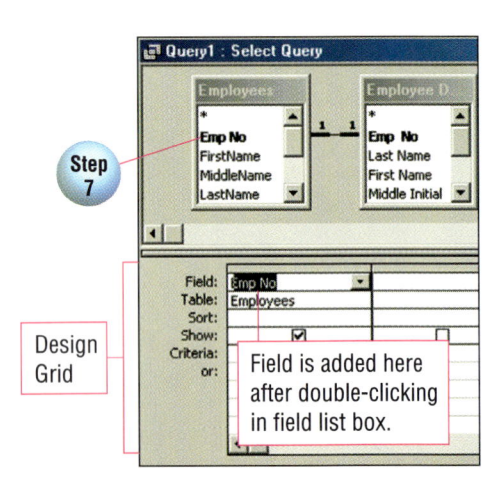

8. Position the mouse pointer on the *FirstName* field in the Employees field list box, hold down the left mouse button, drag the field to the Field row in the second column of the design grid, and then release the mouse button.

9. Click in the Field row in the third column of the design grid, click the down-pointing triangle that appears, and then click *Employees.LastName* in the drop-down list.

10. Using any of the three methods learned in steps 7–9, add the fields *Hire Date*, *Department*, and *Annual Salary* from the Employee Dates and Salaries field list box to the design grid. You may need to scroll down the field list box to see the required field names.

11. Click the Save button on the Query Design toolbar.

12. Key **Trask Employee List** in the Query Name text box in the Save As dialog box and then press Enter or click OK.

13. Click the Run button on the Query Design toolbar.

   The query results are displayed in Datasheet view as shown in Figure A3.1. The query results datasheet can be sorted, edited, or formatted in a manner similar to a datasheet. Data displayed in query results is not stored as a separate entity—the query is simply another interface for viewing and editing data in the associated table(s).

FIGURE A3.1 Query Results Datasheet

Emp No	First Name	Last Name	Hire Date	Department	Annual Salary
1001	Sam	Vestering	7/22/1997	North American Distribution	$67,850.00
1005	Roman	Deptulski	8/15/1998	Overseas Distribution	$67,850.00
1010	Hanh	Postma	1/30/1998	European Distribution	$67,850.00
1015	Lyle	Besterd	5/17/1997	North American Distribution	$44,651.00
1020	Angela	Doxtator	8/3/1997	North American Distribution	$45,178.00
1025	Jorge	Biliski	12/1/1997	North American Distribution	$43,152.00
1030	Thom	Hicks	1/22/1998	Overseas Distribution	$41,624.00
1035	Valerie	Fistouris	3/15/1998	European Distribution	$43,664.00
1040	Guy	Lafreniere	3/10/1998	Overseas Distribution	$44,195.00
1045	Terry	Yiu	4/12/1999	European Distribution	$41,328.00
1050	Carl	Zakowski	2/9/1998	European Distribution	$43,698.00
1055	Edward	Thurston	6/22/1999	Overseas Distribution	$41,498.00
1060	Donald	McKnight	6/22/1998	European Distribution	$41,854.00
1065	Norm	Liszniewski	2/6/2000	North American Distribution	$42,659.00
1070	Balfor	Jhawar	11/22/2000	Overseas Distribution	$43,661.00
1075	Mike	Fitchett	3/19/2001	Overseas Distribution	$41,857.00
1080	Leo	Couture	1/17/2002	European Distribution	$42,185.00

14. Click the Print button on the Query Datasheet toolbar.

15. Close the Trask Employee List : Select Query window.

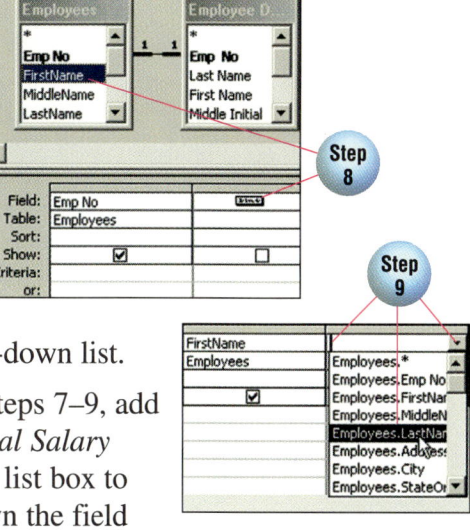

IN BRIEF

Create a Query in Design View
1. Click Queries on the Objects bar.
2. Double-click *Create query in Design view*.
3. Double-click required table(s) in Show Table dialog box.
4. Close Show Table dialog box.
5. Add required field names from field list box(es) to columns in design grid.
6. Click Save button.
7. Key query name and click OK.
8. Click Run button.

3.2 Using the Simple Query Wizard

Access includes the Simple Query Wizard to facilitate creating a query. At the first Simple Query Wizard dialog box, the table(s) and the fields within the table(s) are added to the query. Select a Detail or Summary query in the second dialog box. If you select Summary, click Summary Options to specify which field to group by and whether to calculate the sum, average, minimum, or maximum values in the group. Key the name for the query in the last dialog box.

PROJECT: Using the Simple Query Wizard, you will generate a printout that lists each employee's name, number of dependents, life insurance, vacation entitlement, and pension plan eligibility date.

STEPS

1. With WE Employees3 open and Queries selected on the Objects bar, double-click *Create query by using wizard*.

2. Click the down-pointing triangle next to the Tables/Queries list box and then click *Table: Employees* in the drop-down list.

3. With *Emp No* selected in the Available Fields list box, click the Add Field button > to move *Emp No* to the Selected Fields list box.

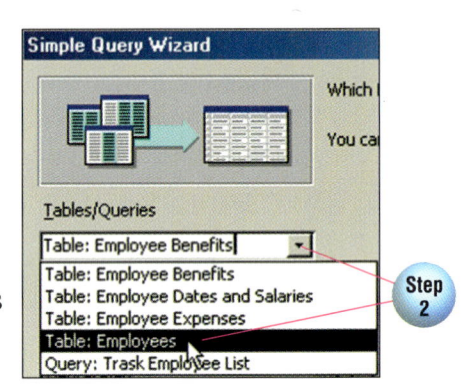

4. Click the Add Field button to move *FirstName* to the Selected Fields list box.

5. Click *LastName* in the Available Fields list box and then click the Add Field button.

6. Click the down-pointing triangle next to the Tables/Queries list box and then click *Table: Employee Benefits* in the drop-down list.

7. Double-click *Dependents* in the Available Fields list box.

   Double-clicking a field name is another way to move a field to the Selected Fields list box.

8. Move the following fields from the Available Fields list box to the Selected Fields list box:

   Life Insurance
   Vacation
   RPP Eligibility Date

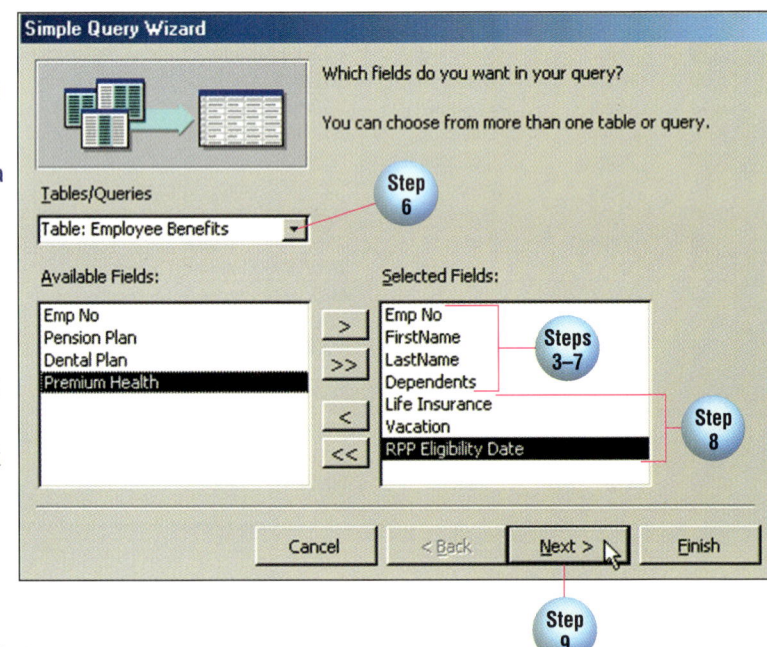

9. Click Next.

10. Click Next at the second Simple Query Wizard dialog box to accept the default Detail report.

SECTION 3: CREATING QUERIES, FORMS, AND REPORTS

ACCESS

11. Key **Employee Ins, Vac, and RPP** in the What title do you want for your query? text box, and then click Finish.

12. View the query results in the datasheet and then click the View button on the Query Datasheet toolbar to switch to Design view.

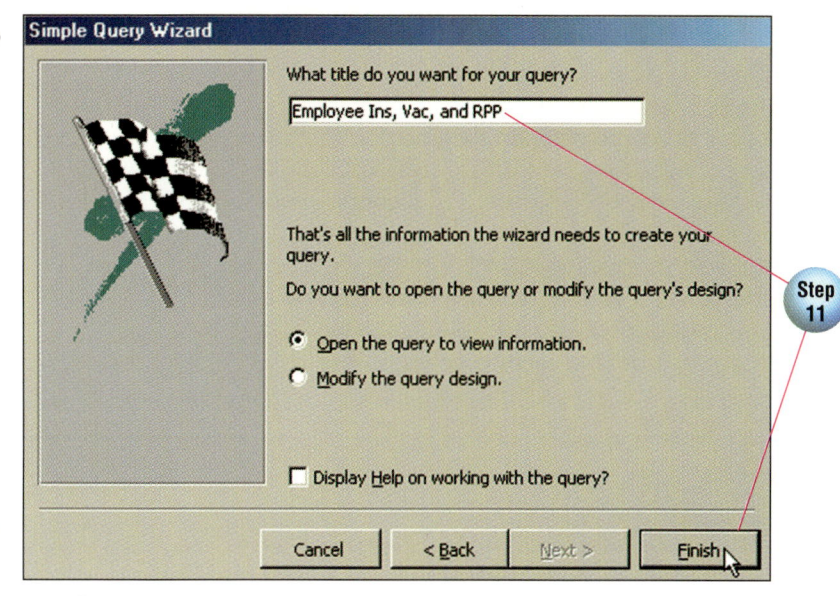

   In the next step you will modify the query design to sort the query results in ascending order by the employee's last name.

13. Click in the Sort row in the *LastName* column in the design grid, click the down-pointing triangle that appears, and then click *Ascending* in the drop-down list.

14. Click the Save button on the Query Design toolbar and then click the Run button.

    The query results datasheet appears with the records sorted by the *LastName* column.

15. View the query results datasheet, change the page orientation to landscape, and then print the query results.

16. Close the Employee Ins, Vac, and RPP Select Query window.

In Addition

Action Queries

In the last topic and in this topic, you have created *select* queries that displayed specific fields from a table. An *action* query makes changes to records in one procedure. There are four types of action queries: delete, update, append, and make-table. A delete query will delete a group of records from one or more tables. An update query is used to make global changes to a group of records in one or more tables. An append query adds a group of records from one or more tables to the end of one or more other tables. A make-table query will create a new table from all or part of the data in existing tables.

In Brief

Create a Query Using the Simple Query Wizard
1. Double-click *Create query by using wizard.*
2. Choose table(s) and field(s) to include in the query.
3. Click Next.
4. Choose Detail or Summary query.
5. Click Next.
6. Key title for query.
7. Click Finish.

SECTION 3: CREATING QUERIES, FORMS, AND REPORTS

ACCESS 69

3.3 Extracting Records Using Criteria Statements

All of the records in the tables were displayed in the query results datasheet in the two queries you have done so far. Adding a criterion statement to the query design grid will cause Access to display only those records that meet the criterion. For example, you could generate a list of employees who are entitled to four weeks of vacation. Extracting specific records from the tables is where the true power in creating queries is found since you are able to separate out only those records that serve your purpose.

PROJECT: Rhonda Trask has requested a list of employees who receive either three or four weeks of vacation. Since you already have the employee names and vacation fields in an existing query, you will modify the query to add the criteria statement.

STEPS

1. With WE Employees3 open and Queries selected on the Objects bar, right-click the Employee Ins, Vac, and RPP query and then click <u>D</u>esign View at the shortcut menu.

2. Maximize the query window if it is not already maximized.

3. Click in the Criteria row in the *Vacation* column in the design grid.

4. Key **4 weeks** and then press Enter.

    The insertion point moves to the Criteria row in the next column and Access inserts quotation marks around *4 weeks* in the *Vacation* column. Since quotation marks are required in criteria statements for text fields, Access automatically inserts them if they are not keyed into the Criteria text box.

5. Click in the or row in the *Vacation* column in the design grid (blank row below *4 weeks*), key **3 weeks**, and then press Enter.

    Including a second criteria statement below the first one instructs Access to display records that meet either of the two criteria.

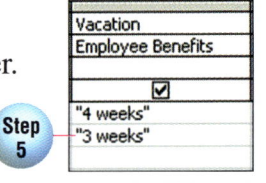

6. Click <u>F</u>ile and then Save <u>A</u>s. Key **Employees with 3 or 4 weeks vacation** in the Save Query 'Employee Ins, Vac, and…' To text box in the Save As dialog box, and then click OK.

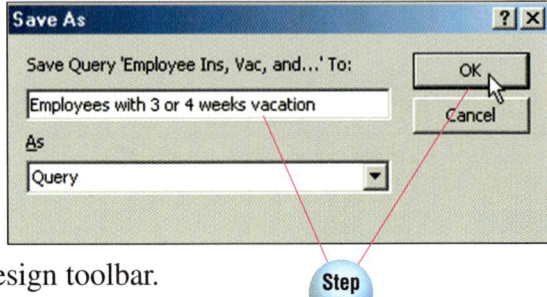

7. Click the Run button on the Query Design toolbar.

PROBLEM? Is the query results datasheet blank? Check the criteria statement in Design view. A keying error, such as **4 weks** instead of **4 weeks**, can cause a blank datasheet to appear.

8. View the query results in the datasheet and then click the View button on the Query Datasheet toolbar to switch to Design view.

    Since Rhonda Trask is interested only in the employee names and vacation weeks, you will instruct Access not to display the other fields in the query results datasheet.

9. Click the check box in the Show row in the *Dependents* column to remove the check mark.

   Deselecting the check box instructs Access to hide the column in the query results datasheet.

10. Deselect the Show check boxes in the *Life Insurance* and *RPP Eligibility Date* columns in the design grid.

11. Run the query.

12. Print the query results datasheet.

13. Close the Employees with 3 or 4 weeks vacation : Select Query window. Click Yes to save changes to the design of the query.

    Examples of other criteria statements are listed in Table A3.1.

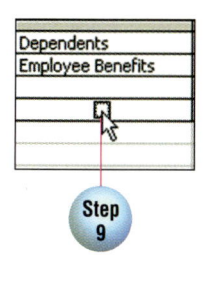

TABLE A3.1 Criteria Examples

Criteria Statement	Records That Would Be Extracted
"Finance Department"	Those with *Finance Department* in the field
Not "Finance Department"	All *except* those with *Finance Department* in the field
"Fan*"	Those that begin *Fan* and end with any other characters in the field
>15000	Those with a value greater than 15,000 in the field
>=15000 And <=20000	Those with a value from 15,000 to 20,000 in the field
#05/01/03#	Those that contain the date May 1, 2003 in the field
>#05/01/03#	Those that contain dates after May 1, 2003 in the field

In Addition

Extracting Based on Two or More Criteria Statements

A query can be created that extracts records based on meeting two or more criteria statements at the same time. In the query design grid shown below, Access will display the records of employees who work in the North American Distribution department *and* who earn over $40,000. Keying two criteria in the same row means the record will have to satisfy *both* criteria to be displayed in the query results datasheet.

Field:	FirstName	LastName	Department	Annual Salary
Table:	Employees	Employees	Employee Dates and Salaries	Employee Dates and
Sort:				
Show:	☑	☑	☑	☑
Criteria:			"North American Distribution"	>40000
or:				

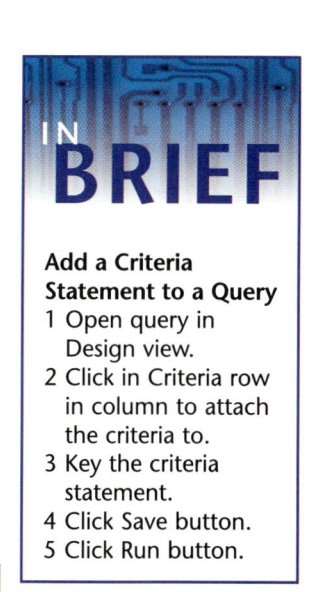

In Brief

Add a Criteria Statement to a Query
1. Open query in Design view.
2. Click in Criteria row in column to attach the criteria to.
3. Key the criteria statement.
4. Click Save button.
5. Click Run button.

SECTION 3: CREATING QUERIES, FORMS, AND REPORTS

3.4 Performing Calculations in a Query

A calculated field can be included in the query design grid. To do this, in a blank Field text box in the design grid key a field name followed by a colon and then the mathematical expression for the calculated values. Field names included in the mathematical expression are encased in square brackets. For example, the entry *Total Salary:[Base Salary]+[Commission]* would add the value in the field named *Base Salary* to the value in the field named *Commission*. The result would be placed in a new column in the query datasheet with the column heading *Total Salary*. The values in the *Total Salary* column do not exist in the table used to create the query; they are dynamically calculated each time the query is run.

PROJECT: Worldwide Enterprises contributes 6% of each employee's annual salary to a registered pension plan. You will modify the Trask Employee List query to include a calculation for the employer pension contribution.

STEPS

1. With WE Employees3 open and Queries selected on the Objects bar, open the Trask Employee List query in Design view.

2. Click File and then Save As.

3. Key **Employer Pension Contributions** and then click OK in the Save As dialog box.

    In the next step you will delete the *Hire Date* and *Department* columns in the design grid, since they are not required in the new query.

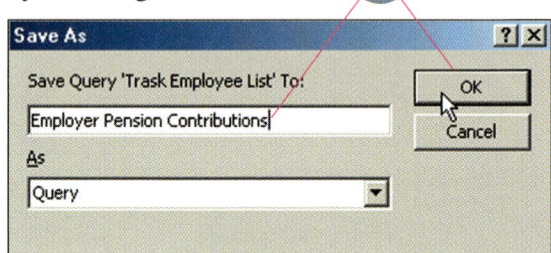

4. Position the mouse pointer in the gray field selector bar above the *Hire Date* field in the design grid until the pointer changes to a downward-pointing black arrow, hold down the left mouse button, drag right to select both the *Hire Date* and *Department* columns, and then release the mouse button.

5. Click Edit and then Cut.

    The selected columns are deleted from the design grid.

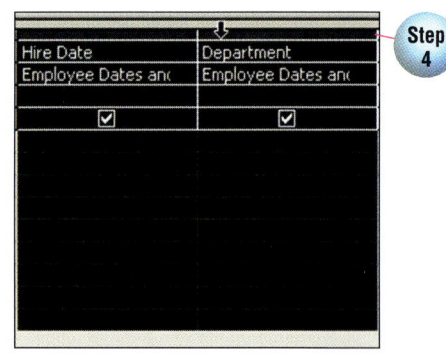

6. Click in the blank Field row next to the *Annual Salary* column in the design grid.

7. Key **Pension Contribution:[Annual Salary]*.06** and then press Enter.

   PROBLEM? Message appears stating expression has invalid syntax? Check that you have used the correct type of brackets, keyed a colon, and that there are no other keying errors.

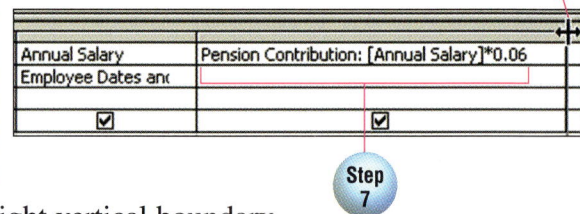

8. Position the mouse pointer on the right vertical boundary line in the gray field selector bar above the *Pension Contribution* column until the pointer changes to a black vertical line with a left- and right-pointing arrow, and then double-click the left mouse button.

    Double-clicking the right field boundary line adjusts the width of the column to the length of the text in the field row.

SECTION 3: CREATING QUERIES, FORMS, AND REPORTS

ACCESS

9 Click the Save button and then click the Run button.

PROBLEM? Does an Enter Parameter Value dialog box appear? A mistake in keying of *[Annual Salary]* in the calculated field will cause Access to display this dialog box, since it does not recognize the field name.

10 Best Fit the *Pension Contribution* column in the query results datasheet.

The values in the calculated column need to be formatted to display a consistent number of decimal values.

11 Switch to Design view.

12 Click the insertion point anywhere within the *Pension Contribution* field row in the design grid and then click the Properties button on the Query Design toolbar.

13 Click in the Format property box, click the down-pointing triangle that appears, and then click *Currency* in the drop-down list.

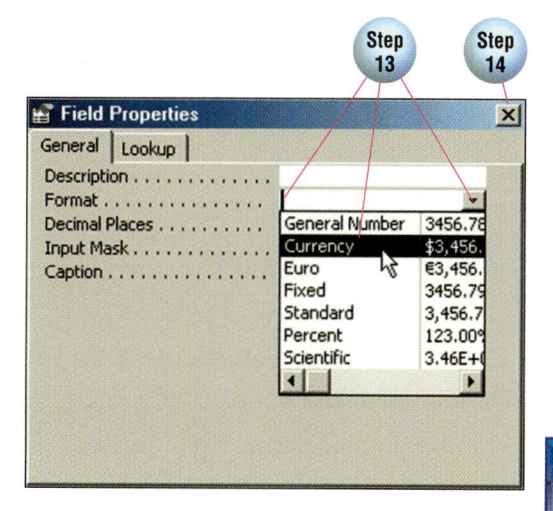

14 Click the Close button on the Field Properties Title bar.

15 Click the Save button and then click the Run button.

16 Print the query results datasheet.

17 Close the Employer Pension Contributions query.

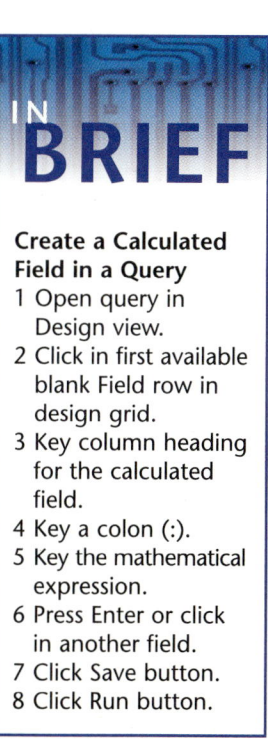

IN BRIEF

Create a Calculated Field in a Query
1. Open query in Design view.
2. Click in first available blank Field row in design grid.
3. Key column heading for the calculated field.
4. Key a colon (:).
5. Key the mathematical expression.
6. Press Enter or click in another field.
7. Click Save button.
8. Click Run button.

SECTION 3: CREATING QUERIES, FORMS, AND REPORTS

ACCESS 73

3.5 Creating a Parameter Query

A parameter query displays a dialog box when the query is run asking the user which records to extract from the table. The user keys the criteria in the dialog box and then Access displays the query results. A parameter query is useful if you frequently want to query a table for different values within the same field. For example, you could create a parameter query that asks the user which state they want to view. This query could then be used for producing lists of records that have different state values in the field without the user having to modify the criteria statement in the design grid each time.

PROJECT: Rhonda Trask has decided she would like separate lists of employees for each vacation entitlement of one week, two weeks, three weeks, or four weeks. You will modify the Employees with 3 or 4 weeks vacation query to create a parameter query that will allow you to enter the vacation criteria when the query is run.

STEPS

1. With WE Employees3 open and Queries selected on the Objects bar, open the Employees with 3 or 4 weeks vacation query in Design view.

2. Click File and then Save As.

3. Key **Employee Vacation Entitlements** and then click OK in the Save As dialog box.

4. Select the text in the Criteria row for the *Vacation* column.

5. Press Delete.

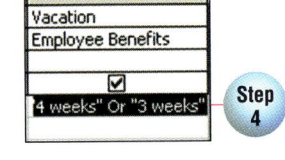

   To create a parameter query, in the Criteria row of the field that will contain the variable data key a question or phrase encased in square brackets. The text within the square brackets is displayed in a dialog box when the query is run.

6. With the insertion point positioned in the Criteria row of the *Vacation* column, key **[Which vacation entitlement do you want?]** and then press Enter or click in another field.

7. Position the mouse pointer on the right vertical boundary line in the field selector bar above *Vacation* until the pointer changes to a vertical line with a left- and right-pointing arrow, and then double-click the left mouse button.

8. Click the Save button and then click the Run button.

   The Enter Parameter Value dialog box appears with the question text *Which vacation entitlement do you want?*

9. Key **1 week** in the Enter Parameter Value dialog box and then press Enter or click OK.

   PROBLEM Enter Parameter Value dialog box does not appear? Check the design grid and make sure you keyed the question text in square brackets.

   The query results datasheet appears with only those records of employees with a field value of *1 week* in the *Vacation* column.

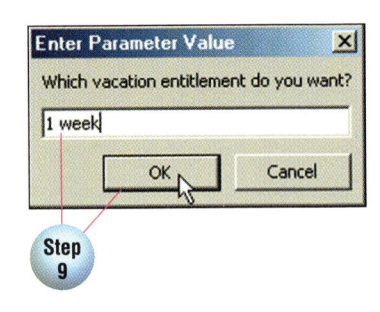

10. Print and then close the Employees Vacation Entitlements query.

11. With Queries selected on the Objects bar, double-click *Employee Vacation Entitlements*.

12. Key **2 weeks** in the Enter Parameter Value dialog box and then press Enter or click OK.

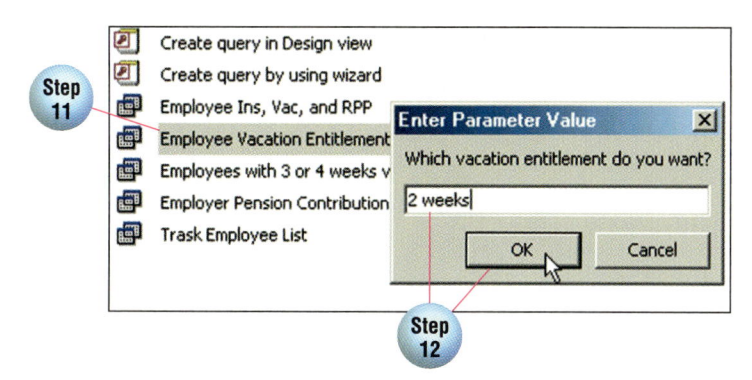

The query results datasheet appears with only those records of employees with a field value of *2 weeks* in the *Vacation* column.

13. Print and then close the Employee Vacation Entitlements query.

14. Repeat steps 11–13 to produce a list of employees with a field value of *3 weeks* in the *Vacation* column.

15. Repeat steps 11–13 to produce a list of employees with a field value of *4 weeks* in the *Vacation* column.

In Addition

Creating Two or More Parameters

A parameter query is not limited to displaying only one Enter Parameter Value dialog box. For each field that will be variable, enter in the Criteria row in the design grid a question or phrase in square brackets. Access will display a separate Enter Parameter Value for each field. For example, in the design grid shown below, Access will display first the question *What date was the costume taken out?* in an Enter Parameter Value dialog box. Once the user keys the date and clicks OK, Access will then display the question *What date was the costume returned?* in a second Enter Parameter Value dialog box.

In Brief

Create a Parameter Query
1. Open query in Design view.
2. Click in Criteria row of field to create parameter for.
3. Key question text in square brackets.
4. Press Enter or click in another field.
5. Click Save button.
6. Click Run button.

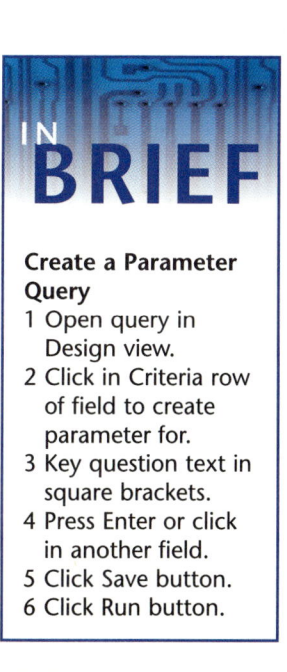

SECTION 3: CREATING QUERIES, FORMS, AND REPORTS

3.6 Creating a Form Using the Form Wizard

In the previous section, you learned how to create a form using the AutoForm Wizard. AutoForm automatically includes all of the fields in the selected table. The layout and style are predefined based on the selection of AutoForm: Columnar, AutoForm: Tabular, or AutoForm: Datasheet in the New Form dialog box. The Form Wizard provides more choices for the form design than AutoForm. In the Form Wizard the user is guided through a series of dialog boxes to generate the form, including selecting the table and fields that will be used to make up the form; choosing a layout for the fields; selecting the form style from various colors and backgrounds; and entering a title for the form.

PROJECT: You will create a form for the Employee Dates and Salaries table; a form for the Employee Benefits table; and a form with a subform for the Employees and Employee Expenses tables using the Form Wizard.

STEPS

1. With WE Employees3 open, click Forms on the Objects bar, and then double-click *Create form by using wizard*.

2. Click the down-pointing triangle next to the Tables/Queries list box and then click *Table: Employee Dates and Salaries* in the drop-down list.

   The list of fields in the Available Fields list box changes to the field names for the Employee Dates and Salaries table. In the next step you will choose which fields to include in the form.

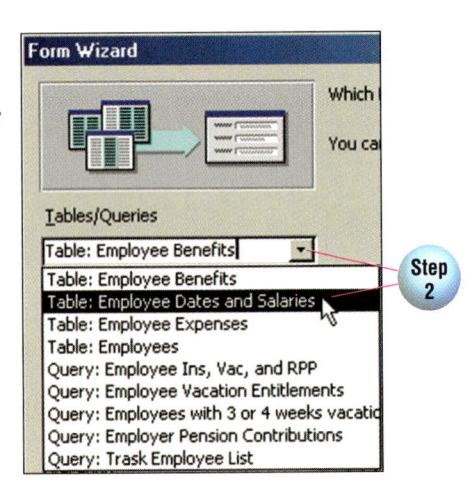

3. Click the Add All Fields button >> to move all of the fields in the Available Fields list box to the Selected Fields list box, and then click Next.

4. Click Tabular in the second Form Wizard dialog box to view the tabular layout in the preview window.

5. Click Datasheet to preview the datasheet layout.

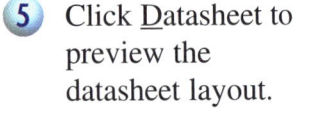

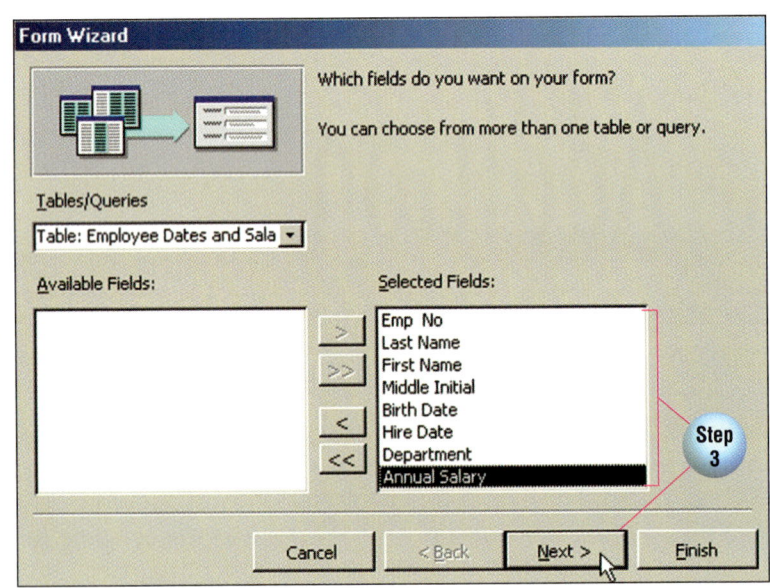

6. Click Justified to preview the justified layout.

ACCESS

76

SECTION 3: CREATING QUERIES, FORMS, AND REPORTS

ACCESS

7 Click Columnar and then click Next.

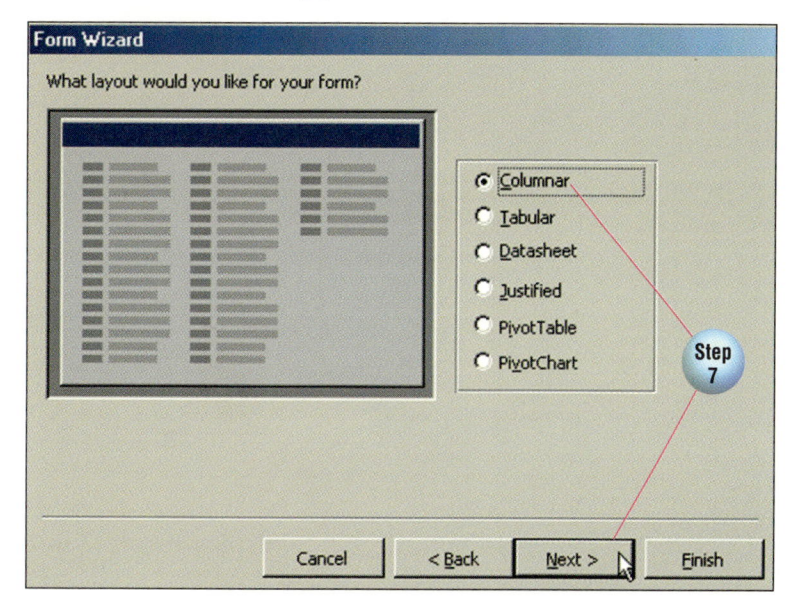

8 Click each of the styles in the list box in the third Form Wizard dialog box to preview each style's colors and backgrounds in the preview window.

9 Click Industrial and then click Next.

10 Click Finish at the last Form Wizard dialog box to accept the default title of *Employee Dates and Salaries* and *Open the form to view or enter information*.

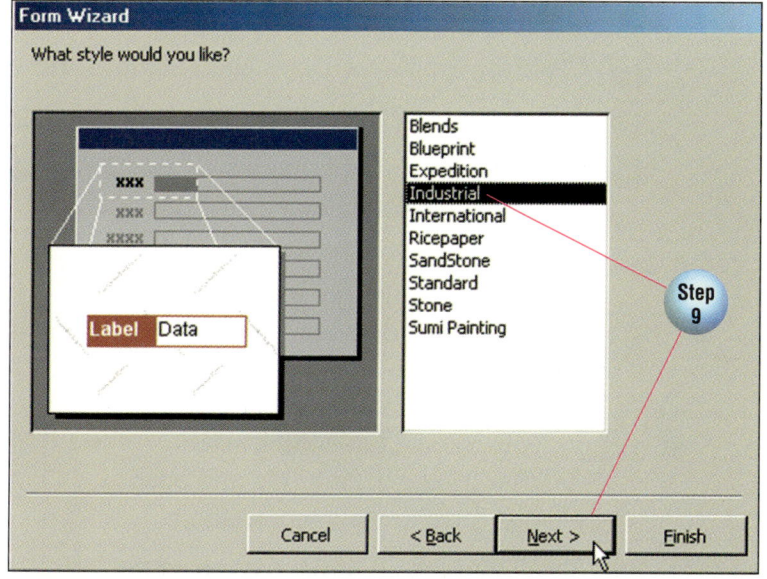

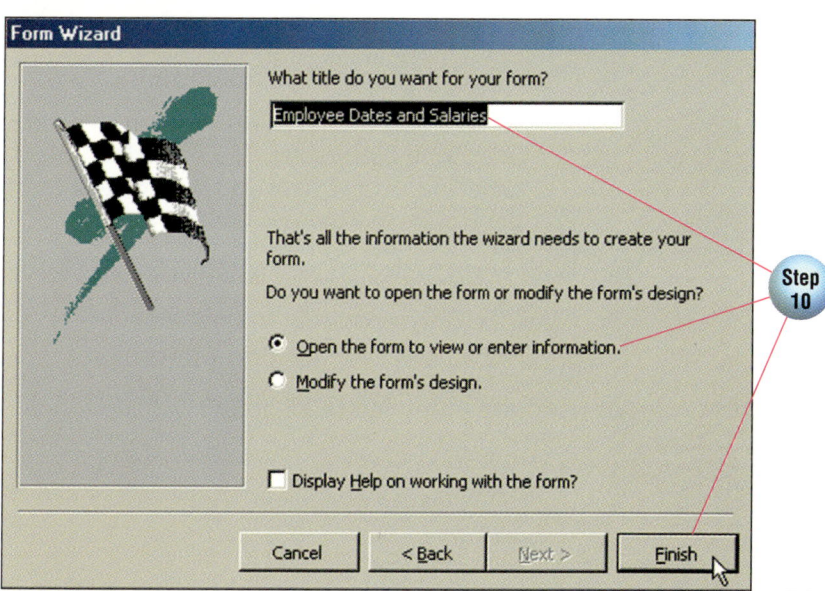

> In a few seconds the Employee Dates and Salaries form appears with the data displayed for record 1 as shown in Figure A3.2 on page 78.

(continued)

SECTION 3: CREATING QUERIES, FORMS, AND REPORTS

ACCESS
77

FIGURE A3.2 Employee Dates and Salaries Form

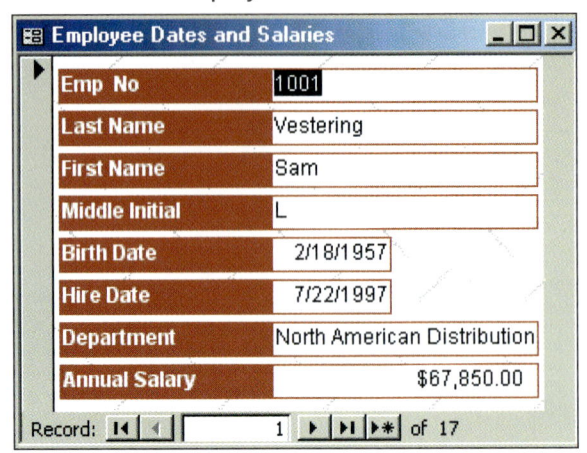

⑪ Click the Next Record button to display record 2 in the form.

⑫ Continue clicking the Next Record button until you have viewed all of the records in the form.

⑬ Close the Employee Dates and Salaries form.

⑭ With Forms selected on the Objects bar, double-click *Create form by using wizard*.

⑮ Create a new form for the Employee Benefits table using the following specifications:

- Add all of the fields in the Employee Benefits table to the form.
- Choose the columnar layout.
- Choose the Expedition style.
- Accept the default title and open the form to view information.

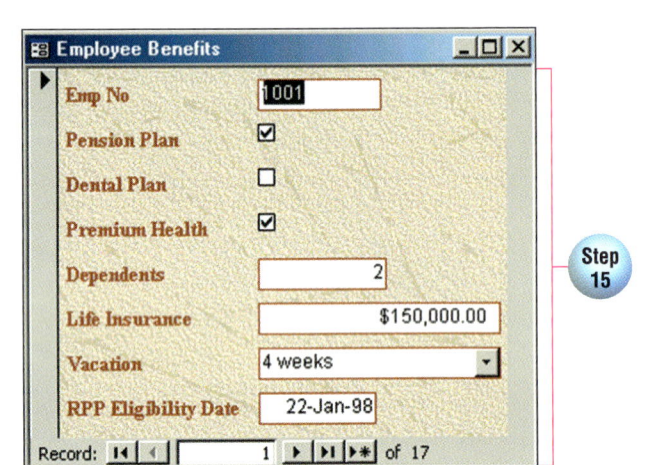

⑯ Scroll through all of the records in the Employee Benefits form.

⑰ Close the Employee Benefits form.

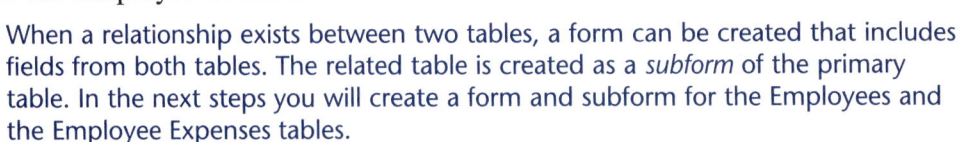

When a relationship exists between two tables, a form can be created that includes fields from both tables. The related table is created as a *subform* of the primary table. In the next steps you will create a form and subform for the Employees and the Employee Expenses tables.

⑱ With Forms selected on the Objects bar, double-click *Create form by using wizard*.

⑲ Click the down-pointing triangle next to the Tables/Queries list box and then click *Table: Employees* in the drop-down list.

⑳ Add the following fields to the Selected Fields list box:

Emp No
FirstName
LastName

SECTION 3: CREATING QUERIES, FORMS, AND REPORTS

㉑ Click the down-pointing triangle next to the Tables/Queries list box and then click *Table: Employee Expenses* in the drop-down list.

㉒ Add the following fields to the Selected Fields list box:

Date
Amount
Description

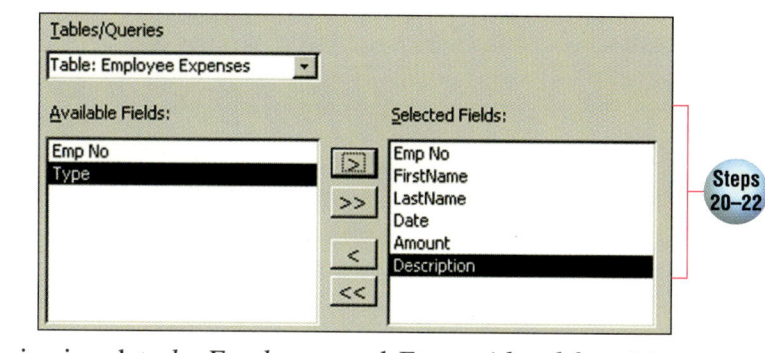

㉓ Click Next.

㉔ Click Next at the second Form Wizard dialog box to accept the default options of viewing data *by Employees* and *Form with subform(s)*.

㉕ Complete the remaining steps in the Form Wizard as follows:

- Accept the default layout of Datasheet for the subform.
- Choose the Blends style.
- Accept the default titles for the Form and Subform and open the form to view information.

   The form and subform appear as shown in Figure A3.3. Notice a separate Record Navigation bar exists for each form. The Record Navigation bar in the subform is used to scroll the records in the Employee Expenses table for the employee shown in the Employees form. The Record Navigation bar in the Employees form will move to the specified record in the Employees table and automatically display the related record(s) in the Employee Expenses table in the subform.

FIGURE A3.3 Employees Form with Employee Expenses Subform

A separate Record Navigation bar appears for each table.

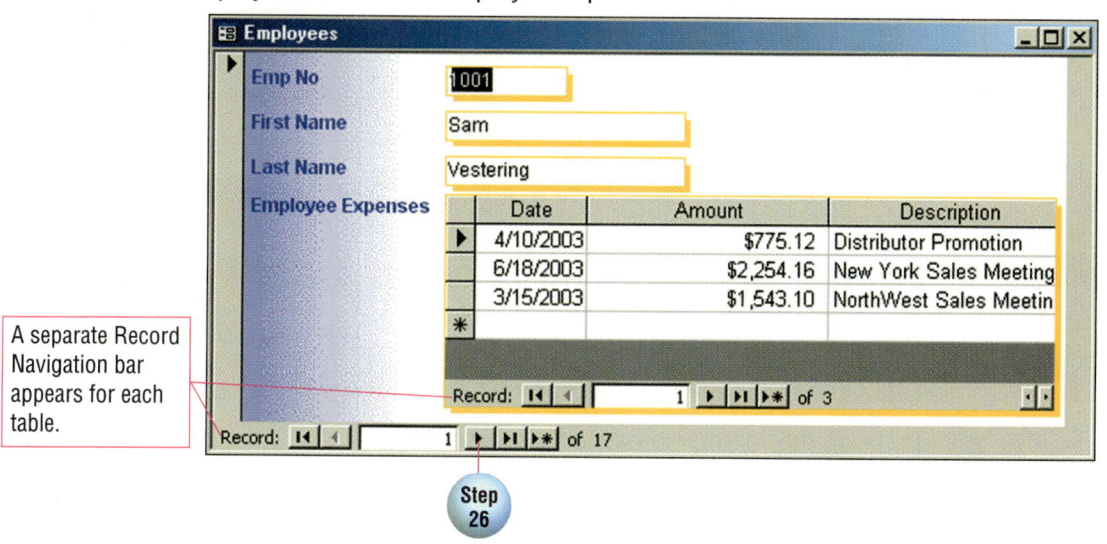

㉖ Click the Next Record button on the Record Navigation bar for the Employees form to view record 2. Notice the subform automatically changes to display the related record for Roman Deptulski in the Employee Expenses table.

㉗ Continue clicking the Next Record button on the Record Navigation bar for the Employees form until you have viewed all of the records in the form.

㉘ Close the Employees form.

   Notice the two forms added to the Forms object list: Employees and Employee Expenses Subform.

SECTION 3: CREATING QUERIES, FORMS, AND REPORTS

3.7 Modifying Controls in a Form

Once a form has been created using AutoForm or the Form Wizard, the form can be modified by opening it in Design view. A form is comprised of a series of objects referred to as *controls*. A form created with the Form Wizard contains a label control and a text box control for each field included from the specified table. The label control contains the field name and is used to describe the data that will be entered or viewed in the adjacent text box control. The text box control is the field placeholder where data is entered or edited. The controls can be moved, resized, or deleted from the form.

PROJECT: Some of the controls in the Employee Dates and Salaries form are wider than necessary for the data that will be entered or viewed. You will open the form in Design view, resize these controls, and modify the format properties.

STEPS

FIGURE A3.4 Employee Dates and Salaries Form Design View

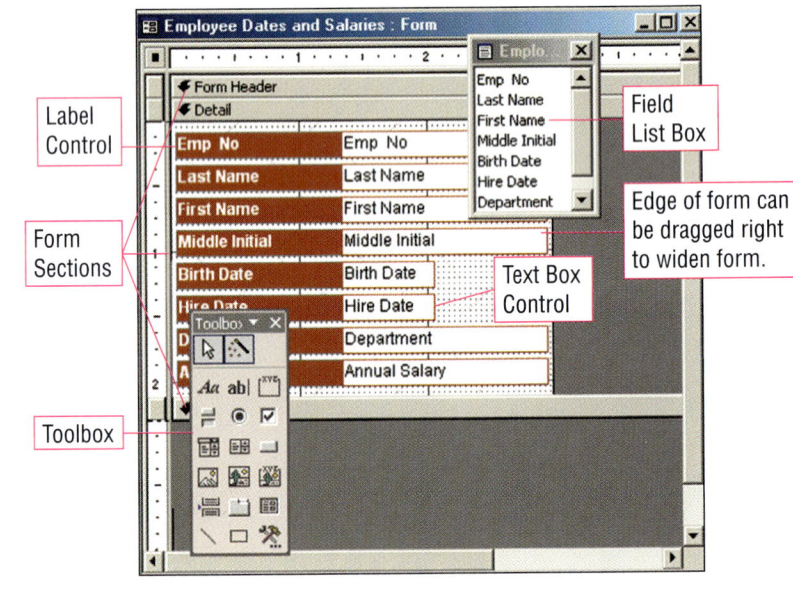

1. With WE Employees3 open and Forms still selected on the Objects bar, right-click *Employee Dates and Salaries* and then click Design View at the shortcut menu.

   A form contains three sections, as shown in Figure A3.4: Form Header, Detail, and Form Footer. The control objects for the fields in the table are displayed in the Detail section. A Field List box and a Toolbox palette display in the window. These can be dragged out of the way or closed.

2. Click the Emp No text box control. This is the control object with the white background and red border, containing the text *Emp No*. Eight sizing handles display around the object.

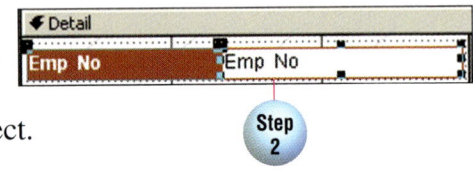

3. Position the mouse pointer on the middle sizing handle at the right edge of the control object until the pointer changes to a left- and right-pointing double arrow, hold down the left mouse button, drag left until the right border is at position 2 on the horizontal ruler, and then release the left mouse button.

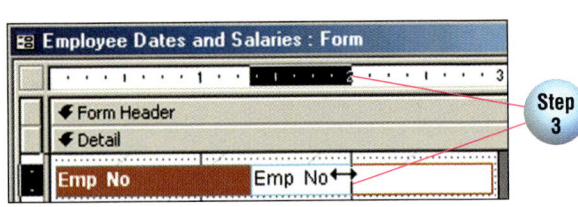

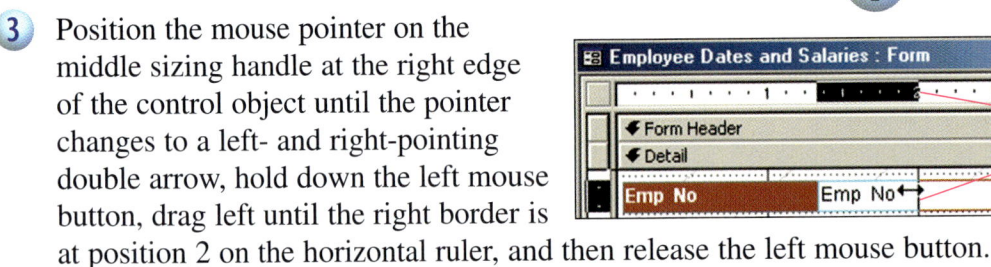

4. Resize the Annual Salary text box control to position 2.5 on the horizontal ruler by completing steps similar to those in steps 2–3.

5. Click Edit and then Select All.

   All of the controls in the form are selected. You can also use the Shift key and click control objects to select multiple controls.

ACCESS
80

SECTION 3: CREATING QUERIES, FORMS, AND REPORTS

ACCESS

6 Click the Properties button on the Form Design toolbar.

> This opens the Multiple selection property sheet for the selected controls. Each control object in the form has a property sheet that can be opened to change formats such as font, font size, color, and so on.

7 Click the Format tab in the Multiple selection property sheet.

8 Scroll down the property sheet, click in the Font Name property box, click the down-pointing triangle that appears, scroll down the font list, and then click *Times New Roman* in the drop-down list.

9 Click in the Font Size property box, click the down-pointing triangle that appears, and then click *10* in the drop-down list.

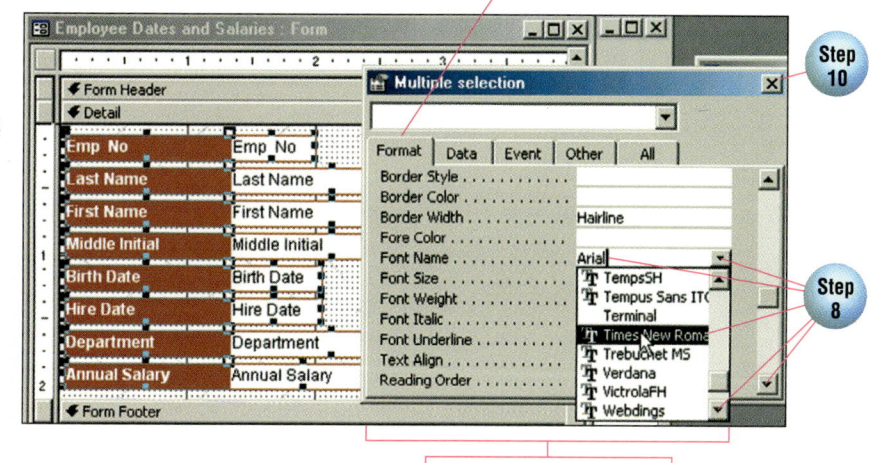

Changes made will affect all selected objects.

10 Close the Multiple selection property sheet.

11 Click in the gray shaded area within the Form window to deselect the objects and then click the Save button.

12 Click the View button on the Form Design toolbar to switch to Form view.

13 Scroll through the records in the form.

14 Close the Employee Dates and Salaries form.

In Addition

Deleting and Moving Control Objects

A selected control object can be deleted from the form by pressing the Delete key. To move a selected object, position the mouse pointer on the border of the selected control object until the pointer changes to a hand. Hold down the left mouse button, drag the control to the desired location, and then release the mouse button. To move a text box control separately from its corresponding label control, drag the large black handle that appears in the top left corner of the control object.

Move a control by dragging the border of the selected object. The label and text box move simultaneously.

IN BRIEF

Resize Form Control Objects
1 Right-click form name, click Design View.
2 Click object to be resized.
3 Drag sizing handles to increase or decrease the size of the object.
4 Click Save button.
5 Close the form.

Modify Form Control Properties
1 Right-click form name, click Design View.
2 Click object to be modified.
3 Click Properties button.
4 Change properties as required.
5 Close property sheet.
6 Click Save button.
7 Close the form.

SECTION 3: CREATING QUERIES, FORMS, AND REPORTS

3.8 Adding Controls to a Form

The Toolbox that displays when the form is opened in Design view contains a palette of control object buttons that are used to add controls to a form. To add a control to a form, click the control object button in the Toolbox for the type of control you want to add, and then drag the outline of the object in the design grid the approximate height and width you want the control to be. Depending on the control object created, key the text or expression for the object and modify properties as required.

PROJECT: You will add label control objects that add descriptive text to the Employee Dates and Salaries form in the Form Header and Form Footer sections.

STEPS

1. With WE Employees3 open and Forms still selected on the Objects bar, open the Employee Dates and Salaries form in Design view.

2. Position the mouse pointer at the top of the gray Detail border line until the pointer changes to a black horizontal line with an up- and down-pointing arrow, hold down the left mouse button, drag the pointer down approximately 1 inch, and then release the mouse button.

   PROBLEM? Form Header/Form Footer sections not visible? Right-click the Employee Dates and Salaries : Form Title bar and then click Form Header/Footer at the shortcut menu.

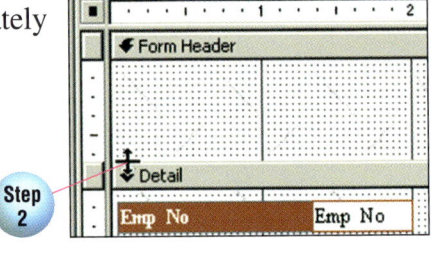

3. Click the Label object button [Aa] in the Toolbox.

   PROBLEM? Toolbox not visible? Click the Toolbox button on the Form Design toolbar.

4. Position the crosshairs pointer with the label icon attached to it at the top left edge of the Form Header section, drag the mouse down to the approximate height and width shown at the right, and then release the mouse button.

   A label box will appear with the insertion point at the top left edge of the box.

5. Key **Employee Dates and Salaries Form** and then click outside the box.

6. Click the label control object in the Form Header section to select it.

7. Click the Center button on the Formatting (Form/Report) toolbar. If the toolbar is not visible, click View, point to Toolbars, and then click Fomatting (Form/Report).

Crosshairs pointer with label icon.

SECTION 3: CREATING QUERIES, FORMS, AND REPORTS

ACCESS

8) With the label control still selected, click the Properties button on the Form Design toolbar to open the Label property sheet.

9) Click the Format tab, if necessary, and then change the font name to Times New Roman and the font size to 12.

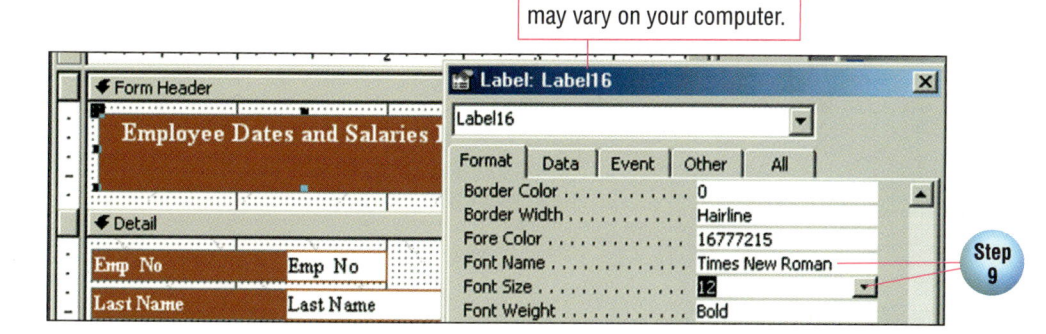

> Label number in Title bar may vary on your computer.

Step 9

10) Close the Label property sheet.

11) Maximize the Form window if it is not currently maximized.

12) Position the mouse pointer on the Form Footer bottom gray border line until the pointer changes to a black horizontal line with an up- and down-pointing arrow, drag the bottom of the form down until the Form Footer section is approximately 1 inch in height, and then release the mouse button.

13) Add a label control object to the Form Footer section as shown using the following specifications. *(Hint: Review steps 3–6 if you need assistance creating this object.)*

- Substitute your first and last name for *Student Name*.
- Change the font name to Times New Roman and the font size to 10 using the drop-down list buttons on the Formatting (Form/Report) toolbar.

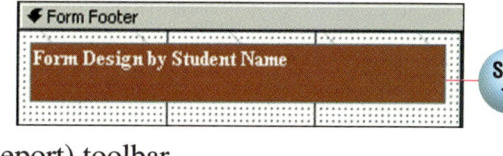

Step 13

14) Click the Save button.

15) Switch to Form view. Click File and then Print. Click Selected Record(s) in the Print Range section of the Print dialog box and then click OK.

16) Scroll through the remaining records in the form.

17) Close the Employee Dates and Salaries form.

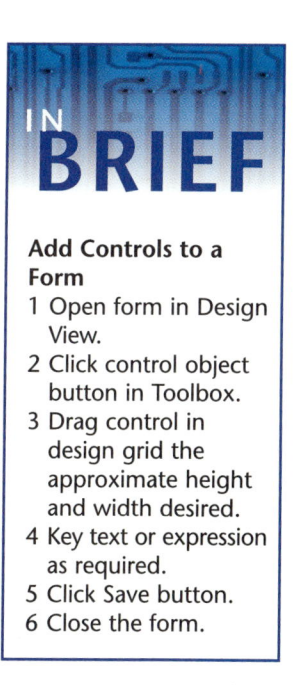

IN BRIEF

Add Controls to a Form
1. Open form in Design View.
2. Click control object button in Toolbox.
3. Drag control in design grid the approximate height and width desired.
4. Key text or expression as required.
5. Click Save button.
6. Close the form.

SECTION 3: CREATING QUERIES, FORMS, AND REPORTS

3.9 Creating, Previewing, and Printing a Report

Information from the database can be printed while viewing tables in Datasheet view or while viewing a query results datasheet by clicking the Print button on the toolbar. In these printouts all of the fields are printed in a tabular layout, with the fields displayed in rows. Create a report when you want to specify which fields to print and to have more control over the report layout and format. Access includes the Report Wizard, which generates the report based on selections made in a series of dialog boxes.

PROJECT: You will use the Report Wizard to create a report that will list the mailing addresses of the employees in a columnar format.

STEPS

1. With WE Employees3 open, click Reports on the Objects bar.
2. Double-click *Create report by using wizard*.
3. Click the down-pointing triangle next to the Tables/Queries list box and then click *Table: Employees* in the drop-down list.
4. Click the Add All Fields button >> to move all of the fields in the Employees table from the Available Fields list box to the Selected Fields list box.
5. Click *Emp No* in the Selected Fields list box and then click the Remove Field button < to move *Emp No* back to the Available Fields list box.
6. Click *MiddleName* in the Selected Fields list box and then click < to move *MiddleName* back to the Available Fields list box.
7. Click Next.

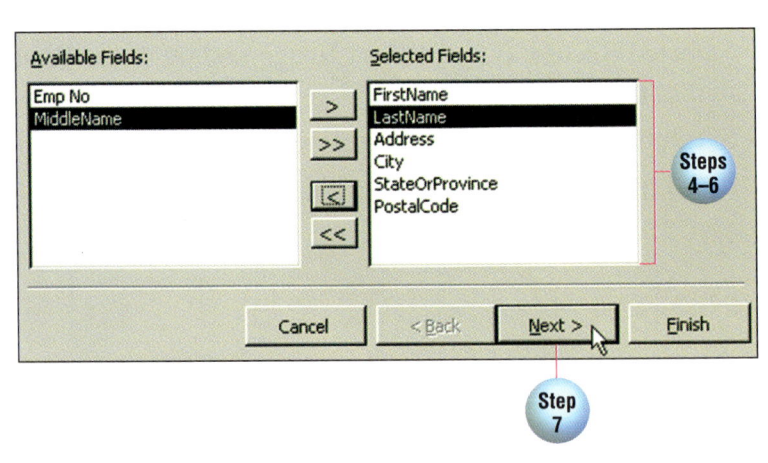

SECTION 3: CREATING QUERIES, FORMS, AND REPORTS

8. Click Next at the second Report Wizard dialog box to indicate that there is no grouping in the report.

> A grouping level in a report allows you to print records by sections within a table. For example, in an employee report you could print the employees grouped by city. In this example, you would double-click the *City* field to define the grouping level. The buttons with the up- and down-pointing arrows are used to modify the position of a field in the grouping level to increase or decrease its priority level if there is grouping by multiple fields.

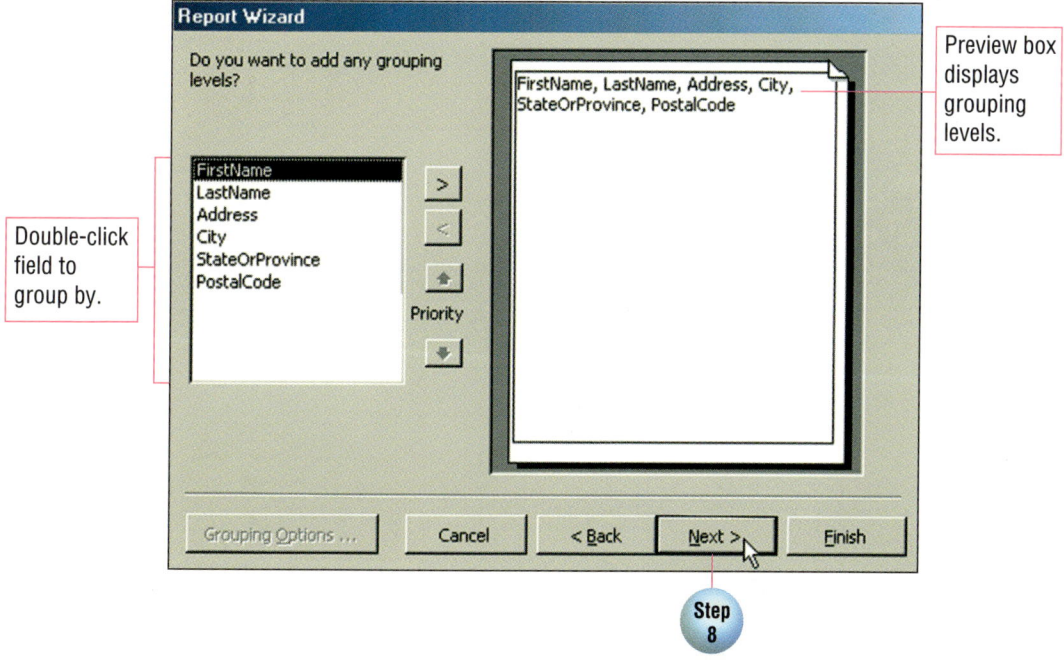

9. Click the down-pointing triangle next to the first text box in the third Report Wizard dialog box and then click *LastName* in the drop-down list.

   > You can sort a report by up to four fields in the table.

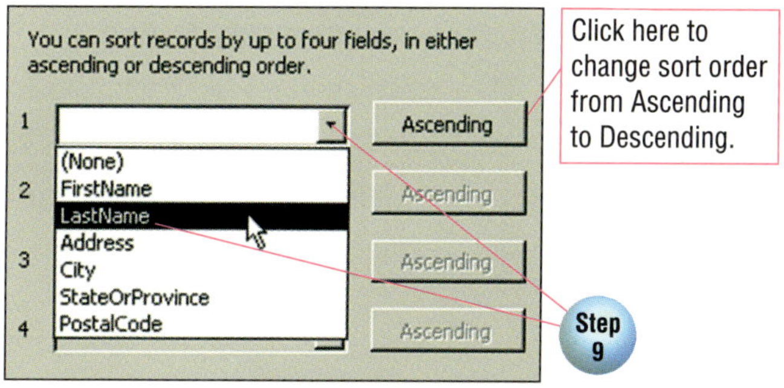

10. Click Next.

11. Click Columnar in the Layout section in the fourth Report Wizard dialog box and then click Next.

    > Use the preview box to view the selected layout before clicking the Next button.

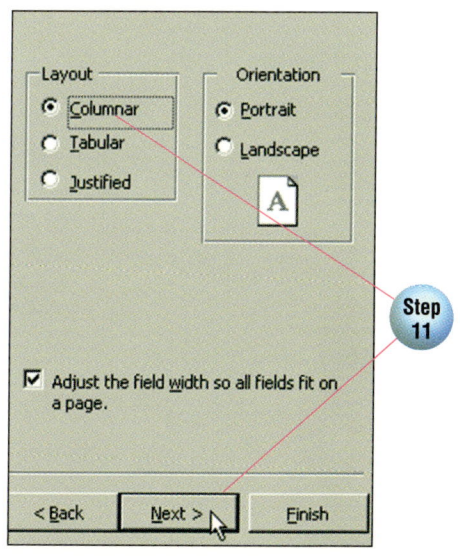

(continued)

SECTION 3: CREATING QUERIES, FORMS, AND REPORTS

12. Click *Corporate* in the style list box in the fifth Report Wizard dialog box and then click Next.

13. Key **Employee Mailing Addresses** in the title text box in the sixth Report Wizard dialog box and then click Finish.

    In a few seconds the report will appear in the Print Preview window.

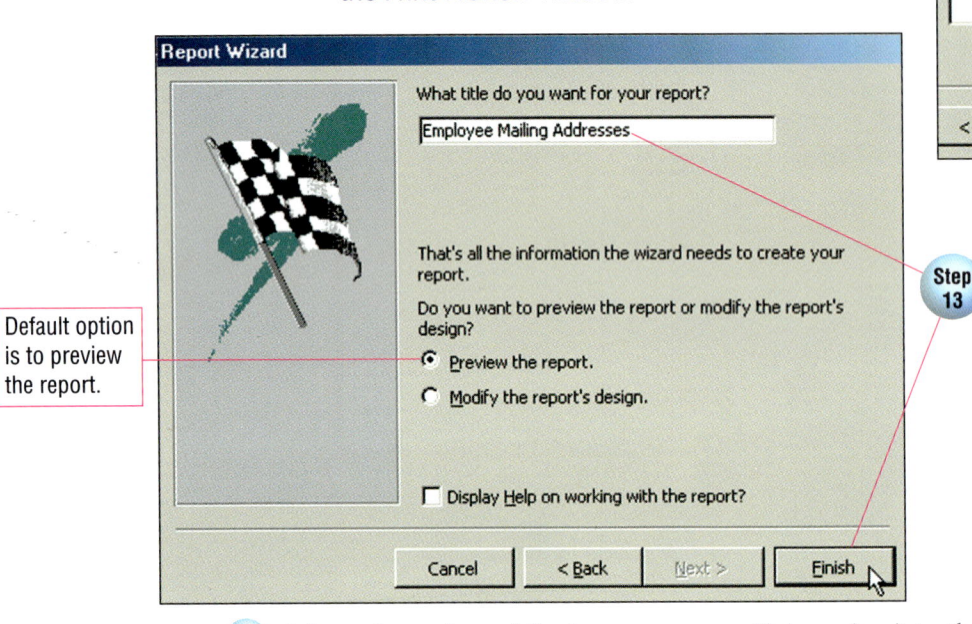

Default option is to preview the report.

14. Move the pointer (displays as a magnifying glass) to the middle of the report and then click the left mouse button.

    The zoom changes to *Fit* and the entire page is displayed in the Print Preview window, as shown in Figure A3.5.

FIGURE A3.5 Report Page in Print Preview

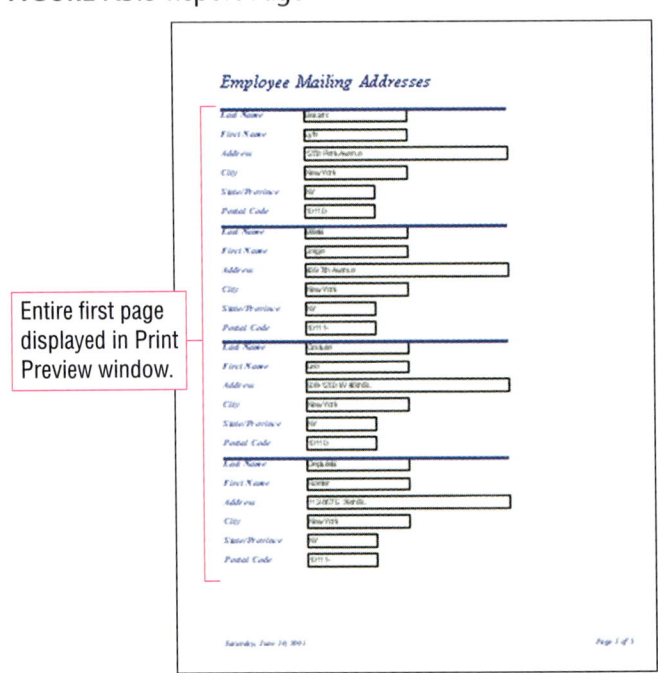

Entire first page displayed in Print Preview window.

SECTION 3: CREATING QUERIES, FORMS, AND REPORTS

15. Click the Next Page button ▶ on the Page navigation bar to display page 2 of the report.
16. Continue clicking the Next Page button until you have viewed all of the pages in the report.
17. Click File and then Print.
18. Click Pages in the Print Range section.
19. With the insertion point positioned in the From text box, key **1** and then press Tab.
20. With the insertion point positioned in the To text box, key **1**.
21. Click OK.

   In a few seconds, the first page only of the five-page *Employee Mailing Addresses* report will print.

22. Click the Close button on the Print Preview toolbar.

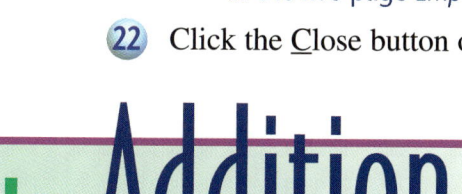

In Addition

Creating a Report in Design View

A report can be created in a blank Design view window as shown below. Initially, the Field List box is blank until a table or query is associated with the report. Double-click the Report Selector button to display the Report property sheet. Click the Data tab and then click the down-pointing triangle in the Record Source property box to select a table or query name. To add fields to the design grid, drag the field name from the Field List box to the position in the grid where you want the field to appear.

In Brief

Create a Report Using Report Wizard
1. Click Reports on the Objects bar.
2. Double-click *Create report by using wizard*.
3. Choose table(s) and field(s) to include in report.
4. Click Next.
5. Choose a grouping level and click Next.
6. Choose a field to sort by and click Next.
7. Choose a report layout and click Next.
8. Chose a report style and click Next.
9. Key report title and click Finish.

SECTION 3: CREATING QUERIES, FORMS, AND REPORTS

3.10 Resizing Controls in a Report

Once a report has been created using the Report Wizard, the report can be modified by opening it in Design view. A report is similar to a form in that it is comprised of a series of objects referred to as controls. A report can be modified using similar techniques to those learned in topics 3.7 and 3.8 on Modifying Controls and Adding Controls to a Form.

PROJECT: Some of the controls in the *Employee Mailing Addresses* report are wider than necessary for the data that will be printed. You will open the report in Design view, resize these controls, and then print the first page only of the report.

STEPS

1. With WE Employees3 open and Reports selected on the Objects bar, right-click *Employee Mailing Addresses* and then click <u>D</u>esign View at the shortcut menu.

   A report contains five sections, as shown in Figure A3.6: Report Header, Page Header, Detail, Page Footer, and Report Footer. The control objects for the fields in the table are displayed in the Detail section. In a tabular report layout, the Page Header section contains the label control objects for the fields placed in the report. In Addition at the end of this topic explains the purpose of each report section.

   FIGURE A3.6 *Employee Mailing Addresses* Report Design View

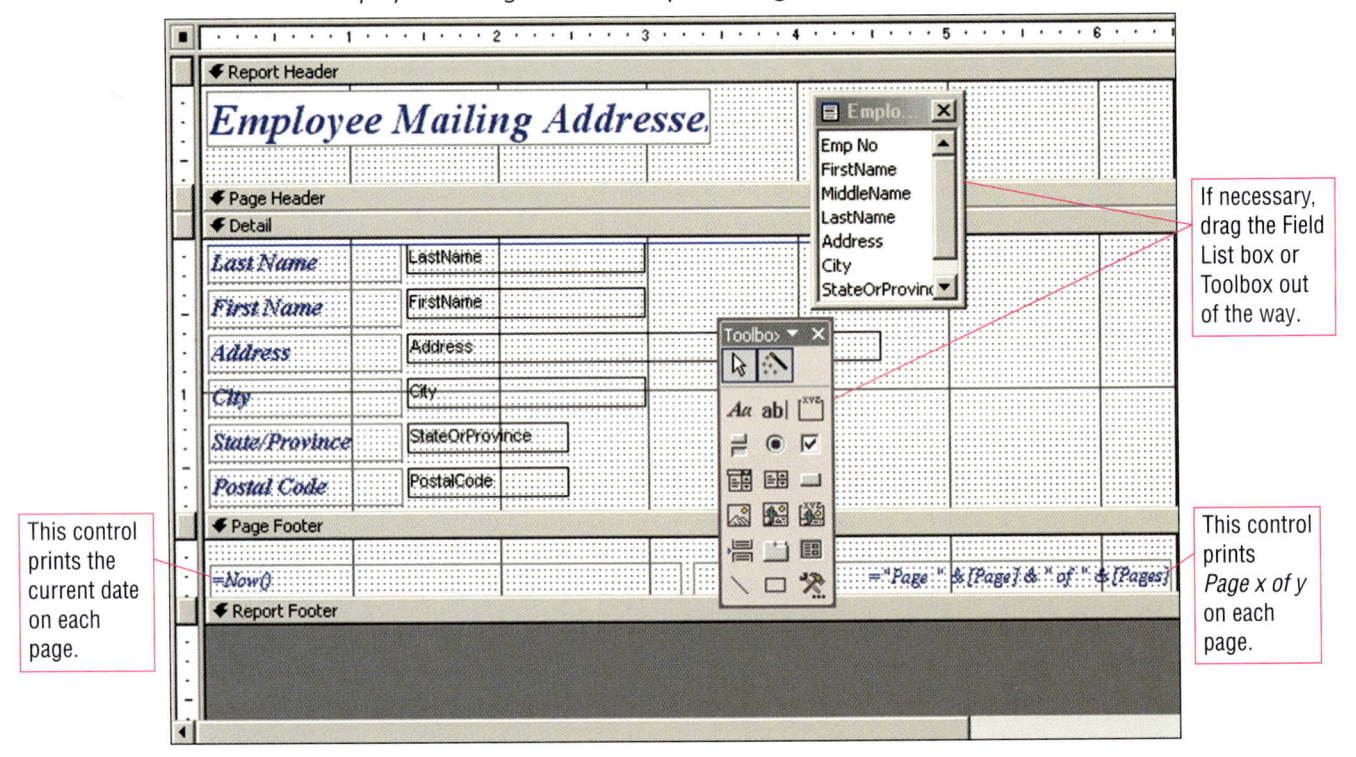

   This control prints the current date on each page.

   If necessary, drag the Field List box or Toolbox out of the way.

   This control prints Page x of y *on each page.*

2. Click the Address text box control object to select it.

3. Position the mouse pointer on the right middle sizing handle until the pointer displays as a left- and right-pointing arrow, hold down the left mouse button, drag left until the control is resized to position 3.25 on the horizontal ruler, and then release the mouse button.

4. Resize the City and StateOrProvince controls to position 2.25 on the horizontal ruler.

5. Resize the PostalCode control to position 2 on the horizontal ruler.

6. Click the Save button.

7. Click the Print Preview button on the Report Design toolbar.

8. Preview all of the pages in the report.

9. Click File and then Print.

10. Click Pages in the Print Range section, key **1**, press Tab, key **1**, and then click OK or press Enter.

11. Close the Print Preview window.

12. Close the WE Employees3 database.

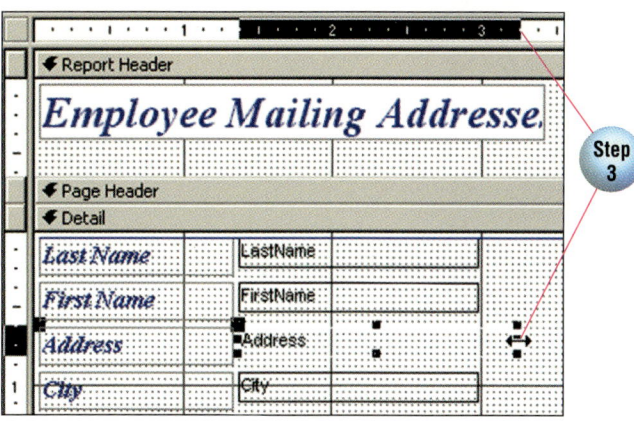

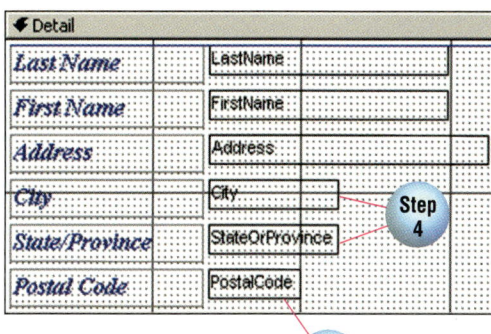

In Addition

Controls and Report Sections

All of the techniques you learned for modifying controls and adding controls to a form in Design view can be applied to a report. The five sections of the report are detailed below.

Report Header:	Controls in this section are printed once at the beginning of the report.
Page Header:	Controls in this section are printed at the top of each page in the report.
Detail:	Controls in this section make up the body of the report.
Page Footer:	Controls in this section are printed at the bottom of each page in the report.
Report Footer:	Controls in this section are printed once at the end of the report.

In Brief

Resize Control Objects in Design View
1. Right-click report name, click Design View.
2. Click object to be resized.
3. Drag sizing handles to increase or decrease size of object.
4. Click Save button.
5. Close the report.

SECTION 3: CREATING QUERIES, FORMS, AND REPORTS

FEATURES SUMMARY

Feature	Button	Menu	Keyboard
Design View		View, Design View	
Form View		View, Form View	
Form Wizard		Insert, Form, Form Wizard	
Property sheet		View, Properties	F4
Report Wizard		Insert, Report, Report Wizard	
Run a query		Query, Run	
Select all controls		Edit, Select All	Ctrl + A
Simple Query Wizard		Insert, Query, Simple Query Wizard	

PROCEDURES CHECK

Completion: In the space provided at the right, indicate the correct term or command.

1. This is the name of the wizard used to facilitate creating a query to select records from a table. _____
2. Key this entry in the Annual Salary criteria row in Query Design view to extract records of employees who earn more than $40,000. _____
3. Click the check box in this row in the query design grid to prevent a column from being displayed in the query results. _____
4. This type of query allows the user to key the criteria statement in a dialog box when the query is run. _____
5. Use this method of creating a form if you want to choose the layout and style of the form. _____
6. The label control object button is located in this palette. _____
7. Click this button on the Form Design toolbar to change the formats of a selected control object. _____
8. Click this option in the Print dialog box to print only the active form. _____
9. A report is comprised of a series of objects referred to as this. _____

10. Provide the entry you would key in a blank Field row in the Query Design grid to calculate the total cost of an item given the following information:

    - the total cost is calculated by multiplying the units ordered by the unit price.
    - the units ordered is stored in a field named *UnitsOnOrder*.
    - the unit cost is stored in a field named *UnitCost*.
    - the new column should have the column heading *Total Cost*.

    _____

List the names of the five sections found in a report.

11. _____   14. _____

12. _____   15. _____

13. _____

FIGURE A3.7

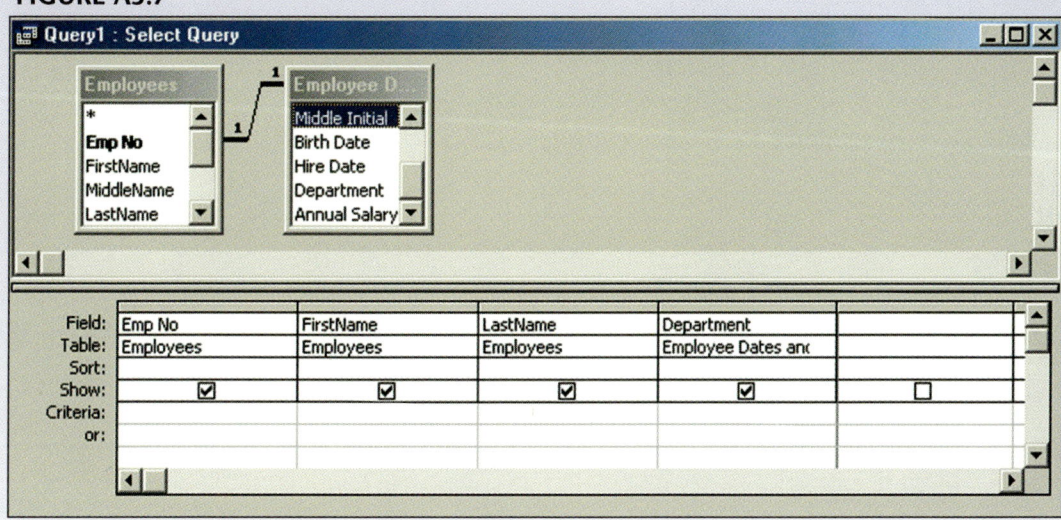

Use the Query Design window shown in Figure A3.7 to answer questions 16–18.

16. List the steps you would complete to sort the query results by the *LastName* field.
    _____
    _____
    _____

17. List the steps you would complete to add the field named *Annual Salary* in the Employee Dates and Salaries table to the blank column after *Department* in the query design grid.
    _____
    _____
    _____

18. List the steps you would complete to extract records of employees who work in the Overseas Distribution department.
    _____
    _____
    _____

SECTION 3: CREATING QUERIES, FORMS, AND REPORTS

SKILLS REVIEW

Activity 1: CREATING A QUERY USING THE SIMPLE QUERY WIZARD

1. Open the WE Employees3 database.
2. Use the Simple Query Wizard to create a query that will display the fields from the Employees, Employee Dates and Salaries, and Employee Benefits tables as follows:

Employees	Employee Dates and Salaries	Employee Benefits
Emp No	Hire Date	Life Insurance
FirstName	Annual Salary	
LastName		

3. Accept the default Detail query and then key **Salaries and Life Insurance** as the title for the query.
4. View the query results datasheet.
5. Print the query results datasheet.
6. Close the Salaries and Life Insurance query.

Activity 2: SORTING A QUERY; ADDING A CRITERIA STATEMENT; CREATING A CALCULATED FIELD

1. With WE Employees3 open, open the Salaries and Life Insurance query in Design view.
2. Sort the query results by the *LastName* field in ascending order.
3. Add a criteria statement in the *Annual Salary* field that will extract the records of employees who earn more than $44,000. *(Hint: Numeric fields do not require quotation marks and should not include any currency symbols or commas.)*
4. Create a calculated field in the column after *Life Insurance* that will divide the *Annual Salary* column by 12 to display the monthly salary. Label the new column *Monthly Salary*.
5. Format the *Monthly Salary* column to display the calculated values in Currency format.
6. Use the Save As command to save the revised query as *Employees Earning Over 44,000*.
7. Run the query.
8. Preview, and then print the query results datasheet.
9. Close the Employees Earning Over 44,000 query.

Activity 3: CREATING A FORM USING THE FORM WIZARD; ENTERING RECORDS

1. With WE Employees3 open, create a new form for the Employee Expenses table using the following specifications:
   - Add all of the fields in the Employee Expenses table to the form.
   - Choose the Columnar layout.
   - Choose the Sumi Painting style.
   - Accept the default title for the form.

2. Add the following records to the Employee Expenses table using the form created in step 1:

Emp No	**1045**	*Emp No*	**1025**
Date	**5/13/03**	*Date*	**6/18/03**
Amount	**1510.45**	*Amount*	**1123.41**
Type	**Sales**	*Type*	**Sales**
Description	**Spring Promotion**	*Description*	**Sales Conference**

3. Print all records in the table using the form.
4. Close the Employee Expenses form.

Activity 4: MODIFYING A FORM

1. With WE Employees3 open, open the Employee Expenses form created in Activity 3 in Design view.
2. Maximize the form window.
3. Expand the Form Header section approximately 1 inch and then insert the title *Expenses Form* in a label control object in the Form Header. Center the text in the label control object and then change the font size to 16 point.
4. Expand the Form Footer section approximately 1 inch and then insert the text *Form Design by Student Name* in a label control object in the Form Footer. Substitute your first and last name for *Student Name*.
5. Decrease the width of the Amount text box control to position the right edge of the control at approximately 2.25 on the horizontal ruler.
6. Decrease the width of the Type text box control to position the right edge of the control at approximately 2.5 on the horizontal ruler.
7. Drag the right edge of the form design grid to approximately 3.5 on the horizontal ruler and then increase the width of the Description text box control to position the right edge of the control at approximately 3.25 on the horizontal ruler.
8. Switch to Form view.
9. Print the first record only in the form.
10. Close the Employee Expenses form saving the changes.

Activity 5: CREATING A REPORT; RESIZING CONTROLS

1. With WE Employees3 open, use the Report Wizard to create a report based on the Salaries and Life Insurance query as follows:
   - Add all of the fields from the query to the report.
   - Do not include any grouping or sorting.
   - Select the Tabular layout.
   - Select the Bold style.
   - Accept the default title for the report.
2. Preview and then print the report.
3. Display the report in Design View and then resize controls as follows:
   a. Drag the right edge of the Last Name label control object in the Page Header section to position 3 on the horizontal ruler.
   b. Drag the left edge of the Hire Date label control object in the Page Header section to approximately position 3.25 on the horizontal ruler.

4. Preview and then print the report.
5. Close the *Salaries and Life Insurance* report. Click Yes to save changes to the report design.
6. Close the WE Employees3 database.

PERFORMANCE PLUS

Activity 1: CREATING A QUERY IN DESIGN VIEW; ADDING CRITERIA

1. The Bursary Selection Committee at Niagara Peninsula College would like you to provide them with the names of students who have achieved an A+ in all three of their courses.
2. Open NPC Grades3.
3. Create a query in Design view that will extract the records of those students who have an A+ in all three courses. Include student numbers, first names, last names, and grades. Sort the query in ascending order by student's last name. *(Hint: Key A+ encased in quotation marks in the Criteria row to indicate the plus symbol is not part of an expression.)*
4. Save the query and name it A+ Students.
5. Run the query.
6. Best Fit the columns in the query results datasheet.
7. Print the query results datasheet in landscape orientation.
8. Close the A+ Students query.
9. Close NPC Grades3.

Activity 2: CREATING A QUERY AND REPORT

1. Bobbie Sinclair, business manager of Performance Threads, would like a report that lists the costumes that were rented in August 2003.
2. Open PT Costume Inventory3.
3. Create a new query in Design view using the Costume Inventory table that will list the fields in the following order: *Costume No., Date Out, Date In, Character, Daily Rental Fee.*
4. Key the following criteria statement in the *Date Out* column that will extract the records for costumes that were rented in the month of August 2003:

    Between August 1, 2003 and August 31, 2003

5. Expand the column width of the *Date Out* column to view the entire criteria statement.
6. Notice Access converted the long dates to short dates and added pound symbols to the dates in the criteria statement. Dates in Access queries are encased in pound symbols (#).
7. Sort the query results first by *Date Out*, then by *Date In*, and then by *Character* in ascending order.
8. Save the query and name it August 2003 Rentals.
9. Run the query. Close the query after viewing the query results datasheet.
10. Create a report based on the August 2003 Rentals query. Add all of the fields to the report. You determine the layout, style, and title for the report.
11. Add your name in a label object control at the right side of the Report Header section.
12. Preview and then print the report.
13. Close PT Costume Inventory3.

Activity 3: CREATING A PARAMETER QUERY

1. Dana Hirsch, manager of The Waterfront Bistro, has asked for your assistance in creating a query that will allow for extracting records based on different supplier codes. Dana does not wish to modify the criteria statement each time the query is run to change the desired supplier code list.
2. Open WB Inventory3.
3. Create a select query using the Simple Query Wizard using the following specifications:
    - Include all of the fields in the Inventory List table.
    - Key **Inventory by Supplier Code** as the query title.
4. View and then close the query results datasheet.
5. Open the Inventory by Supplier Code query in Design view.
6. Add a criteria in the *Supplier Code* column that will prompt the user to enter the supplier code they want to extract.
7. Sort the query in ascending order by the *Item* column.
8. Save and then run the query. Key **1** as the supplier code.
9. Print and then close the query results datasheet.
10. Open the Inventory by Supplier Code query and then key **4** as the supplier code.
11. Print and then close the query results datasheet.
12. Close WB Inventory3.

Activity 4: CREATING AND MODIFYING A FORM

1. Staff at Performance Threads have mentioned that looking up a costume in the costume inventory datasheet is difficult, since there are so many records in the table. You decide to create a form for the staff in which they see only one record on the screen at a time as they are browsing the inventory.
2. Open PT Costume Inventory3.
3. Create a new form using the Form Wizard for the Costume Inventory table. You determine the layout, style, and title of the form. Include all of the fields in the form.
4. Modify the form as follows.
    a. Add the title *Costume Inventory* in a label control object in the Form Header.
    b. Add the text *Check for damage/repairs upon return* in a label control object in the Form Footer.
    c. Resize the Daily Rental Fee text box control so that the right edge of the control aligns with the right edge of the Date Out and Date In objects below it.
    d. Move and/or resize any other controls to improve the appearance of the form.
5. Change the font and font size of all the control objects in the form to a font and size of your choosing.
6. Display the form in Form view.
7. Print the first record only in the form.
8. Close the form. Choose Yes to save changes to the form design.
9. Close PT Costume Inventory3.

Activity 5: FINDING INFORMATION ON ADDING A PICTURE TO A FORM

1. Use Access's Help feature to find out how to insert a picture that doesn't change from record to record in a form. *(Hint: Start by keying the phrase "add a picture to a form" in the Ask a Question box and then click the link that describes how to use an image control to add an unbound picture.)*
2. Print the Help topic that you find.
3. Open WE Employees3.
4. Open the Employee Expenses form in Design view.
5. Decrease the size of the label control object in the Form Header section so that the title only requires one-half of the width of the form.
6. Insert the company logo to the other half of the Form Header section. The logo file name is Worldwide.tif. If the logo is not completely visible within the control object, display the property sheet and then change the Size Mode property box to Zoom. Adjust the sizes of the objects in the Form Header section as necessary.
7. Print the first record only in the form.
8. Close the Employee Dates and Salaries form. Choose Yes to save the changes to the form design.
9. Close WE Employees3.

Activity 6: RESEARCHING TRAVEL DESTINATIONS ON THE INTERNET

1. You are considering taking a one-week vacation at the end of the term. The destination is flexible and will depend on available flights, costs, and activities.
2. Search the Internet for flight information to at least four destinations to which you might like to travel. Determine departure times, arrival times, and air fares for the week following the end of the current term.
3. Search the Internet for additional travel costs that you might incur for the destinations you used in step 2. Include hotel accommodations, car rentals, and any tours or other activities that you might like to purchase.
4. Create a new database named Travel Destinations to store your travel data. Design and create a table within the database that will include all of the data you collected.
5. Design and create a form to be used to enter the data into the tables.
6. Enter data using the form created in step 5.
7. Print all of the records in the form.
8. Close the form.
9. Close Travel Destinations.

ACCESS SECTION 4

Modifying Tables and Reports, Performing Calculations, and Viewing Data

Moving, inserting, and deleting fields can modify the structure of a table and field properties can be used to control how data is displayed in the tables. Forms and reports can be customized to move objects to a different position or add objects that cause Access to perform mathematical computations as the form or report is viewed or printed. The Label Wizard generates mailing labels preformatted to print on a variety of commercially available adhesive labels. Data in related tables can be viewed together using subdatasheets. Filtering records allows the user to view a portion of the table data that meets a specific criterion. Tables and queries can be converted to a Web page to post on the Internet or a company's intranet by saving data in a data access page. In this section you will learn the skills and complete the projects described here.

Note: Before beginning this section, delete from your disk any database files you created in Section 3. Next, copy to your disk as you need them the database files contained in the Access S4 *subfolder in the* Access *folder on the CD that accompanies this textbook. Remove the read-only attribute from each database as you copy it.*

Skills
- Move a field in a table
- Insert and delete fields in a table
- Modify field properties
- Create a calculated control object in a form and report
- Move and resize control objects in a report
- Modify properties of report controls
- Add objects to the report using the Toolbox
- Create mailing labels
- Display records in a subdatasheet
- Apply and remove filters to a table
- Save a table and a query as a Web page
- Add a hyperlink to a Web page

Projects

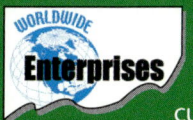

Worldwide Enterprises Move, insert, and delete fields in tables and modify field properties; modify a form and report to include a calculated control and custom design; create mailing labels for distributors; display subdatasheets for records in a related table; filter records to display employees in only one department and by vacation; save a table and query as a Web page and insert hyperlinks.

The Waterfront Bistro Modify the structure of the Inventory List table and display data from the Purchases table in the inventory datasheet. Create a Web page for the Purchases table.

Performance Threads Modify a form for browsing the costume inventory to include a calculation that will display the rental fee including tax.

Niagara Peninsula College Filter records of students who achieved A+ in a course.

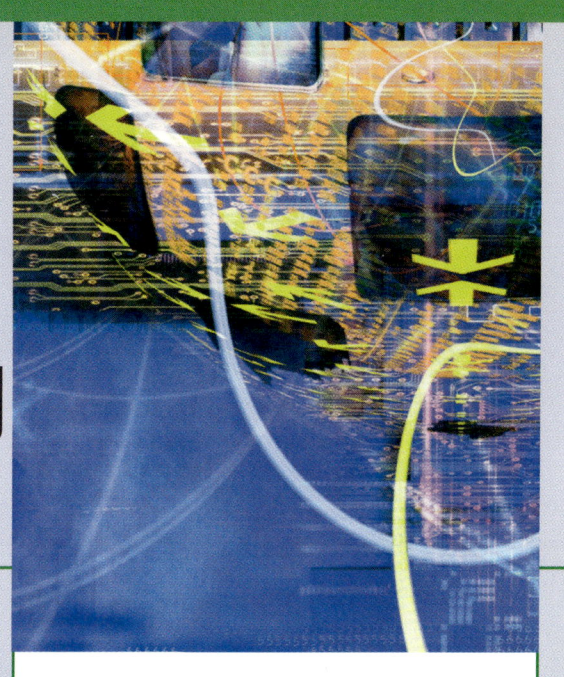

4.1 Moving Fields

Display a table in Design view to move a field from its current location in the table to another position. For example, you may realize after entering a few records that the flow of data is more logical if the layout is changed. In a previous section, you learned how to move columns in the datasheet for sorting purposes. Although the column can be moved in the datasheet, the position of the field in the table structure will remain where it was originally created unless the field is modified in Design view.

PROJECT: After consultation with Rhonda Trask, human resources manager of Worldwide Enterprises, you have decided to move the *Annual Salary* field in the Employee Dates and Salaries table between the *Birth Date* and *Hire Date* fields, to coincide with existing forms used in the department.

STEPS

1. Open WE Employees4.

2. Open the Employee Dates and Salaries table in Design view.

3. Move the mouse pointer in the field selector bar beside *Annual Salary* until the pointer changes to a right-pointing black arrow and then click the left mouse button.

    This selects the *Annual Salary* field.

    Step 3

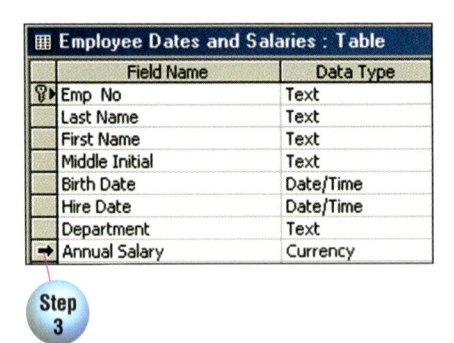

4. Move the mouse pointer in the field selector bar for the *Annual Salary* field until the pointer displays as a white arrow, hold down the left mouse button, drag the pointer up between the *Birth Date* and *Hire Date* fields, and then release the left mouse button.

    As you drag the mouse, a black line appears between existing field names, indicating where the selected field will be repositioned when the mouse button is released and the white arrow pointer displays with a gray shaded box attached to it.

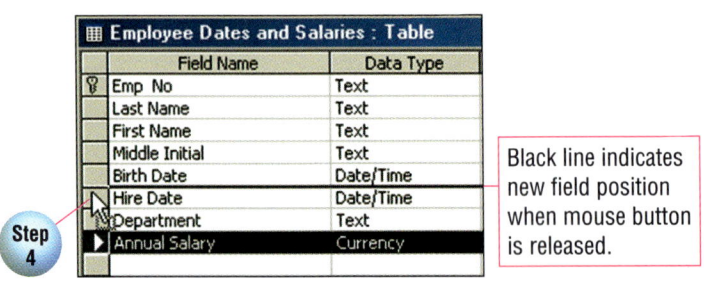

    Step 4

    Black line indicates new field position when mouse button is released.

5. Click in any field to deselect the Annual Salary row and then click the Save button.

ACCESS
98   SECTION 4: MODIFYING TABLES AND REPORTS, PERFORMING CALCULATIONS, AND VIEWING DATA

ACCESS

6. Move the mouse pointer in the field selector bar beside the *Department* field and then click the left mouse button to select the Department row.

7. Move the mouse pointer in the field selector bar for the *Department* field until the pointer changes to a white arrow, drag the *Department* field up between the *Birth Date* and *Annual Salary* fields, and then release the left mouse button.

8. Click the Undo button on the Table Design toolbar.

   Undo restores the *Department* field to the end of the table.

9. Click in any field to deselect the Department row and then click the Save button.

10. Switch to Datasheet view and then view the records in the Employee Dates and Salaries table, as shown in Figure A4.1.

    FIGURE A4.1 Employee Dates and Salaries Table

Emp	Last Name	First Name	Middle Initial	Birth Date	Annual Salary	Hire Date	Department
1001	Vestering	Sam	L	2/18/1957	$67,850.00	7/22/1997	North American Distribution
1005	Deptulski	Roman	W	3/12/1948	$67,850.00	8/15/1998	Overseas Distribution
1010	Postma	Hanh	A	12/10/1952	$67,850.00	1/30/1998	European Distribution
1015	Besterd	Lyle	C	10/15/1959	$44,651.00	5/17/1997	North American Distribution
1020	Doxtator	Angela	B	5/22/1963	$45,178.00	8/3/1997	North American Distribution
1025	Biliski	Jorge	N	6/18/1970	$43,152.00	12/1/1997	North American Distribution
1030	Hicks	Thom	P	7/27/1977	$41,624.00	1/22/1998	Overseas Distribution
1035	Valerie	Fistouris	E	2/4/1970	$43,664.00	3/15/1998	European Distribution
1040	Lafreniere	Guy	F	9/14/1972	$44,195.00	3/10/1998	Overseas Distribution
1045	Yiu	Terry	M	6/18/1961	$41,328.00	4/12/1999	European Distribution
1050	Zakowski	Carl	W	5/9/1967	$43,698.00	2/9/1998	European Distribution
1055	Thurston	Edward	S	1/3/1960	$41,498.00	6/22/1999	Overseas Distribution
1060	McKnight	Donald	Z	1/6/1964	$41,854.00	6/22/1998	European Distribution
1065	Liszniewski	Norm	M	11/16/1970	$42,659.00	2/6/2000	North American Distribution
1070	Jhawar	Balfor	R	9/3/1973	$43,661.00	11/22/2000	Overseas Distribution
1075	Fitchett	Mike	L	4/18/1966	$41,857.00	3/19/2001	Overseas Distribution
1080	Couture	Leo	S	1/8/1978	$42,185.00	1/17/2002	European Distribution

    New location of *Annual Salary* field.

11. Close the Employee Dates and Salaries table.

In Addition

Using Undo in Access

The Undo button in Microsoft Access contains a down-pointing triangle that will display a list of the last 20 actions that can be undone. When you undo an action that is not the first action in the list, all of the actions above the selected action are also undone. The Undo list is cleared when you switch views. If you decide you did not want to undo the action, click the Redo button on the toolbar.

IN BRIEF

Move a Field
1. Open table in Design view.
2. Select field to be moved.
3. Drag field to the new location.
4. Save and close the table.

SECTION 4: MODIFYING TABLES AND REPORTS, PERFORMING CALCULATIONS, AND VIEWING DATA

4.2 Inserting and Deleting Fields

Fields can be added to or deleted from the table after the table has been created. Exercise caution when making changes to the table structure after records have been entered. Data in deleted fields will be lost and existing records will have null values in new fields that have been added.

PROJECT: Rhonda Trask has suggested that the *Last Name*, *First Name*, and *Middle Initial* fields in the Employee Dates and Salaries table contain redundant information, since the table is related to the Employees table where this information already exists. You will delete these three fields and add a new field for the employee performance review date.

STEPS

1. With WE Employees4 open, open the Employee Dates and Salaries table in Design view.

2. Click the insertion point in any text in the Last Name row.

3. Click the Delete Rows button on the Table Design toolbar.

    You can also click Edit and then Delete Rows if you prefer to use the Menu bar.

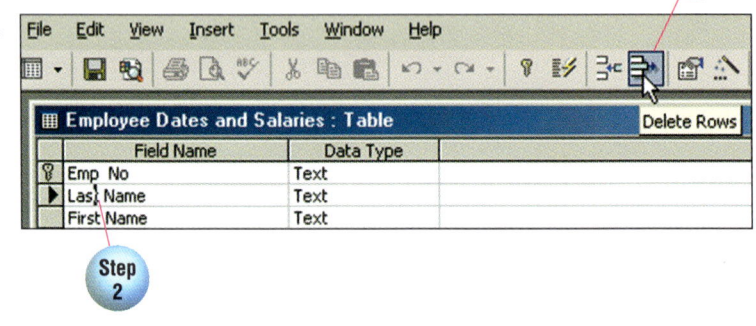

4. Click Yes at the Microsoft Access message asking you to confirm your wish to permanently delete the selected field(s) and all the data in the field(s).

    Multiple fields can be deleted in one operation. In the next step, you will select both the First Name and Middle Initial fields, and in step 6 you will delete both fields at the same time.

5. Position the mouse pointer in the field selector bar for the *First Name* field until the pointer changes to a right-pointing black arrow, hold down the left mouse button, and then drag the pointer down until both the *First Name* and *Middle Initial* fields are selected.

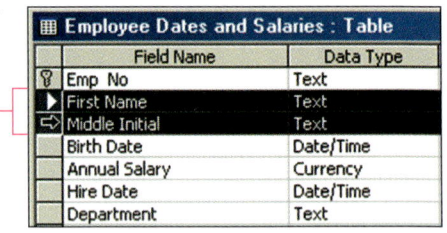

6. Click the Delete Rows button on the Table Design toolbar.

7. Click Yes at the Microsoft Access message.

8. Click the insertion point in any text in the *Department* field row.

    New rows are inserted above the active field.

ACCESS
100 SECTION 4: MODIFYING TABLES AND REPORTS, PERFORMING CALCULATIONS, AND VIEWING DATA

ACCESS

⑨ Click the Insert Rows button on the Table Design toolbar.

You can also click Insert and then Rows if you prefer to use the Menu bar. The new row is positioned between the *Hire Date* and *Department* fields.

New row is inserted above the selected field.

Field Name	Data Type
Emp No	Text
Birth Date	Date/Time
Annual Salary	Currency
Hire Date	Date/Time
Department	Text

⑩ Key **Annual Review Date** in the *Field Name* column, and then change the data type to Date/Time.

⑪ Click the Save button.

⑫ Switch to Datasheet view and then view the records in the Employee Dates and Salaries table.

⑬ Best Fit the *Annual Review Date* column.

Emp	Birth Date	Annual Salary	Hire Date	Annual Review Date	Department
1001	2/18/1957	$67,850.00	7/22/1997		North American Distribution
1005	3/12/1948	$67,850.00	8/15/1998		Overseas Distribution
1010	12/10/1952	$67,850.00	1/30/1998		European Distribution
1015	10/15/1959	$44,651.00	5/17/1997		North American Distribution
1020	5/22/1963	$45,178.00	8/3/1997		North American Distribution
1025	6/18/1970	$43,152.00	12/1/1997		North American Distribution
1030	7/27/1977	$41,624.00	1/22/1998		Overseas Distribution
1035	2/4/1970	$43,664.00	3/15/1998		European Distribution
1040	9/14/1972	$44,195.00	3/10/1998		Overseas Distribution
1045	6/18/1961	$41,328.00	4/12/1999		European Distribution
1050	5/9/1967	$43,698.00	2/9/1998		European Distribution
1055	1/3/1960	$41,498.00	6/22/1999		Overseas Distribution
1060	1/6/1964	$41,854.00	6/22/1998		European Distribution
1065	11/16/1970	$42,659.00	2/6/2000		North American Distribution
1070	9/3/1973	$43,661.00	11/22/2000		Overseas Distribution
1075	4/18/1966	$41,857.00	3/19/2001		Overseas Distribution
1080	1/8/1978	$42,185.00	1/17/2002		European Distribution
		$0.00			

⑭ Print and then close the Employee Dates and Salaries table. Click Yes when prompted to save changes to the layout of the table.

In Addition

Adding Data in a New Field

Consider the following tips for entering data in the datasheet for a new field that has been inserted into a table after several records have already been created.

- Click in the new column (i.e., *Annual Review Date*) in the first row of the table, key the data for the new field, and then press the down arrow key to remain in the same column for the next record.

- Press Ctrl + ' (apostrophe) if the data for the current record is the same field value as the data in the field immediately above the current record. Microsoft Access will automatically duplicate the entry that is above the active field.

In BRIEF

Delete a Field
1. Open table in Design view.
2. Select field to be deleted.
3. Click Delete Rows button on Table Design toolbar.
4. Click Yes.
5. Click Save button.

Insert a Field
1. Open table in Design view.
2. Click in the field row immediately below where new field is to be located.
3. Click Insert Rows button on Table Design toolbar.
4. Key field name, assign data type, and modify properties as needed.
5. Click Save button.

SECTION 4: MODIFYING TABLES AND REPORTS, PERFORMING CALCULATIONS, AND VIEWING DATA

4.3 Modifying Field Properties

In Section 2 you learned how to add entries to field properties by creating an input mask, changing the date format, changing the field size, entering a default value, entering a validation rule, and creating *Lookup* field properties. To add or edit entries to a field property after the table has been created, open the table in Design view, add or edit the property as required, and then save the table.

PROJECT: You will add a caption to the *Emp No* field and format the *FirstName*, *MiddleName*, *LastName*, and *StateOrProvince* fields in the Employees table to convert the existing data to uppercase letters.

STEPS

1. With WE Employees4 open, open the Employees table in Design view.

2. With the insertion point positioned in the *Emp No* field, click in the Caption field property box, and then key **Employee Number**.

   An entry in the caption property box becomes the column heading for the field in Datasheet view. If no entry exists in the caption property box, Access displays the field name as the label. Use the Caption property box to enter a user-friendly label for a field if the field name has been abbreviated, does not include a space between words, or is otherwise unsuitable as a column heading.

3. Click the Save button and then click the View button to switch to Datasheet view.

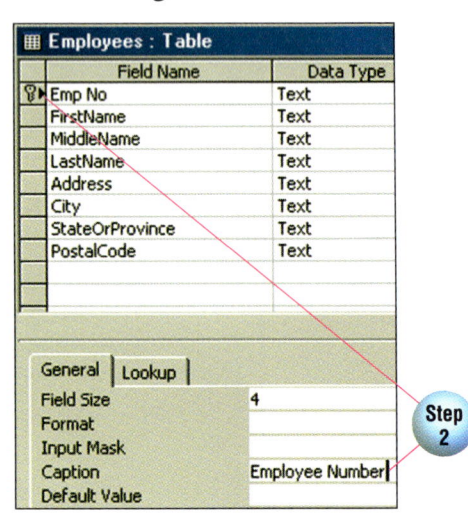

   Notice the first column is now labeled *Employee Number* instead of *Emp No*.

4. Best Fit the first column in the datasheet.

5. Switch to Design view and then click the insertion point in any text in the *FirstName* field row.

6. Click in the Format field property box, and then key **>**.

   PROBLEM? The *greater than* symbol (>) is located in the uppercase position on the period key in the alphabetic section of the keyboard. Hold down the Shift key and type period (.).

   The *greater than* symbol in the Format field property box for a Text field instructs Access to convert all data in the field to uppercase. New data will be converted to uppercase letters regardless of how it is keyed in the field.

7. Click the insertion point in any text in the *MiddleName* field row, click in the Format field property box, and then key **>**.

8. Key **>** in the Format field property box for the *LastName* and *StateOrProvince* fields.

ACCESS
102   SECTION 4: MODIFYING TABLES AND REPORTS, PERFORMING CALCULATIONS, AND VIEWING DATA

⑨ Click the Save button and then switch to Datasheet view.

The existing data in the *First Name*, *Middle Name*, *Last Name*, and *State/Province* columns has been converted to uppercase, as shown in Figure A4.2.

FIGURE A4.2 Data Converted to Uppercase

Employee Number	First Name	Middle Name	Last Name	Address	City	State/Province
1001	SAM	LAWRENCE	VESTERING	287-1501 Broadway	New York	NY
1005	ROMAN	WILLIAM	DEPTULSKI	112-657 E 39th St.	New York	NY
1010	HANH	ASTER	POSTMA	259 Lexington Avenu	New York	NY
1015	LYLE	CAMERON	BESTERD	1258 Park Avenue	New York	NY
1020	ANGELA	BONNIE	DOXTATOR	201-654 W 50th St.	New York	NY
1025	JORGE	NAIRN	BILISKI	439 7th Avenue	New York	NY
1030	THOM	PETER	HICKS	329-5673 W 63rd St.	New York	NY
1035	VALERIE	ELIZABETH	FISTOURIS	210 York Avenue	New York	NY
1040	GUY	FALLON	LAFRENIERE	329-8745 E 41st St.	New York	NY
1045	TERRY	MICHAEL	YIU	398-90 Little Brazil S	New York	NY
1050	CARL	WAYLON	ZAKOWSKI	65 Dyer Avenue	New York	NY
1055	EDWARD	SAMUEL	THURSTON	900-321 10th Avenue	New York	NY
1060	DONALD	ZAVIER	MCKNIGHT	43-874 Beekman Pla	New York	NY
1065	NORM	MATTHEW	LISZNIEWSKI	78-824 Madison Aver	New York	NY
1070	BALFOR	RICHARD	JHAWAR	54-908 WcHandys P	New York	NY
1075	MIKE	LYLE	FITCHETT	329-1009 W 23rd St.	New York	NY
1080	LEO	SAUNDERS	COUTURE	908-1200 W 46th St.	New York	NY

⑩ Add the following new record to the table. Key the data exactly as shown below. Access will automatically convert the name and state data to uppercase.

Employee Number	**1085**
First Name	**Cassandra**
Middle Name	**Rose**
Last Name	**Gauthier**
Address	**18-3142 Center Drive**
City	**New York**
State/Province	**ny**
Postal Code	**10111**

When you press Enter or Tab to move to the next field, Access converts the data to uppercase.

Step 10

⑪ Best Fit all of the columns.

⑫ Change the page orientation to landscape and then print the table.

⑬ Save and then close the Employees table.

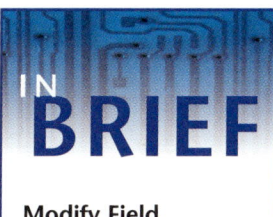

In Brief

Modify Field Properties
1. Open table in Design view.
2. Select field to be modified.
3. Add and/or edit field properties as required.
4. Click Save button.

SECTION 4: MODIFYING TABLES AND REPORTS, PERFORMING CALCULATIONS, AND VIEWING DATA

4.4 Adding a Calculated Control to a Form

A calculated control displays the results of a mathematical operation in a control object. The mathematical operation is performed on existing fields in the table. The results are displayed in the object in a similar manner as a field entry displays; however, the calculated results do not exist in the underlying table associated with the form. For example, if the table used to create the form is opened in Datasheet view, the calculated results will not appear in a column in the datasheet, since a calculated control is not stored as a field.

PROJECT: Worldwide Enterprises pays its employees 4% of their annual salary as vacation pay each year. You will add a calculated control object to the Employee Dates and Salaries form that will display the vacation pay entitlement for each employee.

STEPS

1. With WE Employees4 open, click Forms on the Objects bar, and then open the Employee Dates and Salaries form in Design view.

2. Maximize the Form window if it is not already maximized.

3. Position the mouse pointer at the top of the gray Form Footer border line until the pointer changes to a black horizontal line with an up- and down-pointing arrow, and then drag the Form Footer section down approximately 1 inch.

   This will create additional space at the bottom of the Detail section of the form.

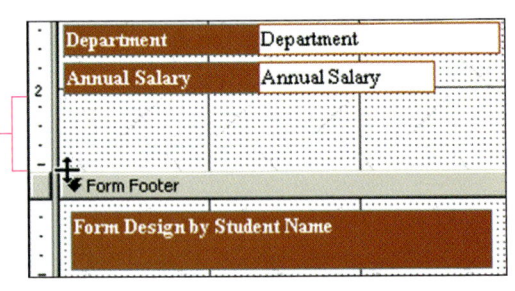

4. Click the Text Box object button [ab|] in the Toolbox.

5. Position the crosshairs pointer with the text box icon attached to it below the Annual Salary text box control, drag to create the object the approximate height and width shown at the right, and then release the mouse button.

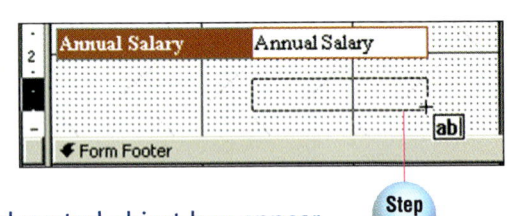

   A text box label control object and an unbound control object box appear. An *unbound* control contains data that is not stored anywhere. A control that displays a field value in a table is referred to as a *bound* control object since the object contents are bound to the table.

6. Click the Properties button on the Form Design toolbar to display the property sheet, and then click the Data tab in the Text Box property sheet.

7. Click in the Control Source property box, key **=[Annual Salary]*0.04**, and then press Enter.

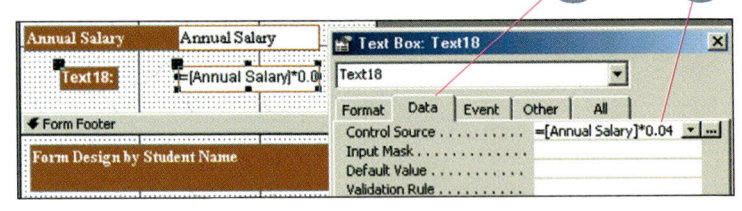

   A mathematical expression in a text box control begins with the equals sign (=) and field names are encased in square brackets. Use +, -, *, and / as mathematical operators within the expression.

8. Click the Format tab in the Text Box property sheet.

ACCESS
104 SECTION 4: MODIFYING TABLES AND REPORTS, PERFORMING CALCULATIONS, AND VIEWING DATA

ACCESS

9. With the insertion point positioned in the Format property box, click the down-pointing triangle that appears, scroll down the drop-down list, and then click *Currency*.

10. Scroll down the Format property sheet, click in the Font Name property box, click the down-pointing triangle that appears, scroll down the font list, and then click *Times New Roman*.

11. Click in the Font Size property box, click the down-pointing triangle that appears, and then click *10* in the drop-down list.

12. Close the Text Box property sheet.

    Do not be concerned if a portion of the mathematical formula no longer appears inside the text box control object. The increased font size prevents the entire formula from displaying within the control. This object will be displaying values in Form view that will fit within the current size.

13. Click the label control object adjacent to the text box control (currently displays *Text##* [where ## is the number of the label object]) to select it.

14. Click a second time inside the selected label control object to display the insertion point, delete the current text, and then key **Vacation Pay**. The width of the box will increase as you key the text.

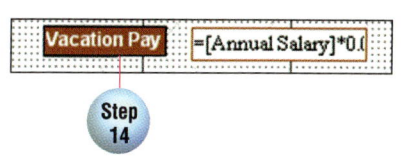

15. With the insertion point positioned inside the Vacation Pay label control object, click the Properties button on the Form Design toolbar, change the Font Name to Times New Roman, the Font Size to 10, and then close the property sheet.

16. Position the mouse pointer on the large black handle at the top left of the Vacation Pay label control object until the pointer changes to a black hand with the index finger pointing upward, drag left as shown at the right, and then release the mouse button.

    Dragging the large black handle moves the label control object separately from the text box control.

17. Drag the right middle sizing handle on the Vacation Pay label control object to extend the width equal to the label control objects above Vacation Pay.

18. Click the Save button, switch to Form view, scroll through the records to view the vacation pay for each employee, and then print the last record only in the form.

19. Close the Employee Dates and Salaries form. Click <u>Y</u>es to save changes to the form design.

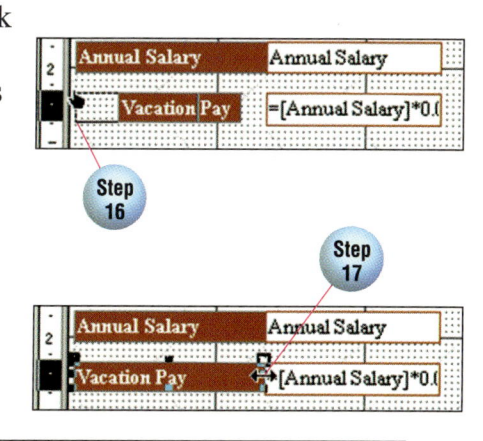

SECTION 4: MODIFYING TABLES AND REPORTS, PERFORMING CALCULATIONS, AND VIEWING DATA

ACCESS
105

4.5 Modifying a Report; Creating a Calculated Control

Modifying a report by resizing, moving, and formatting controls is often required to fine-tune the appearance after the Report Wizard creates the report. A calculated control object can be created in a report by completing steps similar to those learned in the previous topic. The results are displayed and printed in the report. The calculations are not stored in the table, but are dynamically calculated each time the report is previewed or printed.

PROJECT: Worldwide Enterprises estimates that it incurs benefit costs of an additional 20% of an employee's annual salary to cover employer cost of the pension contribution, vacation pay, health insurance, and so on. You will create a report to print a list of employees based on a query and add a control to calculate the estimated benefit cost.

STEPS

1. With WE Employees4 open, click Reports on the Objects bar and then create a new report using the Report Wizard as follows.
   - Add all fields from the Trask Employee List query.
   - Double-click the *Department* field in the second Report Wizard dialog box to group the entries in the report by department.
   - Sort the report by the employee's last name in Ascending order.
   - Choose the block layout in landscape orientation.
   - Choose the Soft Gray style.
   - Key **Employee Benefit Cost** as the title of the report.

2. Click the Close button on the Print Preview toolbar after viewing the report to display the report in Design view.

   The report contains an additional section named Department Header since the report is grouped by the *Department* field.

3. Maximize the report window if it is not already maximized.

4. Click the Employee Number label control object in the Page Header section.

5. Hold down Shift and then click the Emp No control in the Detail section.

   Both controls are now selected.

6. Press Delete.

7. Click the Last Name label control object in the Page Header section, Shift + click the LastName field control in the Detail section, and then resize the controls to position 3 on the horizontal ruler.

   With both controls selected, dragging the right sizing handle of one control will also resize the other control.

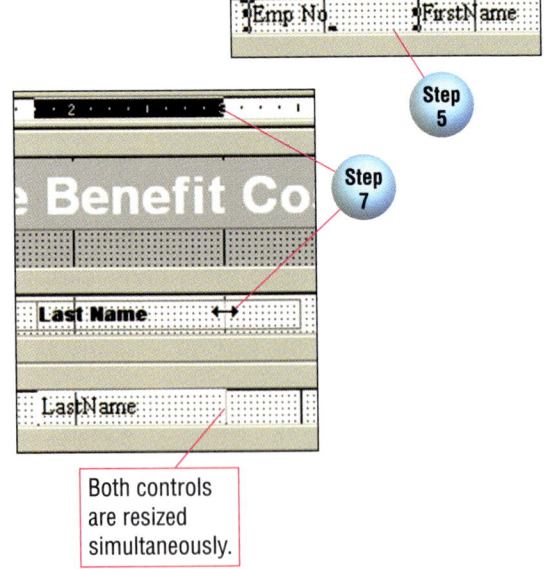

   Both controls are resized simultaneously.

SECTION 4: MODIFYING TABLES AND REPORTS, PERFORMING CALCULATIONS, AND VIEWING DATA

8. Select both First Name controls. Position the mouse pointer on the border of one of the selected controls until the pointer changes to a black hand, and then drag the controls left to align the left edge at position 3.25 on the horizontal ruler.

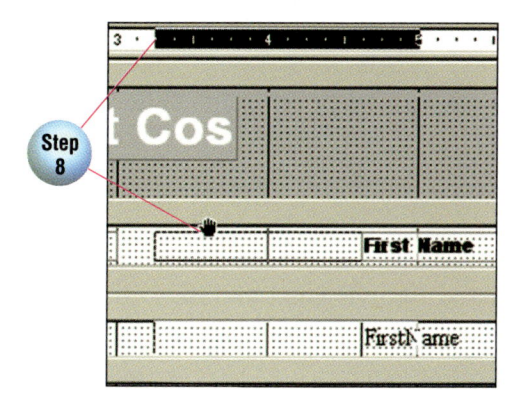

9. With both First Name controls still selected, drag the right middle sizing handle to resize the controls so that the right edge is at position 4.25 on the horizontal ruler.

10. Select both Hire Date controls and then drag the border left to align the left edge at position 4.5 on the horizontal ruler.

11. Select both Annual Salary controls and then drag the border left to align the left edge at position 5.5 on the horizontal ruler.

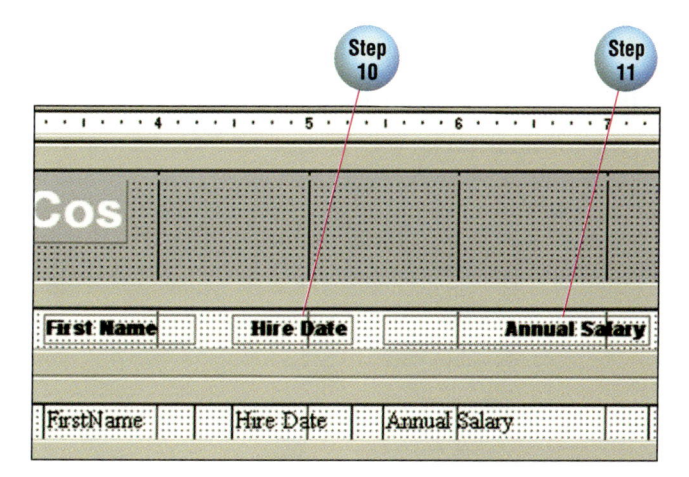

12. Click the right scroll arrow until you can see the right edge of the report.

13. Click the Label object button in the Toolbox.

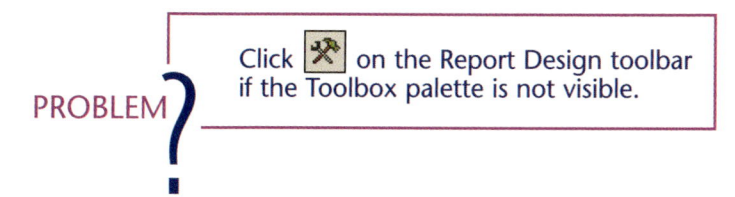

PROBLEM? Click on the Report Design toolbar if the Toolbox palette is not visible.

(continued)

SECTION 4: MODIFYING TABLES AND REPORTS, PERFORMING CALCULATIONS, AND VIEWING DATA

14. Position the crosshairs pointer with the label icon attached in the Page Header section to the right of Annual Salary, drag to create the outline the approximate height and width shown below, and then release the mouse button.

    An insertion point is positioned in the top left corner of the label control.

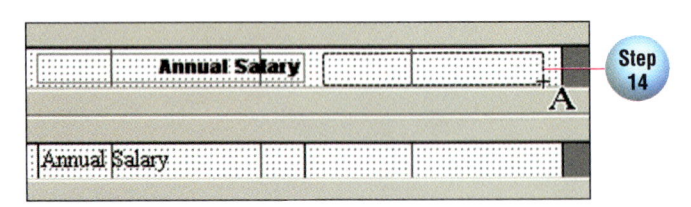

15. Key **Estimated Benefit Cost** and then click outside the label control object to deselect it.

16. Click the Annual Salary control, click the Format Painter button on the Report Design toolbar, and then click the Estimated Benefit Cost label control. Widen the control if necessary to display the entire label contents.

    Format Painter copies the formatting attributes for the Annual Salary label to the Estimated Benefit Cost label.

17. Click the Text Box object button in the Toolbox palette.

18. Position the crosshairs pointer with the text box icon attached in the Detail section below the Estimated Benefit Cost label, drag to create an object the same height and width as the label, and then release the mouse button.

19. Click in the text box control (displays *Unbound*), key **=[Annual Salary]*0.2**, and then click outside the control to deselect it.

    In the previous topic, you learned how to enter a mathematical expression by displaying the property sheet and keying the formula in the Control Source property box. Alternatively, you can key the expression directly into the control object.

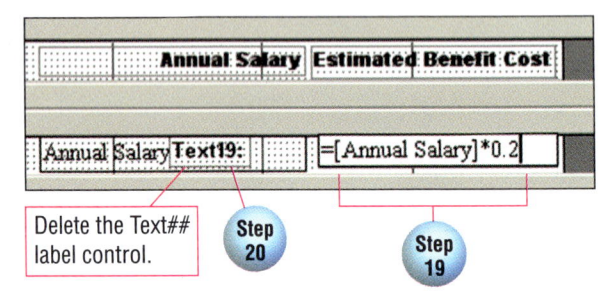

20. Click the label control to the left of the text box control (displays *Text##* [where ## is the text box label number]) and press Delete.

21. Click the Print Preview button to preview the report. If necessary, scroll right to view the right edge of the report where the calculated values display.

    Notice the calculated values are aligned at the left edge of the column, do not display a consistent number of decimal places, and the border lines are not surrounding the values as in the remainder of the report.

22. Close the Print Preview window.

23. Click the Annual Salary control in the Detail section, click the Format Painter button on the Report Design toolbar, and then click the calculated control object containing the mathematical expression.

    The border attributes are copied to the calculated control object.

ACCESS

24. Click to select the calculated control object and then click the Properties button on the Report Design toolbar.

25. Change the following properties on the Format tab in the property sheet:
    - Format property to Currency.
    - Text Align property to Right.

PROBLEM? Scroll down the Format property sheet to locate the Text Align property box.

26. Close the Text Box property sheet.

27. Preview the *Employee Benefit Cost* report. If necessary, adjust controls by moving and/or resizing objects as necessary to fine-tune the report.

Employee Benefit Cost

Department	Last Name	First Name	Hire Date	Annual Salary	Estimated Benefit Cost
European Distribution	COUTURE	LEO	1/17/2002	$42,185.00	$8,437.00
	FISTOURIS	VALERIE	3/15/1998	$43,664.00	$8,732.80
	MCKNIGHT	DONALD	6/22/1998	$41,854.00	$8,370.80
	POSTMA	HANH	1/30/1998	$67,850.00	$13,570.00
	YIU	TERRY	4/12/1999	$41,328.00	$8,265.60
	ZAKOWSKI	CARL	2/9/1998	$43,698.00	$8,739.60

Step 27

28. Print and then close the *Employee Benefit Cost* report. Click <u>Y</u>es to save changes to the report design.

29. Close WE Employees4.

In Addition

Report and Section Properties

A property sheet is available for the report and for each section in the report. Open the report or section property sheet to change formats, control page breaks, and so on. To display the property sheet for the report, double-click the Report Selector button ■ at the top left corner of the horizontal and vertical rulers in Design view. To display the property sheet for a section, double-click the section name in the gray section bar. The Format tab in the Detail property sheet is shown at the right.

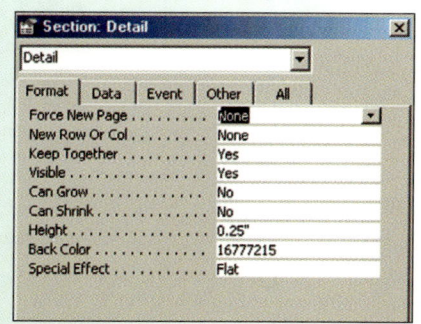

IN BRIEF

Modify Control Properties
1. Display report in Design view.
2. Click control object to be modified.
3. Click Properties button on Report Design toolbar.
4. Change properties as required.
5. Close property sheet.
6. Click Save button.

SECTION 4: MODIFYING TABLES AND REPORTS, PERFORMING CALCULATIONS, AND VIEWING DATA

ACCESS 109

4.6 Using the Label Wizard

Access includes the Label Wizard as one of the reports that can be used to generate mailing labels. Using the Label Wizard is very similar to using the Report Wizard, with the exception that you insert the required name and address fields into a prototype label in one of the wizard dialog boxes. The Label Wizard includes preformatted reports for many of the popular commercially available adhesive labels.

PROJECT: The summer movie release list is ready for mailing. You will generate mailing labels to the U.S. distributors using the Label Wizard.

STEPS

1. Open WE Distributors4.

2. Click Reports on the Objects bar and then click the New button on the WE Distributors4 : Database toolbar.

3. Click *Label Wizard* in the New Report dialog box.

4. Click the down-pointing triangle next to the Choose the table or query where the object's data comes from list box, click *US Distributors* in the drop-down list, and then click OK.

5. If necessary, scroll down the Product number list box, click *5163*, and then click Next.

    The default options for the label size dialog box are English for Units of Measure and Sheet feed for Label Type. The Filter by manufacturer is set to Avery.

6. Click the down-pointing triangle next to the Font size list box, click *12* in the drop-down list, and then click Next.

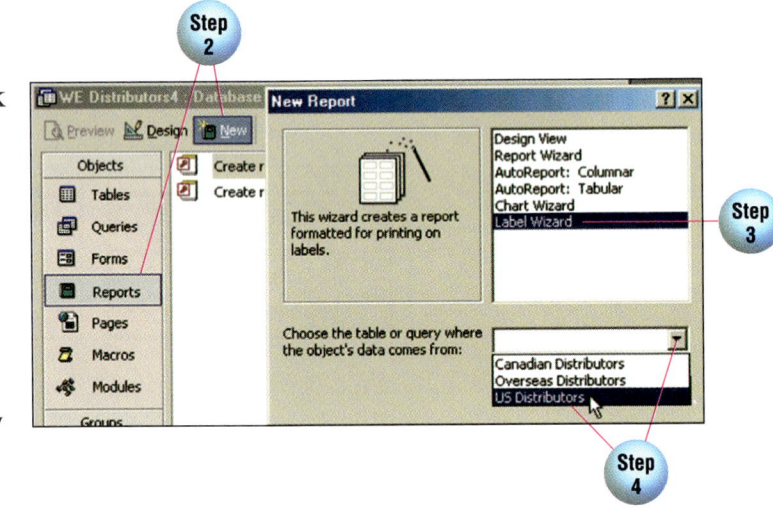

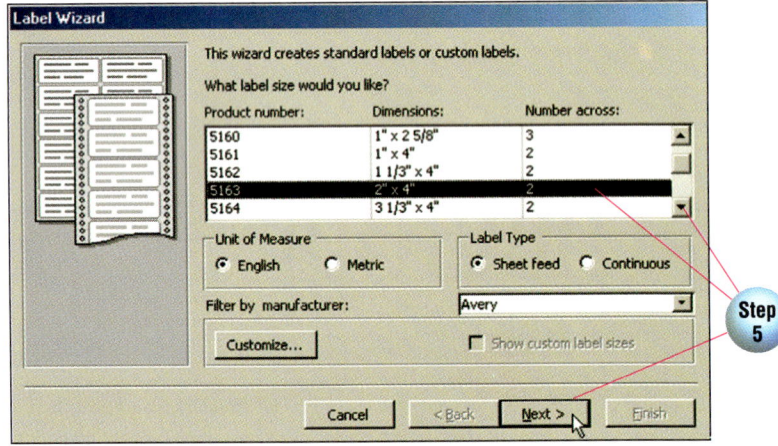

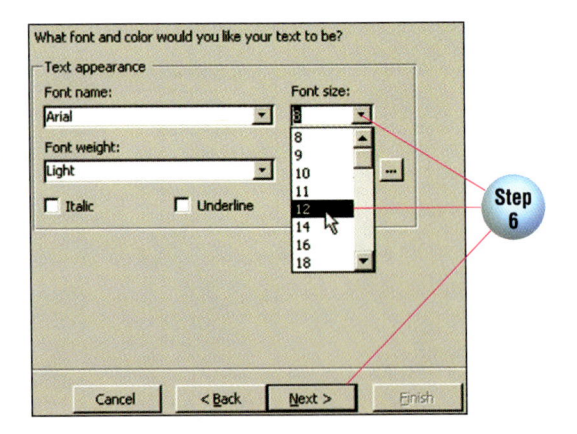

ACCESS

110 SECTION 4: MODIFYING TABLES AND REPORTS, PERFORMING CALCULATIONS, AND VIEWING DATA

ACCESS

7. With the insertion point positioned at the top left of the Prototype label, double-click *Name* in the Available fields list box to move *Name* to the Prototype label, and then press Enter.

   Access inserts the field code {Name} on the Prototype label and moves the insertion point to the next line. The Prototype label is the template that Access uses to determine how to position data from the name and address fields in the selected table onto the mailing labels.

8. Double-click *Street Address1* in the Available fields list box, and then press Enter.

9. Double-click *Street Address2* in the Available fields list box, and then press Enter.

10. Double-click *City*, key a comma (,), press the spacebar, double-click *State*, press the spacebar, and then double-click *Zip Code*.

11. Click Next.

12. Click Next to proceed without specifying a field to sort by.

13. Click Finish at the last Label Wizard dialog box to accept the default title of *Labels US Distributors* and preview the mailing labels in the Print Preview window.

   PROBLEM? Click OK if a message box appears stating that some data may not be displayed.

   The labels appear in the Print Preview window as shown below.

14. Scroll the two-page mailing label report in the Print Preview window, then click File and then Print. Click OK in the Print dialog box. Click OK if a message box appears stating that some data may not be displayed.

15. Click the Close button on the Print Preview toolbar.

16. Close WE Distributors4.

IN BRIEF

Generate Mailing Labels
1. Click Reports on the Objects bar.
2. Click New, Label Wizard.
3. Choose table to create labels from.
4. Click OK.
5. Choose label size.
6. Click Next.
7. Choose font and font size.
8. Click Next.
9. Insert fields on prototype label.
10. Click Next.
11. Choose field to sort by.
12. Click Next.
13. Key name for report.
14. Click Finish.

SECTION 4: MODIFYING TABLES AND REPORTS, PERFORMING CALCULATIONS, AND VIEWING DATA

4.7 Displaying Records in a Subdatasheet

When two tables are joined by establishing a relationship, you can view the two tables at the same time by displaying the subdatasheet. To do this, open the primary table in Datasheet view. A column between the record selector bar and the first field in each row displays a plus symbol (+). Click the plus symbol (referred to as the *expand indicator*) next to the record for which you want to view the data in the related table. A subdatasheet will appear within the primary datasheet. To remove the subdatasheet, click the minus symbol (–) to collapse it (the plus symbol changes to a minus symbol after the record has been expanded).

PROJECT: The Employees table is joined to the Employee Expenses table in a one-to-many relationship. You will open the Employees table in Datasheet view, expand records to display expenses for an employee, display the subdatasheets for several other employees, and then close the subdatasheets.

S T E P S

1. Open WE Employees4, and then open the Employees table in Datasheet view.

2. Click the plus symbol (expand indicator) between the record selector bar and *1001* in the first row in the datasheet.

    The subdatasheet (see Figure A4.3) opens to display the records for the same employee (Sam Vestering) in the related table (Employee Expenses). The record navigation bar at the bottom of the datasheet becomes active for the subdatasheeet.

FIGURE A4.3 Datasheet and Subdatasheet

3. Click the New Record button on the Table Datasheet toolbar. An insertion point appears in the blank row at the bottom of the subdatasheet. Key the following data in the new record:

Date	**6/27/03**
Amount	**955.67**
Type	**Professional Development**
Description	**E-Commerce Conference**

ACCESS

112   SECTION 4: MODIFYING TABLES AND REPORTS, PERFORMING CALCULATIONS, AND VIEWING DATA

4. Click the minus symbol (collapse indicator) between the record selector bar and *1001* in the first row in the datasheet.

   The subdatasheet closes.

5. Click the plus symbol next to employee number *1005* to display the subdatasheet for Roman William Deptulski.

6. Click the plus symbol next to employee number *1010* to display the subdatasheet for Hanh Aster Postma.

7. Collapse the subdatasheets for employee numbers *1005* and *1010*.

8. Click F̲ormat, point to S̲ubdatasheet, and then click E̲xpand All.

   All subdatasheets open.

   Step 8

9. Maximize the datasheet if it is not already maximized and then scroll down and view the records and related records in the subdatasheets.

10. Click F̲ormat, point to S̲ubdatasheet, and then click C̲ollapse All.

    All of the open subdatasheets close.

11. Close the Employees table.

12. Open the Employee Benefits table.

13. Click the plus symbol next to employee number *1001*.

    The subdatasheet opens showing the employee's name and address.

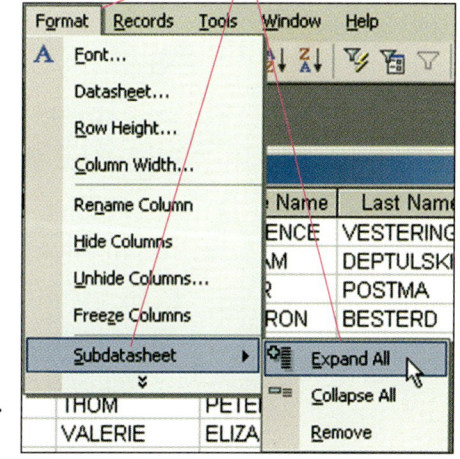

14. Click the plus symbol next to the first name *SAM* in the subdatasheet.

    The data in the Employee Expenses table for Sam Vestering appears within another subdatasheet as shown below.

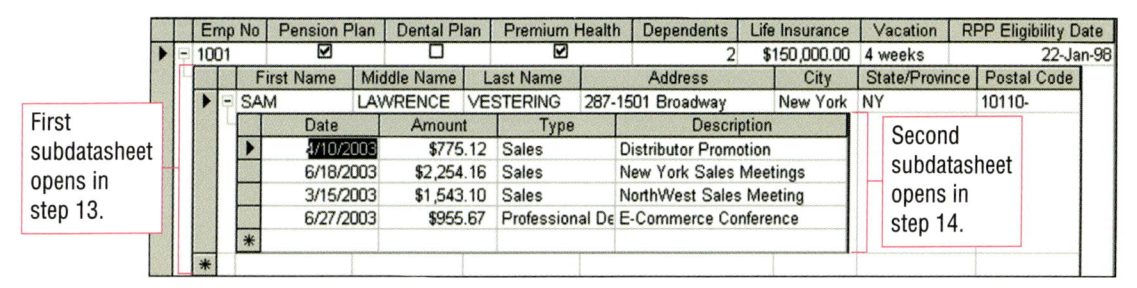

    First subdatasheet opens in step 13.

    Second subdatasheet opens in step 14.

15. Click the minus symbol next to the first name *SAM* in the first subdatasheet to collapse the Employee Expenses subdatasheet.

16. Click the minus symbol next to employee number *1001* to collapse the Employees subdatasheet.

17. Close the Employee Benefits table.

SECTION 4: MODIFYING TABLES AND REPORTS, PERFORMING CALCULATIONS, AND VIEWING DATA

ACCESS
113

4.8 Applying and Removing Filters

A *filter* is used to view only those records in a datasheet that meet a specified criteria. For example, you might want to view only those records of employees who work in a specific department. Once the filter has been applied, you can view, edit, and print the filtered records. The records that do not meet the criteria are temporarily removed from the datasheet. Click the Remove Filter button on the Table Datasheet toolbar to redisplay all records in the table. Records can be filtered using two methods—Filter By Selection, and Filter By Form. The difference between a filter and a query is that the query can be saved for future use, whereas the filter has to be redone each time.

PROJECT: You will use the Filter By Selection method in the Employee Dates and Salaries table to display and print records of employees who work in the European Distribution department. In the Employee Benefits table, you will use the Filter By Form method to print a list of employees who receive four weeks of vacation.

STEPS

1. With WE Employees4 open, open the Employee Dates and Salaries table in Datasheet view.

2. Select the text *European Distribution* in the *Department* column in the third row of the datasheet.

3. Click the Filter By Selection button on the Table Datasheet toolbar.

   Only records of employees in the European Distribution department are displayed, as shown in Figure A4.4.

FIGURE A4.4 Filtered Datasheet

	Emp	Birth Date	Annual Salary	Hire Date	Annual Review Date	Department
▶+	1010	12/10/1952	$67,850.00	1/30/1998		European Distribution
+	1035	2/4/1970	$43,664.00	3/15/1998		European Distribution
+	1045	6/18/1961	$41,328.00	4/12/1999		European Distribution
+	1050	5/9/1967	$43,698.00	2/9/1998		European Distribution
+	1060	1/6/1964	$41,854.00	6/22/1998		European Distribution
+	1080	1/8/1978	$42,185.00	1/17/2002		European Distribution
*			$0.00			

4. Print the table.

5. Click the Remove Filter button on the Table Datasheet toolbar.

   All records in the table are redisplayed.

6. Close the Employee Dates and Salaries table. Click No if prompted to save changes.

7. Open the Employee Benefits table in Datasheet view.

8. Click the Filter By Form button on the Table Datasheet toolbar.

   All records are temporarily removed from the datasheet and a blank row appears. Specify the field and the field value you want to filter by using the fields in the blank row.

ACCESS

⑨ Click in the *Vacation* column, click the down-pointing triangle that appears, and then click *4 weeks* in the drop-down list.

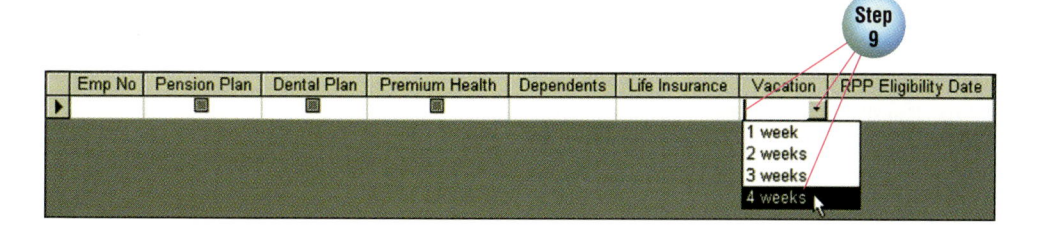

⑩ Click the Apply Filter button on the Table Datasheet toolbar.

The Apply Filter button changes to the Remove Filter button once a filter has been applied to a table.

⑪ Change the page orientation to landscape and then print the table.

⑫ Click the Remove Filter button on the Table Datasheet toolbar.

⑬ Close the Employee Benefits table. Click <u>N</u>o if prompted to save changes.

In Addition

Filtering by Multiple Criteria

The Filter By Form window contains a tab labeled *Or* at the bottom of the window (shown at the right), just above the Status bar. Use this tab to filter by more than one criterion. For example, you could display records of employees who receive three weeks or four weeks of vacation. To do this, click the Filter By Form button and select *3 weeks* in the *Vacation* field, click the Or tab and select *4 weeks* in the *Vacation* field in the second form. Click the Apply Filter button. Records that meet either the three weeks or four weeks criterion will be displayed.

Use this tab to add a second criterion to filter by.

IN BRIEF

Filter By Selection
1. Open table in Datasheet view.
2. Select field value in field you want to filter by.
3. Click Filter By Selection button.
4. View, print, and/or edit data as required.
5. Click Remove Filter button.

Filter By Form
1. Open the table in Datasheet view.
2. Click Filter By Form button.
3. Click in field you want to filter by.
4. Click down-pointing triangle and click value you want to filter by.
5. Click Apply Filter button.
6. View, print, and/or edit data as required.
7. Click Remove Filter button.

SECTION 4: MODIFYING TABLES AND REPORTS, PERFORMING CALCULATIONS, AND VIEWING DATA

4.9 Creating Data Access Pages

Data access pages are Web pages created from tables or queries that are used for interacting with Microsoft Access databases on the Internet or on a company's intranet. Data access pages are stored outside the database file. Designing and modifying a data access page is similar to designing forms and reports. Access includes a Page Wizard that can be used to create a data access page.

PROJECT: You will create a Web page that will enable employees to view their benefits through a Web browser.

STEPS

1. With WE Employees4 open, click the Pages button on the Objects bar.

2. Double-click *Create data access page by using wizard*.

3. With *Table: Employee Benefits* already selected in the Tables/Queries list box in the first Page Wizard dialog box, click *Emp No* in the Available Fields list box and then click the Add Field button `>`.

4. Double-click *Pension Plan, Dental Plan, Premium Health, Life Insurance,* and *Vacation* to move the fields from the Available Fields list box to the Selected Fields list box.

5. Click Next.

6. Click Next at the second Page Wizard dialog box to continue without adding a grouping level to the page.

7. Click Next at the third Page Wizard dialog box to continue without specifying a field to sort the records by.

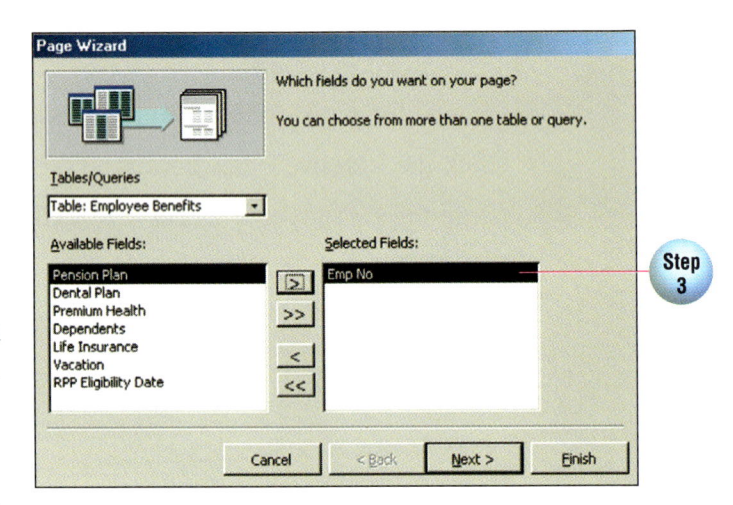

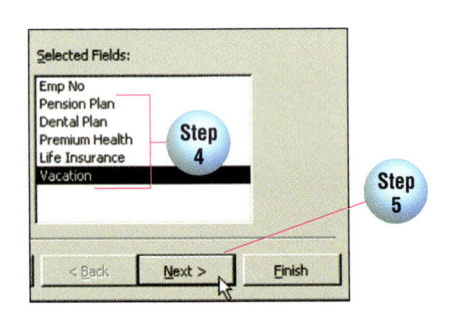

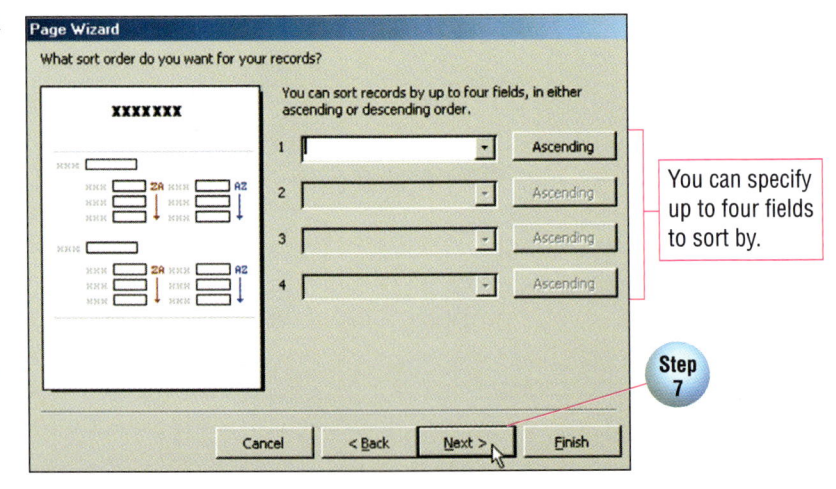

SECTION 4: MODIFYING TABLES AND REPORTS, PERFORMING CALCULATIONS, AND VIEWING DATA

8 Click Finish at the last Page Wizard dialog box to accept the default title Employee Benefits and Modify the page's design.

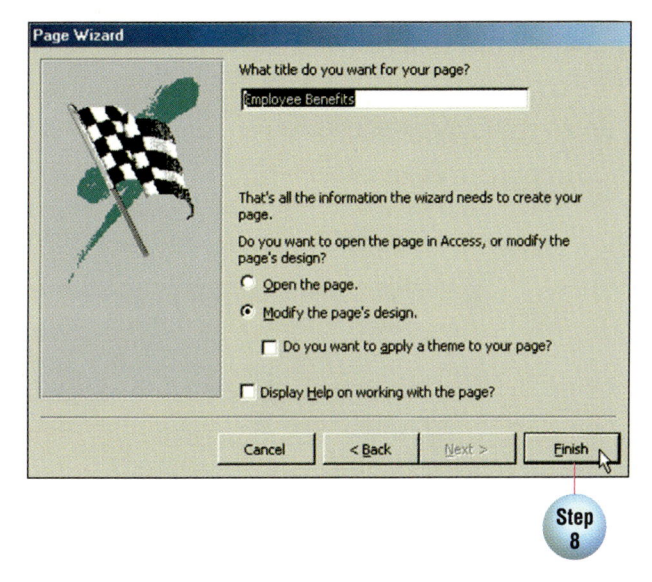

Step 8

In a few seconds the data access page is displayed in Design view, as shown in Figure A4.5.

FIGURE A4.5 Data Access Page Design View

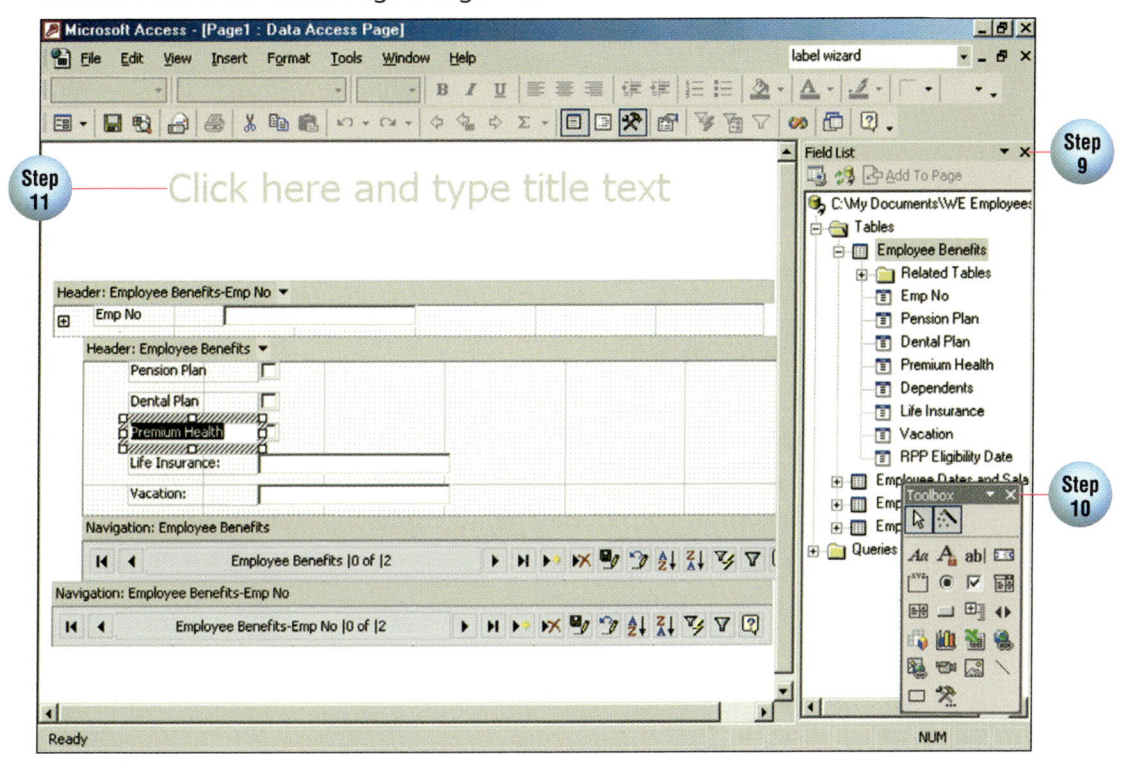

9 Click the Close button at the top right of the Field List Task Pane.

10 Click the Close button on the Toolbox palette Title bar.

11 Click in the text *Click here and type title text* and then key **Worldwide Enterprises Employee Benefits**.

As soon as you click within *Click here and type title text*, the text will disappear and will be replaced with the text you key.

(continued)

SECTION 4: MODIFYING TABLES AND REPORTS, PERFORMING CALCULATIONS, AND VIEWING DATA

12. Click F̲ormat and then T̲heme.

    A *theme* is a group of predefined formats and color schemes for bullets, fonts, horizontal lines, background images, and other data access page elements. Choosing a theme saves a considerable amount of time and allows you to create a Web page that has a professional appearance.

13. Scroll down the Choose a T̲heme list box and then click *Network Blitz*.

    The Sample of theme Network Blitz window displays the selected theme's colors, bullet style, line style, button style, and formats.

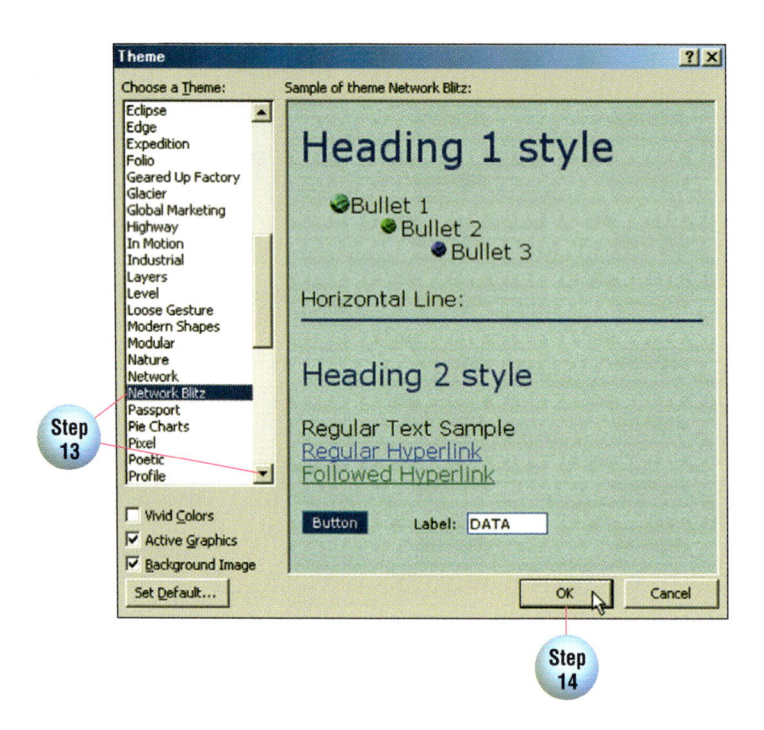

Step 13

Step 14

14. Click OK.

    The Network Blitz theme is applied to the Employee Benefits data access page.

15. Click the Save button on the Page Design toolbar.

16. Key **WE Employee Benefits** in the File n̲ame text box and then click S̲ave. (If a message appears stating that the connection string of this page specifies an absolute path and might not be able to connect to data through the network, click OK.)

17. Click F̲ile and then Web̲ Page Preview.

    The data access page displays in the default Web browser window.

18. Click the plus symbol next to employee number *1001* in the Web browser window.

    The record expands to display the benefits associated with employee number 1001, as shown in Figure A4.6.

SECTION 4: MODIFYING TABLES AND REPORTS, PERFORMING CALCULATIONS, AND VIEWING DATA

FIGURE A4.6 Employee Benefits Data Access Page in Web Browser Window

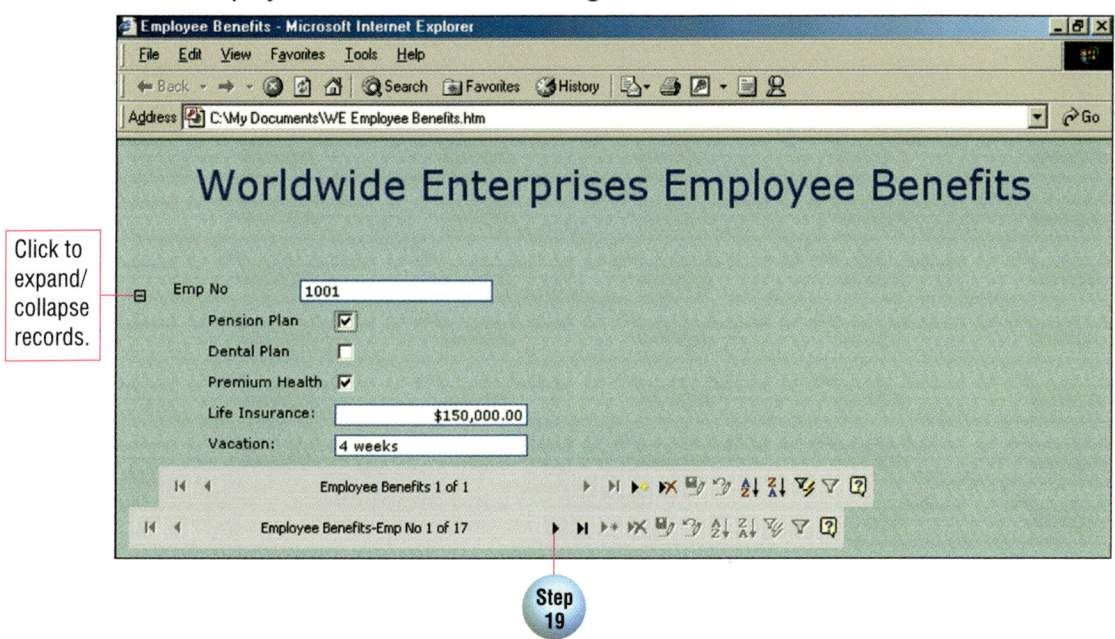

Click to expand/collapse records.

Step 19

19. Scroll through the records in the data access page in the Web browser window by clicking the Next Record button on the lower navigation bar and then expanding the record by clicking the plus symbol.
20. Close the Web browser window.
21. Close the WE Employee Benefits Web Page Data Access Page window.

Data Access pages are stored ouside the database file. The object name in the database window is a shortcut only to the location of the Web files.

In Addition

Using Data Access Pages

When a data access page is created, Access creates a folder in which to store the Web page files. Although the Web pages are not stored directly within the database, the data access page is directly connected to the source database. When a user displays the data access page in the browser, she or he is viewing a copy of the page. Any filtering or sorting that is done to affect the way the data is *displayed* affects only this copy of the page. Changes made to the *content* of the data, however, such as inserting, editing, or deleting field values, are updated immediately in the source database so that everyone viewing the data access page is working with the same information.

In Brief

Create a Data Access Page
1. Click Pages on the Objects bar.
2. Double-click *Create data access page by using wizard*.
3. Choose table or query and field(s) to include in Web page.
4. Click Next.
5. Choose a grouping level and click Next.
6. Choose a field to sort by and click Next.
7. Key page title and click Finish.
8. Modify page in Design view as required.
9. Click Save.
10. Key Web page file name, click Save.

SECTION 4: MODIFYING TABLES AND REPORTS, PERFORMING CALCULATIONS, AND VIEWING DATA

4.10 Inserting Hyperlinks

Hyperlinks can be inserted in data access pages by keying a URL (Uniform Resource Locator) in a label control in the data access page. Access automatically converts the URL to a hyperlink. To hyperlink to other files or Web pages, click the Hyperlink button in the Toolbox palette. Drag to create the outline of a rectangle in the data access page. When you release the mouse button, the Insert Hyperlink dialog box automatically appears. Key the text you want to display for the hyperlink in the Text to display text box and then key the destination for the link in the Type the file or Web page name text box.

PROJECT: You will create a new Web page for displaying employee names and addresses and then create a link in the page to display the employee benefits.

STEPS

1. With WE Employees4 open and Pages selected on the Objects bar, create a new data access page using the Page Wizard as follows.
   - Add all of the fields except *MiddleName* from the Employees table.
   - Click Next at the second Page Wizard dialog box to specify no grouping levels.
   - Choose to sort by the *LastName* field in ascending order at the third Page Wizard dialog box.
   - Accept *Employees* as the title of the Web page.

2. Close the Field List Task Pane in the Data Access Page Design view window.

3. Key **Worldwide Enterprises Employees and Benefits** as the title text.

4. Apply the Nature theme to the data access page.

5. Click the Toolbox button  on the Page Design toolbar and then click the Hyperlink button  in the Toolbox Palette.

6. Position the crosshairs pointer with the hyperlink icon attached to the right of the State/Province text box control, drag to create a box the approximate height and width shown at the right, and then release the mouse.

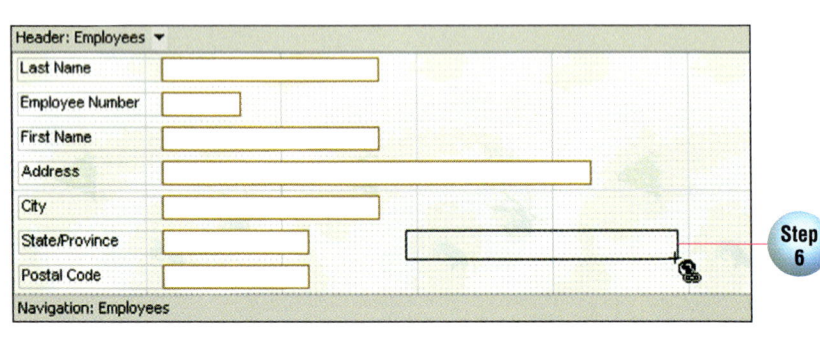

7. At the Insert Hyperlink dialog box, click in the Text to display text box and then key **Employee Benefits**.

8. Click the *Page in This Database* icon on the Link to Objects bar.

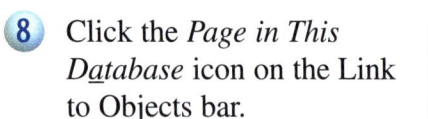

9. Double-click *WE Employee Benefits* in the Select a page in this database list box.

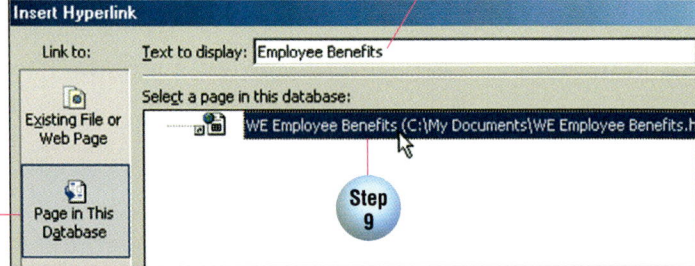

ACCESS
120   SECTION 4: MODIFYING TABLES AND REPORTS, PERFORMING CALCULATIONS, AND VIEWING DATA

⑩ With the hyperlink control object selected, click the down-pointing triangle at the right of the Font Size button on the Formatting (Page) toolbar and then click *10* in the drop-down list.

⑪ Click in the page outside the hyperlink control to deselect the object.

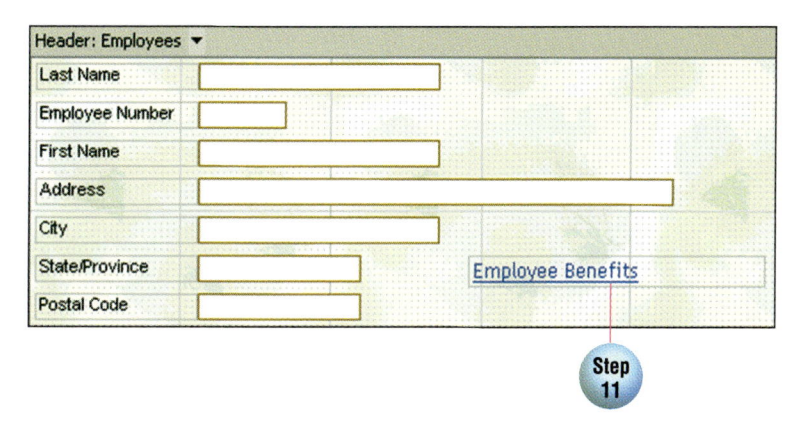

Step 11

⑫ Click the Save button, key **WE Employees** in the File name text box, and then click Save. (Click OK if a message appears stating that the connection string of this page specifies an absolute path and might not be able to connect to data through the network.)

⑬ Click File and then Web Page Preview.

⑭ Click the hyperlink text *Employee Benefits* when the first record displays in the default Web browser.

⑮ Click the Back button on the Web browser toolbar to return to the WE Employees Web page.

⑯ Close the Web browser window.

⑰ Close the WE Employees data access page.

⑱ Close the WE Employees4 database.

In Addition

E-Mail Address Hyperlinks

The Link to Objects bar in the Insert Hyperlink dialog box contains an E-mail Address button. Create an e-mail hyperlink to allow users to create an e-mail message with the correct address entered for them. When the user clicks the link, a message window will open in which he or she can key the subject and content of the message and then click Send. When you click the *E-mail Address* icon on the Link to Objects bar, the Insert Hyperlink dialog box displays as shown at the right.

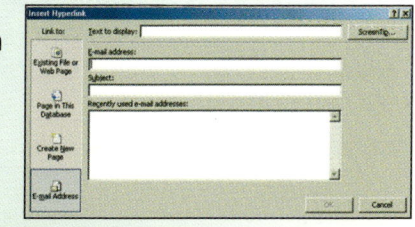

IN BRIEF

Insert a Hyperlink
1 Open data access page in Design view.
2 Click Hyperlink button in Toolbox.
3 Drag to create outline of rectangle in desired location on page.
4 Key display text for the link in the Text to display text box.
5 Key file name or URL in the Address text box.
6 Click OK.
7 Click Save button.

SECTION 4: MODIFYING TABLES AND REPORTS, PERFORMING CALCULATIONS, AND VIEWING DATA

FEATURES SUMMARY

Feature	Button	Menu	Keyboard
Collapse subdatasheet		Format, Subdatasheet, Collapse All	
Delete rows	■	Edit, Delete Rows	
Expand subdatasheet		Format, Subdatasheet, Expand All	
Filter by form	■	Records, Filter, Filter By Form	
Filter by selection	■	Records, Filter, Filter By Selection	
Insert hyperlink	■	Insert, Hyperlink	Ctrl + K
Insert rows	■	Insert, Rows	
Label Wizard		Insert, Report, Label Wizard	
Page Wizard		Insert, Page, Page Wizard	
Property sheet	■	View, Properties	F4
Theme		Format, Theme	
Toolbox palette	■	View, Toolbox	

PROCEDURES CHECK

Completion: In the space provided at the right, indicate the correct term or command.

1. To move, insert, or delete a field in a table, open the table in this view. _____
2. Key this symbol in the Format property box for a Text field to convert all characters to uppercase. _____
3. Click this button in the Toolbox to create a calculated field in a form or report. _____
4. This wizard is used to generate mailing labels. _____
5. Click this symbol next to a record to view the subdatasheet for the related table. _____
6. Click this button on the Datasheet toolbar to temporarily remove all records from the display and then select a criterion from a drop-down list of field values in a field. _____
7. This is the name of the wizard used to facilitate creating a Web page for a table or query. _____
8. This is the name given to a group of predefined formats and color schemes that can be applied to Web pages. _____
9. Click this button in the Toolbox to create a link to another Web page or URL. _____

Identify the following features represented by the buttons.

▽ 10. _____

📇 11. _____

➡ 12. _____

abl 13. _____

⇉ 14. _____

🌐 15. _____

FIGURE A4.7

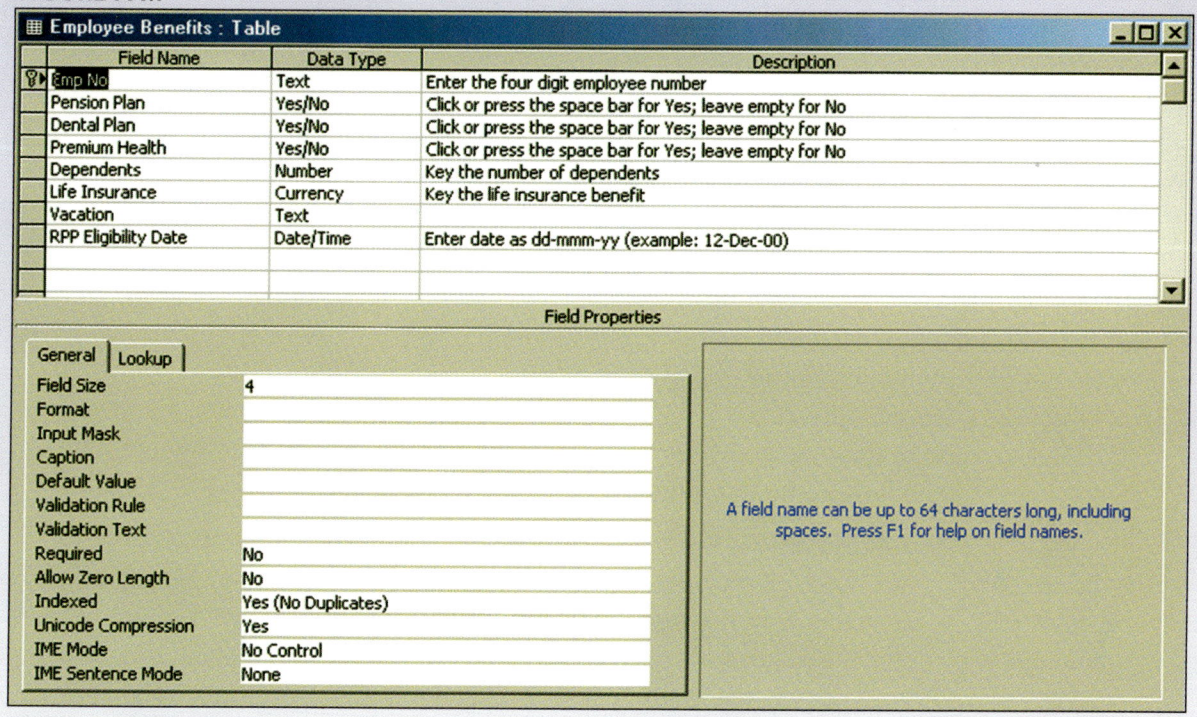

Use the Table Design View window shown in Figure A4.7 to answer questions 16 through 18.

16. List the steps you would complete to move the *RPP Eligibility Date* field between *Pension Plan* and *Dental Plan*.
    _____
    _____

17. List the steps you would complete to insert a new text data field between *Life Insurance* and *Vacation* named *Spousal Life Insurance*. (Assume no description is required.)
    _____
    _____
    _____

18. List the steps you would complete to add a caption property box to the *Emp No* field that would display the column heading *Employee No* in the datasheet.
    _____
    _____
    _____

SECTION 4: MODIFYING TABLES AND REPORTS, PERFORMING CALCULATIONS, AND VIEWING DATA

ACCESS
123

SKILLS REVIEW

Activity 1: MOVING AND DELETING FIELDS; MODIFYING FIELD PROPERTIES

1. Open the WE Employees4 database.
2. Open the Employee Expenses table in Design view.
3. Move the *Amount* field between the *Emp No* and *Date* fields.
4. Delete the *Type* field.
5. Modify the *Description* field so that all text will be converted to uppercase letters.
6. Save the table.
7. Switch to Datasheet view.
8. Best Fit the *Description* column.
9. Print the datasheet.
10. Close the Employee Expenses table. Click Yes to save the layout changes.

Activity 2: CREATING AND MODIFYING A REPORT; CREATING A CALCULATED CONTROL

1. With WE Employees4 open, create a new report using the Report Wizard based on the Trask Employee List query as follows:
    a. Add all of the fields from the query to the report.
    b. Do not include any grouping or sorting.
    c. Select the Columnar layout.
    d. Select the Corporate style.
    e. Accept the default title for the report.
2. Display the Trask Employee List in Design view and then modify the report as follows:
    a. Insert a label control in the Report Header section that will print the text *Report Design by Student Name*. Substitute your first and last names for *Student Name*. Align the control near the right edge of the report header section and change the font size to 12-point. If necessary, resize the control to display the entire text in the label after changing the font size.
    b. Create a calculated control object to the right of the Annual Salary text box control that will calculate the monthly salary as dividing the Annual Salary by 12. Key the label **Monthly Salary** for the calculated control object.
    c. Change the Format property for the calculated control object to *Currency*.
    d. Use the Format Painter to copy the border style from the Annual Salary control object to the Monthly Salary control object.
3. Save and then print the first page only of the report.
4. Close the *Trask Employee List* report.

Activity 3: DISPLAYING SUBDATASHEETS

1. With WE Employees4 open, open the Employee Benefits table in Datasheet view.
2. Expand the first five records in the table.
3. Use the Menu bar to collapse all of the subdatasheets. (*Hint: Make sure a record is not active inside a subdatasheet when you select Collapse All.*)
4. Close the Employee Benefits table.
5. Open the Employee Dates and Salaries table.
6. Expand the first record in the table.
7. Expand the first record in the subdatasheet.
8. Close the Employee Dates and Salaries table.

Activity 4: CREATING A WEB PAGE; INSERTING A HYPERLINK; USING WEB PAGE PREVIEW

1. With WE Employees4 open, use the Page Wizard to create a Web page based on the Employee Dates and Salaries table as follows:
   a. Add all of the fields except *Annual Review Date* from the table to the Web page.
   b. Do not include any grouping or sorting.
   c. Accept the default title for the Web page.
2. Apply a theme of your choosing to the Web page.
3. Key **Worldwide Enterprises Dates and Salaries** as the title text in the Web page.
4. Save the Web page and name it WE Dates and Salaries.
5. Create a hyperlink positioned to the right of the *Emp No* field that will display the WE Employees Web page when the user clicks the link.
6. Save the Web page, display it in the default browser window, and then view two or three records.
7. Print the Web page.
8. Click the link to view the WE Employees Web page.
9. Click the Back button on the browser toolbar to return to the WE Dates and Salaries page and then close the browser window.
10. Close the WE Dates and Salaries Web page.
11. Close WE Employees4.

PERFORMANCE PLUS

Activity 1: MODIFYING A TABLE; DISPLAYING SUBDATASHEETS

1. After reviewing the inventory list with Dana Hirsch, manager of The Waterfront Bistro, you realize some adjustments need to be made to the structure of the table.
2. Open WB Inventory4.
3. Open the Inventory List table in Design view.
4. Make the following changes to the table.
   a. Move the *Unit* field between the *Item No* and *Item* fields.
   b. Edit the properties of the *Unit* and *Item* fields so that all text is automatically converted to uppercase letters.
   c. Move the *Supplier Code* field between the *Item No* and *Unit* fields.
5. Save the table and then switch to Datasheet view.
6. Expand the first three records to display the subdatasheets and Best Fit the *Item* column.
7. Collapse all of the subdatasheets.
8. Print the table.
9. Close the Inventory List table. Click Yes to save changes to the table layout.
10. Close the WB Inventory4 database.

Activity 2: ADDING A CALCULATED CONTROL TO A FORM

1. Staff at Performance Threads have commented positively on the usefulness of the form created for browsing the inventory table. They have asked for a modification to the form that will allow them to tell customers what the daily rental fee is with the tax included.
2. Open PT Costume Inventory4.

SECTION 4: MODIFYING TABLES AND REPORTS, PERFORMING CALCULATIONS, AND VIEWING DATA

3. Open the Costume Inventory form in Form view and review the current form layout and design.
4. Switch to Design view and then make the following changes:
   a. Create a calculated control object to the right of the Daily Rental Fee object that will calculate the Daily Rental Fee with 7% GST included. (GST is the goods and services tax levied on all purchases by the government of Canada.)
   b. Key **Rental fee tax included** as the label for the calculated control.
   c. Format the calculated control object to Currency.
   d. If necessary, adjust the position of the calculated object so that is aligned horizontally with the Daily Rental Fee object at the right side of the form.
   e. If necessary, resize the label and text box control to ensure the text and values are entirely visible.
   f. Make sure the new object is the same font and font size as the other objects on the form.
5. Save the revised form and then switch to Form view.
6. Print the first record only in the form.
7. Close the form.
8. Close PT Costume Inventory4.

Activity 3: CREATING AND MODIFYING A REPORT

1. Heidi Pasqual, financial officer of Worldwide Enterprises, requires a report that will print the names and addresses of the Canadian distributors. Since Heidi is not familiar with Access, she has asked you to create the report for her.
2. Open WE Distributors4.
3. Create a new report using the Report Wizard as follows:
   - Select the *Name, Street Address1, Street Address2, City, Province,* and *PostalCode* fields from the Canadian Distributors table.
   - Do not include any grouping or sorting.
   - Choose the Tabular layout in Portrait orientation.
   - Choose the Corporate style.
   - Accept the default title of Canadian Distributors.
4. Preview the report at 100% magnification. Notice that some of the names and street addresses are truncated on the report.
5. Switch to Design view.
6. Resize and move the City, Province, and Postal Code controls in the Page Header and Detail sections to make enough room on the page to widen the name and address columns.
7. Widen the Name, Street Address1, and Street Address2 controls in the Page Header and Detail sections.
8. View the report in Print Preview.
9. If necessary, switch to Design view and make further adjustments to the size and placement of the controls.
10. Position the pointer on the bottom gray border line for the Report Footer section and then drag the design grid down approximately 0.5 inch. Add a label object in the Report Footer that includes the text *Report Design by Student Name*. Substitute your first and last name for *Student Name*.
11. Save, print, and then close the *Canadian Distributors Addresses* report.
12. Close WE Distributors4.

Activity 4: CREATING MAILING LABELS

1. Heidi Pasqual has reviewed the report you created in Activity 3 and is pleased with the results. She would now like to be able to produce mailing labels for the same distributors.
2. Open WE Distributors4.
3. Use the Label Wizard to generate mailing labels for the Canadian Distributors as follows:
    - Choose the Avery 5160 label size.
    - Click the Italic check box under What font and color would you like your text to be?
    - Construct the prototype label as you would address an envelope.
    - Sort by the *PostalCode* field.
    - Accept the default title Labels Canadian Distributors.
4. Click OK if you receive a message indicating some data may not be displayed.
5. Preview, print, and then close the labels report.
6. Close WE Distributors4.

Activity 5: APPLYING AND REMOVING FILTERS

1. Niagara Peninsula College has received three grants from Performance Threads to be awarded to the top three students in the Theatre Arts Division. Cal Rubine, chair of the Theatre Arts Division of Niagara Peninsula College, has requested a list of students who achieved A+ in a course for review by the selection committee.
2. Open NPC Grades4.
3. Open the ACT104 Grades table.
4. Filter the table to display only those records with an A+ in the *Grade* field.
5. Print and then close the table. Click No to save changes.
6. Open the PRD112 Grades table.
7. Filter the table to display only those records with an A+ in the *Grade* field.
8. Print and then close the table. Click No to save changes.
9. Open the SPE266 Grades table.
10. Filter the table to display only those records with an A+ in the *Grade* field.
11. Print and then close the table. Click No to save changes.
12. Close NPC Grades4.

Activity 6: CREATING AND MODIFYING A WEB PAGE

1. Dana Hirsch, manager of The Waterfront Bistro, has been considering posting the inventory purchases information on the company intranet for the executive chef, who is more familiar with Web browser navigation methods than Access. Dana has asked you to create a Web page from the Purchases table.
2. Open WB Inventory4.
3. Create a Web page using the Page Wizard and adding the fields in the order listed below. Accept all other default settings in the Page Wizard dialog boxes.

Table	Field
Purchases	*Purchase Order No*
Purchases	*Item No*
Inventory List	*Item*
Inventory List	*Supplier Code*
Inventory List	*Unit*
Purchases	*Purchase Date*
Purchases	*Amount*

SECTION 4: MODIFYING TABLES AND REPORTS, PERFORMING CALCULATIONS, AND VIEWING DATA

4. Apply a theme of your choosing to the Web page.
5. Key **The Waterfront Bistro Inventory Purchases** as the title of the page.
6. Save the Web page and name it Inventory Purchases.
7. View the Web page in the Web browser window.
8. Scroll through the records in the Web browser window.
9. Print the last record in the page.
10. Close the Web browser window.
11. Close the Inventory Purchases Web page.
12. Close WB Inventory4.

Activity 7: FINDING INFORMATION ON ADDING FIELDS TO AN EXISTING REPORT

1. Use Access's Help feature to find out how to add a field to an existing report in Design view. *(Hint: A control that will display data from the associated table is considered a bound control.)*
2. Print the Help topic that you find.
3. Open WE Distributors4.
4. Open the *Canadian Distributors* report in Design view.
5. Resize and move controls left to make room for the telephone number to print as the last column in the report. You will need a width of approximately 1 inch at the right edge of the form for the telephone number.
6. Add the *Telephone* field to the report. *(Hint: Cut and paste the label control for the Telephone field from the Detail section to the Page Header section after you have added the field. You may have to edit the control after it is pasted.)*
7. Preview the report.
8. Save, print, and then close the *Canadian Distributors* report.
9. Close WE Distributors4.

Activity 8: RESEARCHING MOVIES ON THE INTERNET

1. Choose four movies that are currently playing in your vicinity that you have seen or would like to see, and then find their Web sites on the Internet. Look for the information listed in step 3 that you will be entering into a new database.
2. Create a new database named Movies.
3. Create a table named Movie Facts that will store the following information:

Movie title	Lead Actor—Female
Director's name	Supporting Actor—Female
Producer's name	Movie category—e.g., drama, action, thriller
Lead Actor—Male	Web site address
Supporting Actor—Male	

4. Design and create a form to enter the records for the movies you researched.
5. Enter the records using the form created in step 4.
6. Print the last form only.
7. Design and create a report for the Movie Facts table. Add your name to the Report Header or Report Footer section in a label control object.
8. Print the *Movie Facts* report.
9. Close the Movies database.

INTEGRATED 2
Integrating Word, Excel, and Access

Data in one program within the Microsoft Office suite can be imported and/or exported to another program. For example, you can export data in an Access table to an Excel worksheet or a Word document. One of the advantages of exporting data to Excel or Word is that formatting can be applied using Excel or Word formatting features. Data can also be imported into an Access database file. If you know that you will update data in a program other than Access, link the data. Changes made to linked data are reflected in both the source and destination programs. In this section you will learn the skills and complete the projects described here.

Note: Before beginning this section, copy to a floppy disk or other folder the Integrated 02 *subfolder from the* Integrated *folder on the CD that accompanies this textbook, and then make* Integrated 02 *the active folder.*

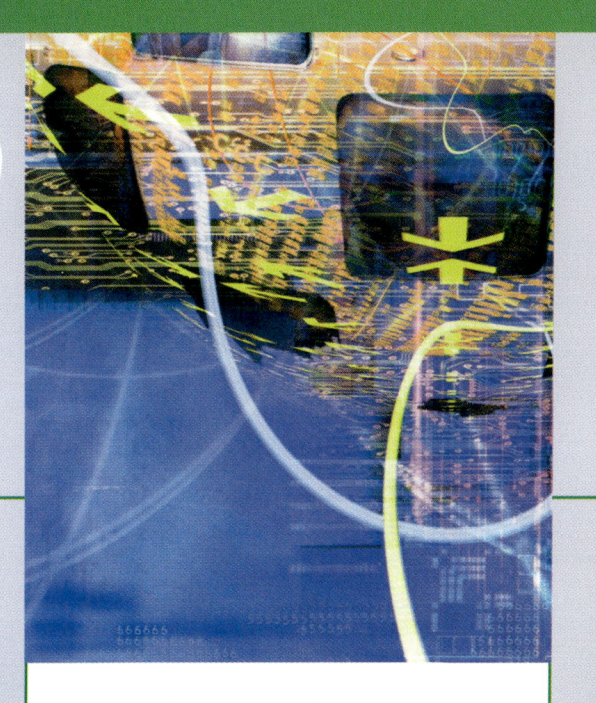

Skills
- Export Access data in a table to Excel
- Export Access data in a table to Word
- Export Access data in a report to Word
- Import Excel data to a new Access table
- Link data between an Excel worksheet and an Access table
- Edit linked data

Projects

Niagara Peninsula COLLEGE — Export grades for PRD 112 from an Access table to an Excel worksheet; import grades for a Beginning Theatre class from an Excel worksheet into an Access database table; link grades for TRA 220 between an Excel worksheet and an Access database table.

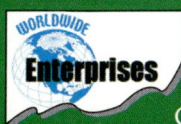

The Waterfront — Export data on inventory from an Access table to a Word document.

WORLDWIDE Enterprises — Export data on overseas distributors from an Access table to a Word document; export data on Canadian distributors from an Access report to a Word document.

FIRST CHOICE Travel — Link data on booking commissions between an Excel worksheet and an Access table and then update the data.

Performance Threads Theatrical Fabrics, Costumes and Supplies — Export data on costume inventory from an Access table to an Excel worksheet; export data on costume inventory from an Access report to a Word document; import data on costume design hours from an Excel worksheet into an Access table.

I-2.1 Exporting Access Data to Excel

One of the advantages of a suite program like Microsoft Office is the ability to exchange data from one program to another. Access, like the other programs in the suite, offers a feature to export data from Access into Excel and/or Word. Export data using the OfficeLinks button on the Database toolbar. Access data saved in a table, form, or report can be exported to Excel. The data is saved as an Excel file in the folder where Access is installed.

PROJECT: You are Katherine Lamont, Theatre Arts Division instructor at Niagara Peninsula College. You want to work on your grades for your PRD 112 class over the weekend and you do not have Access installed on your personal laptop. You decide to export your Access grading table to Excel.

STEPS

1. Open Access and then open the NPC Classes database file. (Remove the read-only attribute.)

2. Click the Tables button on the Objects bar and then click once on *PRD112 Grades* in the list box.

3. Click the down-pointing triangle at the right side of the OfficeLinks button on the Database toolbar.

4. At the drop-down list that displays, click *Analyze It with Microsoft Excel*.

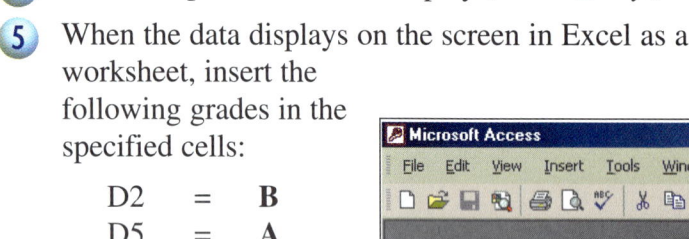

5. When the data displays on the screen in Excel as a worksheet, insert the following grades in the specified cells:

    D2 = B
    D5 = A
    D13 = D
    D15 = C
    D16 = D

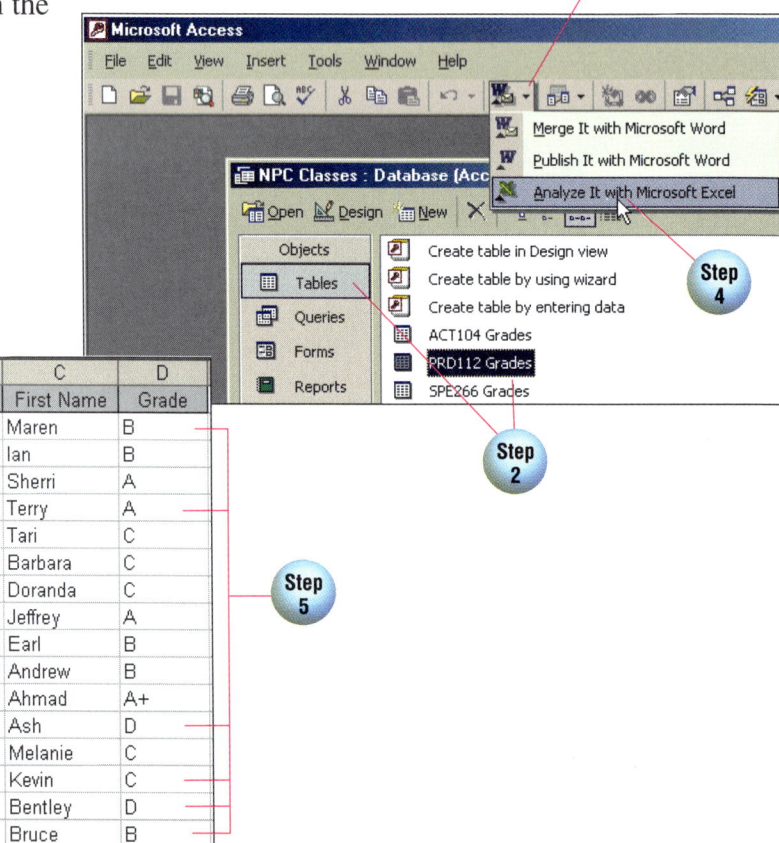

INTEGRATING WORD, EXCEL, AND ACCESS

INTEGRATED 2

6. Select cells A1 through D17.
7. Click Format and then AutoFormat.
8. At the AutoFormat dialog box, scroll down the list of autoformats until *List 1* is visible and then double-click *List 1*.

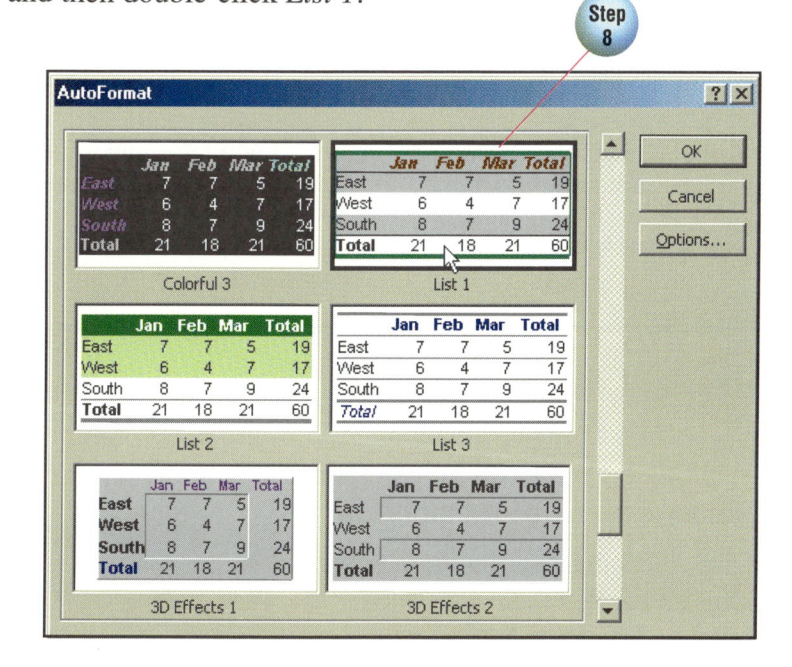

Step 8

9. Deselect the cells by clicking outside the selected cells.
10. Save the worksheet with Save As and name it Int E2-01.
11. Print and then close Int E2-01.
12. Click the button on the Taskbar representing the Access database file NPC Classes and then close the database file.

In Addition

Exporting to Excel

Three methods are available for exporting Access data to an Excel worksheet. You can export data using the Analyze It with Microsoft Excel option from the OfficeLinks drop-down list as you did in this section. You can save the output of a datasheet, form, or report directly as an Excel (*.xls*) worksheet, or you can export the datasheet as unformatted data to Excel.

IN BRIEF

Export Access Table to Excel
1. Open database file.
2. Click Tables button on Objects bar and then click desired table.
3. Click down-pointing triangle at right side of OfficeLinks button.
4. Click *Analyze It with Microsoft Excel*.

INTEGRATING WORD, EXCEL, AND ACCESS

INTEGRATED 2
131

I-2.2 Exporting Access Data to Word

Export data from Access to Word in the same manner as exporting to Excel. To export data to Word, open the database file, select the table, form, or report, and then click the OfficeLinks button on the Database toolbar. At the drop-down list, click *Publish It with Microsoft Word*. Word automatically opens and the data displays in a Word document that is automatically saved with the same name as the database table, form, or report. The difference is that the file extension *.rtf* is added to the name rather than the Word file extension *.doc*. An rtf file is saved in "rich-text format," which preserves formatting such as fonts and styles. A document saved with the *.rtf* extension can be opened in Word and other Windows word processing or desktop publishing programs.

PROJECT: Roman Deptulski, the manager of overseas distribution for Worldwide Enterprises, has asked you to export an Access database table containing information on overseas distributors to a Word document. He needs some of the information for a distribution meeting.

STEPS

1. With Access the active program, open WE Company. (Remove the read-only attribute.)

2. Click the Tables button on the Objects bar and then click once on *Overseas Distributors* in the list box.

3. Click the down-pointing triangle at the right side of the OfficeLinks button on the Database toolbar and then click *Publish It with Microsoft Word* at the drop-down list.

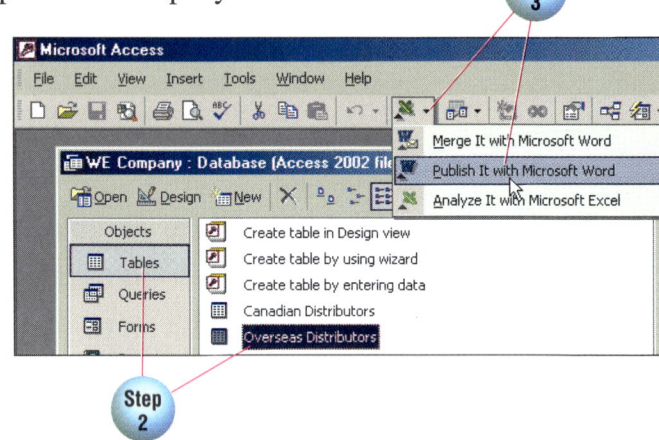

4. When the data displays on the screen in Word, select all of the cells in the two *Street* columns.

5. Delete the selected columns by clicking T<u>a</u>ble, pointing to <u>D</u>elete, and then clicking <u>C</u>olumns.

6. Select all of the cells in the *Postal Code*, *Telephone*, and *Fax* columns, click T<u>a</u>ble, point to <u>D</u>elete, and then click <u>C</u>olumns.

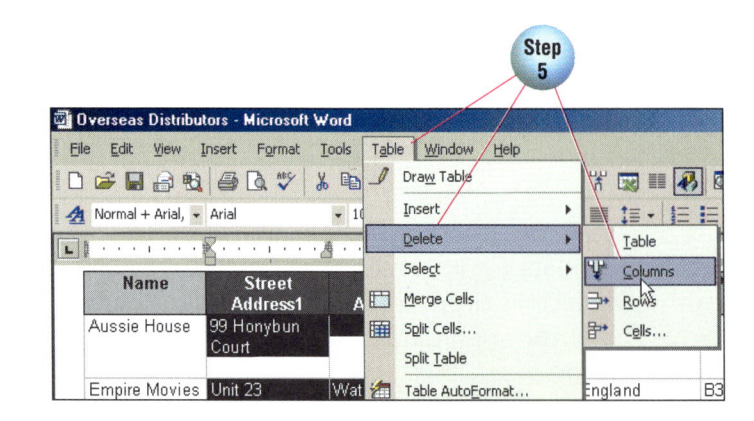

INTEGRATED 2

132

INTEGRATING WORD, EXCEL, AND ACCESS

INTEGRATED 2

7. The Word Table feature has an autofit feature that will automatically adjust the columns' widths to the contents of the columns. Make sure the insertion point is positioned in a cell in the table and then use this feature by clicking Table, pointing to AutoFit, and then clicking AutoFit to Contents.

8. With the insertion point positioned in any cell in the table, click Table and then Table AutoFormat.

9. At the Table AutoFormat dialog box, double-click *Table List 7* in the Table styles list box.

10. Click the Save button to save the document with the same name (Overseas Distributors).

11. Print and then close Overseas Distributors.

12. Click the button on the Taskbar representing the WE Company Access database file and then close the database file.

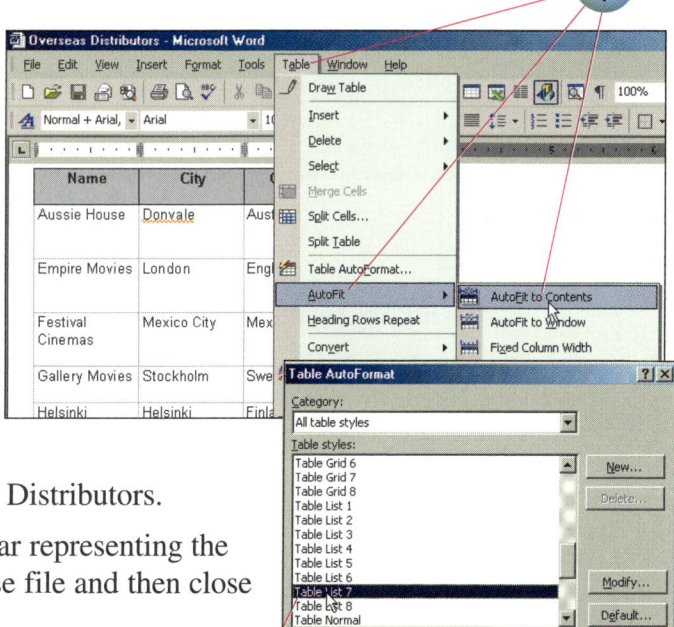

In Addition

Adjusting a Table

In this section, you adjusted the Word table to the cell contents. The Table AutoFit feature contains several options for adjusting table contents. These options are:

Option	Action
AutoFit to Contents	Adjusts table to accommodate the table text
AutoFit to Window	Resizes table to fit within the window or browser. If browser changes size, table size automatically adjusts to fit within window
Fixed Column Width	Adjusts each column to a fixed width using the current widths of the columns
Distribute Rows Evenly	Changes selected rows or cells to equal row height
Distribute Columns Evenly	Changes selected columns or cells to equal column width

IN BRIEF

Export Access Table to Word
1. Open database file.
2. Click Tables button on Objects bar and then click desired table.
3. Click down-pointing triangle at right side of OfficeLinks button.
4. Click *Publish It with Microsoft Word*.

INTEGRATING WORD, EXCEL, AND ACCESS

I-2.3 Exporting an Access Report to Word

An Access report, like an Access table, can be exported to a Word document. Export a report to Word by using the Publish It with Microsoft Word option from the OfficeLinks drop-down list. One of the advantages to exporting a report to Word is that formatting can be applied to the report using Word formatting features.

PROJECT: Sam Vestering, manager of North American distribution for Worldwide Enterprises, needs a list of Canadian distributors. He has asked you to export a report to Word and then apply specific formatting to the report. He needs some of the information for a contact list.

STEPS

1. With Access the active program, open WE Company.
2. At the WE Company : Database window, click the Reports button on the Objects bar.
3. Click *Canadian Distributors Addresses* in the list box.
4. Click the down-pointing triangle at the right side of the OfficeLinks button and then click *Publish It with Microsoft Word*. 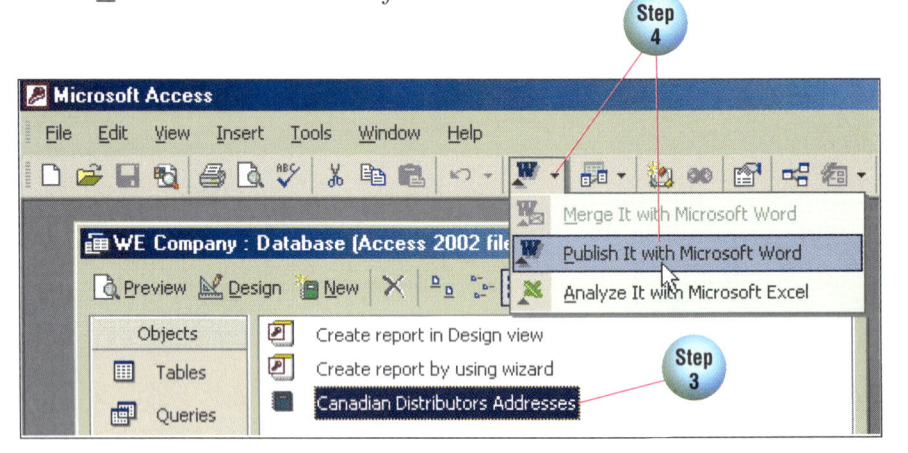
5. When the data displays on the screen in Word, press Ctrl + A to select the entire document.
6. Click the down-pointing triangle at the right side of the Font button on the Formatting toolbar and then click *Arial* at the drop-down list.

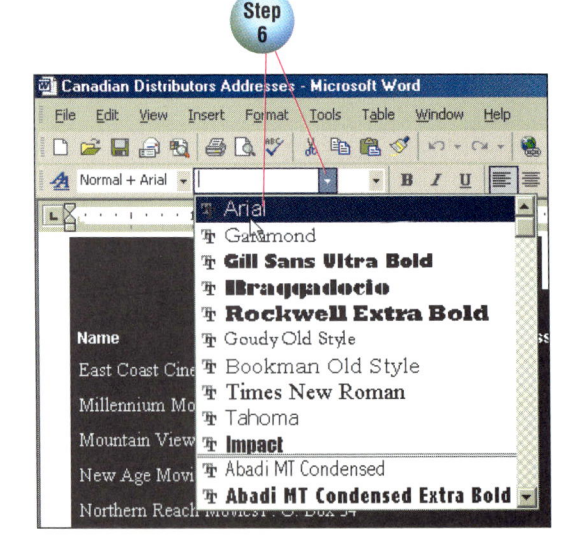

INTEGRATING WORD, EXCEL, AND ACCESS

INTEGRATED 2

7. With the document still selected, click the down-pointing triangle at the right side of the Font Size button on the Formatting toolbar and then click *10* at the drop-down list.

8. Press Ctrl + Home to move the insertion point to the beginning of the document and then key **Worldwide Enterprises**.

9. Press Enter and then key **Canadian Distributors**.

10. Select *Worldwide Enterprises* and then change the font to 22-point Arial bold.

11. Select *Canadian Distributors* and then change the font to 18-point Arial bold.

12. Click the Save button on the Standard toolbar to save the report with the default name (Canadian Distributors Addresses).

13. Print and then close Canadian Distributors Addresses.

    The Canadian Distributors Addresses document prints in landscape orientation and includes a footer at the bottom of the page that prints the current date.

14. Exit Word.

15. In Access, close the WE Company Access database file.

In Addition

Merging Access Data with a Word Document

Word includes a mail merge feature that you can use to create letter and envelopes and much more, with personalized information. Generally, a merge requires two documents—the *data source* and the *main document*. The data source contains the variable information that will be inserted in the main document. Create a data source document in Word or create a data source using data from an Access table. When merging Access data, you can either key the text in the main document or merge Access data with an existing Word document. To merge data in an Access table, open the database file, click the Tables button on the Objects bar, and then click the desired table. Click the OfficeLinks button on the Database toolbar and then click *Merge It with Microsoft Word*. Follow the steps presented in the Mail Merge Task Pane to complete the merge.

In Brief

Export Access Report to Word
1 Open database file.
2 Click Reports button on Objects bar and then click desired report.
3 Click down-pointing triangle at right side of OfficeLinks button.
4 Click *Publish It with Microsoft Word*.

INTEGRATING WORD, EXCEL, AND ACCESS

I-2.4 Importing Data to a New Table

In the previous three sections, you exported Access data to Excel and Word. You can also import data from other programs into an Access table. For example, you can import data from an Excel worksheet and create a new table in a database file. Data in the original program is not connected to the data imported into an Access table. If you make changes to the data in the original program, those changes are not reflected in the Access table.

PROJECT: You are Gina Simmons, Theatre Arts instructor, and have recorded grades in an Excel worksheet for your students in the Beginning Theatre class. You want to import those grades into the NPC Classes database file.

STEPS

1. In Access, open the NPC Classes database file and then click the Tables button on the Objects bar.

2. Import an Excel worksheet by clicking File, pointing to Get External Data, and then clicking Import.

3. At the Import dialog box, change the Files of type option to *Microsoft Excel*, and then double-click *NPC Beg Th Grades* in the list box.

   Your list of documents may vary from what you see in the image below and at the right.

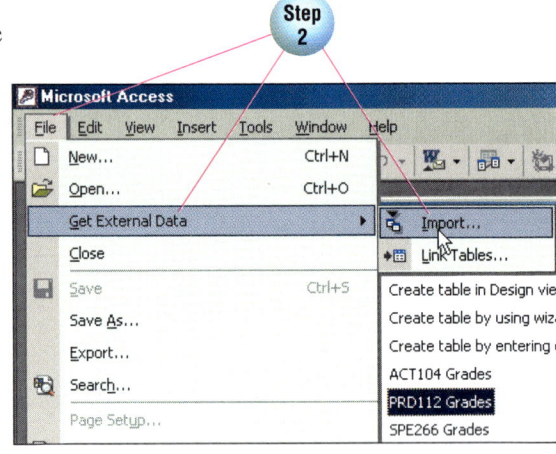

   PROBLEM: If *NPC Beg Th Grades* does not display in the list box, you may need to navigate to another folder. Check with your instructor.

4. At the first Import Spreadsheet Wizard dialog box, click the Next button.

5. At the second dialog box, insert a check mark in the First Row Contains Column Headings option, and then click the Next button.

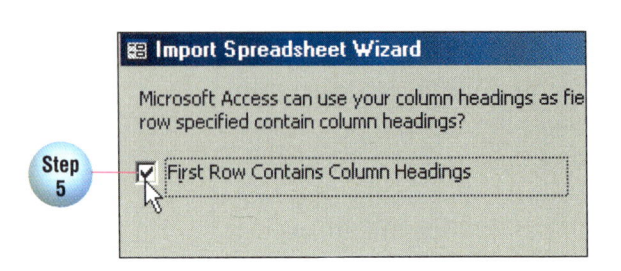

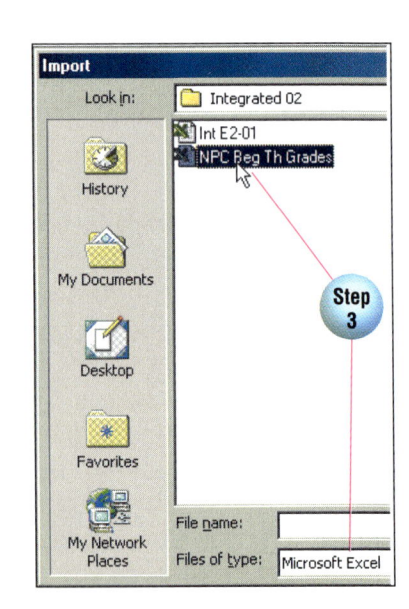

INTEGRATING WORD, EXCEL, AND ACCESS

INTEGRATED 2

6. At the third dialog box, make sure the In a New Table option is selected, and then click the Next button.

7. At the fourth dialog box, click the Next button.

8. At the fifth dialog box, click the Choose my own primary key option (this inserts *Student No* in the text box located to the right of the option), and then click the Next button.

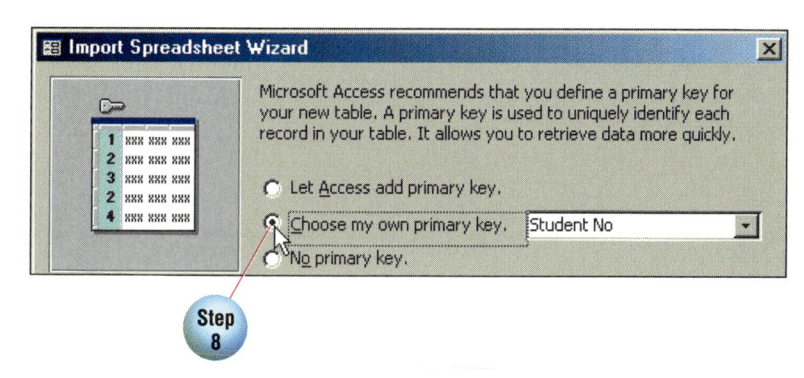

9. At the sixth dialog box, key **Beg Th Grades** in the Import to Table text box, and then click the Finish button.

10. At the message saying the data was imported, click OK.

11. Open the new table by double-clicking *Beg Th Grades* in the list box.

12. Print and then close Beg Th Grades.

13. Close the NPC Classes database file.

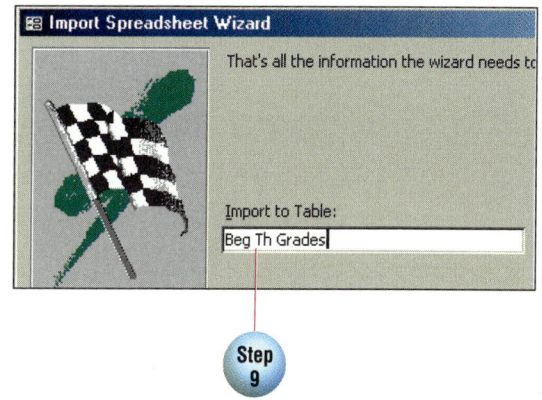

In Addition

Importing or Linking a Table

You can import data from another program into an Access table or you can link the data. Choose the method depending on how you are going to use the data. Import data to a table if you are going to use the data only in Access. Access generally operates faster working with its own tables. Link data to an Access table if the data will be changed or updated in a program other than Access. Changes made to linked data are reflected in both the source and destination programs.

In Brief

Import Data to a New Table
1. Open database file.
2. Click Tables button on Objects bar.
3. Click File, Get External Data, Import.
4. Follow the Import Wizard steps.

INTEGRATED 2
137

I-2.5 Linking Data to a New Table and Editing Linked Data

Imported data is not connected to the source program. If you know that you will use your data only in Access, import it. However, if you want to update data in a program other than Access, link the data. Changes made to linked data are reflected in both the source and destination programs. For example, you can link an Excel worksheet with an Access table and when you make changes in either the Excel worksheet or the Access table, the change is reflected in the other program. To link data to a new table, open the database file, click File, point to Get External Data, and then click Link Tables. At the Link dialog box, double-click the desired document name. This activates the link wizard that walks you through the steps to link the data.

PROJECT: You are Cal Rubine, Theatre Arts instructor at Niagara Peninsula College. You record students' grades in an Excel worksheet and also link the grades to an Access database file. With the data linked, changes you make to either the Excel table or the Access table will be reflected in the other table.

STEPS

1. Open Excel and then open NPC TRA 220.
2. Save the worksheet with Save As and name it Int E2-02.
3. Print and then close Int E2-02.
4. Make Access the active program, open the NPC Classes database file, and then click the Tables button on the Objects bar.
5. Link an Excel worksheet by clicking File, pointing to Get External Data, and then clicking Link Tables.

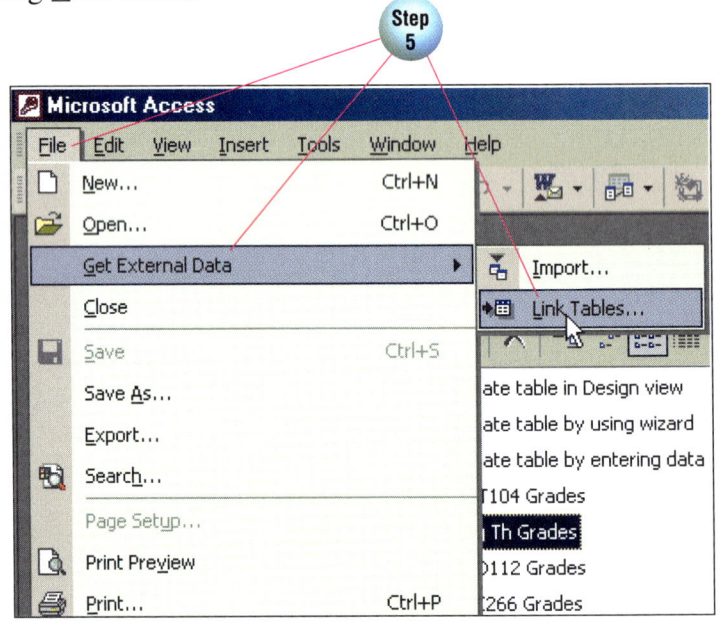

6. At the Link dialog box, change the Files of type option to *Microsoft Excel*, and then double-click *Int E2-02* in the list box.

   Depending on your system configuration, you may need to navigate to the folder containing Int E2-02.

INTEGRATING WORD, EXCEL, AND ACCESS

INTEGRATED 2

7. At the first Link Spreadsheet Wizard dialog box, make sure Show Worksheets is selected, and that *Sheet1* is selected in the list box, and then click the Next button.

8. At the second dialog box, make sure there is a check mark in the First Row Contains Column Headings option, and then click the Next button.

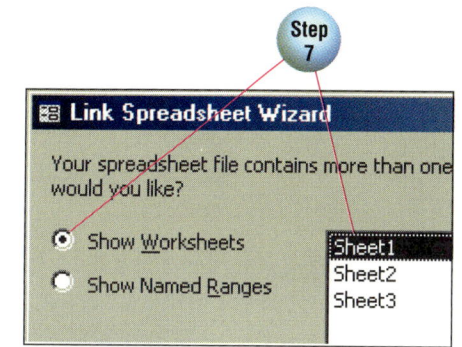

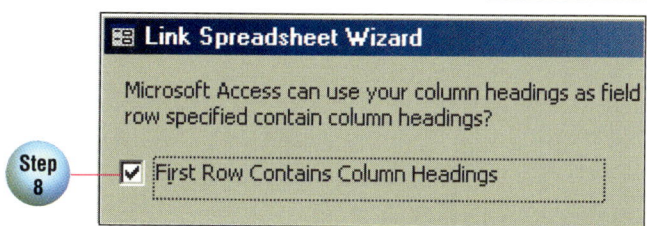

9. At the third dialog box, key **Linked Grades** in the Linked Table Name text box, and then click the Finish button.

10. At the message stating the link is finished, click OK.

    > Access uses different icons to represent linked tables and tables that are stored in the current database. Notice the icon that displays before the Linked Grades table.

11. Open the new Linked Grades table in Datasheet view.

12. As you look at the table, you realize that you need to add a student to the end of the list. Add the following new record in the specified fields (see image below):

    Student No **138-456-749**

    Student **Yui, T.**

    Midterm **3.25**

(continued)

INTEGRATING WORD, EXCEL, AND ACCESS

13. Print and then close the Linked Grades table.

    The new record is automatically saved when the table is closed.

14. Make Excel the active program and then open Int E2-02.

    Notice that the worksheet contains the student, Yui, T., you added to the Access table.

15. You have finished grading student finals and need to insert the grades in the worksheet. Insert the following grades in the specified cells:

    D2 = 2.75
    D3 = 1
    D4 = 3.5
    D5 = 2
    D6 = 3.5
    D7 = 2.5
    D8 = 3
    D9 = 3.5
    D10 = 2.5

	A	B	C	D
1	Student No	Student	Midterm	Final
2	111-75-156	Bastow, M.	3.25	2.75
3	359-845-475	Collyer, S.	1.50	1.00
4	157-457-856	Dwyer, B.	3.50	3.50
5	348-876-486	Ennis, A.	2.25	2.00
6	378-159-746	Gagne, M.	3.00	3.50
7	197-486-745	Koning, J.	2.75	2.50
8	314-745-856	Morgan, B.	3.75	3.00
9	349-874-658	Retieffe, S.	4.00	3.50
10	138-456-749	Yui, T.	3.25	2.50

    Step 15

16. Make cell E2 the active cell and then insert a formula to average scores by clicking the Insert Function button f_x on the Formula bar.

17. At the Insert Function dialog box, double-click *AVERAGE* in the Select a function list box.

PROBLEM?

If *AVERAGE* is not visible in the Select a function list box, click the down-pointing triangle at the right side of the Or select a category option box, and then click *Most Recently Used* at the drop-down list.

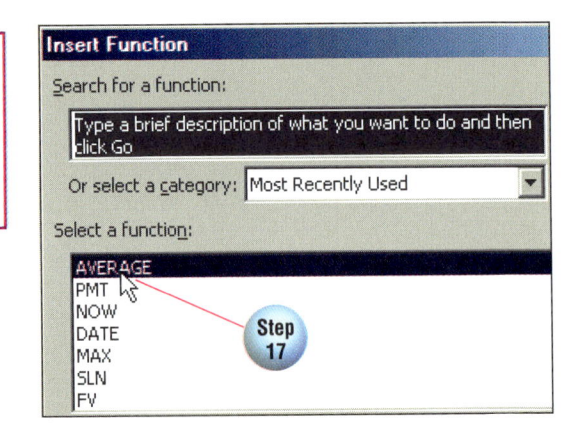

Insert Function

Search for a function:

Type a brief description of what you want to do and then click Go

Or select a category: Most Recently Used

Select a function:

AVERAGE
PMT
NOW
DATE
MAX
SLN
FV

Step 17

INTEGRATED 2

140   INTEGRATING WORD, EXCEL, AND ACCESS

INTEGRATED 2

18. At the formula palette, make sure *C2:D2* displays in the Number1 text box, and then click OK.

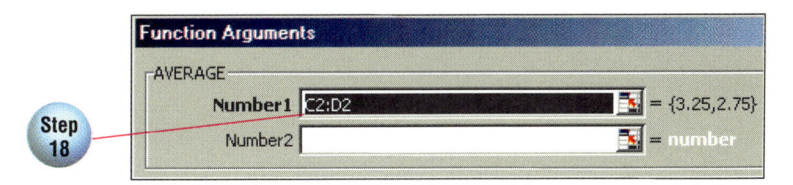

    Function Arguments
    AVERAGE
    Number1: C2:D2 = {3.25,2.75}
    Number2: = number

19. Using the fill handle, copy the formula down to cell E10.

	A	B	C	D	E
1	Student No	Student	Midterm	Final	Average
2	111-75-156	Bastow, M.	3.25	2.75	3.00
3	359-845-475	Collyer, S.	1.50	1.00	1.25
4	157-457-856	Dwyer, B.	3.50	3.50	3.50
5	348-876-486	Ennis, A.	2.25	2.00	2.13
6	378-159-746	Gagne, M.	3.00	3.50	3.25
7	197-486-745	Koning, J.	2.75	2.50	2.63
8	314-745-856	Morgan, B.	3.75	3.00	3.38
9	349-874-658	Retieffe, S.	4.00	3.50	3.75
10	138-456-749	Yui, T.	3.25	2.50	2.88

20. Deselect the cells by clicking outside the selected cells.
21. Save and then print Int E2-02.
22. Click the button on the Taskbar representing the NPC Classes Access database file.
23. Open the Linked Grades table.

    Notice that this linked table contains the final grades and the average scores you inserted in the Excel Int E2-02 worksheet.

24. Print and then close the Linked Grades table.
25. Close the NPC Classes database file and then close Access.
26. With Excel the active program, close Int E2-02, and then close Excel.

In Addition

Deleting the Link to a Linked Table

If you want to delete the link to a table, open the database file, and then click the Tables button on the Objects bar. Click the linked table in the list box and then click the Delete button on the Tables toolbar (or press the Delete key). At the Microsoft question asking if you want to remove the link to the table, click Yes. Access deletes the link and removes the table's name from the list box. When you delete a linked table, you are deleting the information Access uses to open the table, not the table itself. You can link to the same table again, if necessary.

In Brief

Link Data to a New Table
1. Open database file.
2. Click Tables button on Objects bar.
3. Click File, Get External Data, Link Tables.
4. Follow the Link Wizard steps.

SKILLS REVIEW

Activity 1: EXPORTING ACCESS DATA TO EXCEL

1. Open Access and then open the PT Costumes database file. (Remove the read-only attribute.)
2. Click the Tables button on the Objects bar and then export the data in the Costume Inventory table to Excel.
3. When the data displays in Excel, make the following changes in the specified cells:
   - C4 = Change *110.00* to *120.00*
   - C5 = Change *110.00* to *125.00*
   - C7 = Change *99.50* to *105.00*
4. Select cells A1 through E17 and then apply an autoformat of your choosing.
5. Save the worksheet with Save As and name it Int E2-R1.
6. Print and then close Int E2-R1.
7. Click the button on the Taskbar representing the Access database file PT Costumes and then close the database file.

Activity 2: EXPORTING ACCESS DATA TO WORD

1. With Access the active program, open WB Supplies. (Remove the read-only attribute.)
2. Click the Tables button on the Objects bar and then export the data in the Inventory List table to Word.
3. When the data displays on the screen in Word, apply a table autoformat of your choosing to the table.
4. Move the insertion point to the beginning of the document, press Enter three times, and then move the insertion point back to the beginning of the document.
5. Key **The Waterfront Bistro** on the first line and **Inventory List** on the second line.
6. Select *The Waterfront Bistro* and *Inventory List* and then change the font to 22-point Arial bold.
7. Save the Word document with the default name (Inventory List).
8. Print and then close Inventory List.
9. Click the button on the Taskbar representing the Access database file WB Supplies and then close the database file.

Activity 3: EXPORTING AN ACCESS REPORT TO WORD

1. With Access the active program, open PT Costumes.
2. At the PT Costumes : Database window, click the Reports button on the Objects bar and then export the *Costume Inventory* report to a Word document.
3. When the data displays on the screen in Word, move the insertion point to the beginning of the document and then key the company name, **Performance Threads**.
4. Press the Enter key and then key **Costume Inventory**.
5. Increase the size and apply bolding to *Performance Threads* and *Costume Inventory*.
6. Save the Word document with the default name (Costume Inventory).
7. Print and then close Costume Inventory.
8. Exit Word.
9. With Access the active program, close the PT Costumes database file.

Activity 4: IMPORTING DATA TO A NEW TABLE

1. In Access, open the PT Costumes database file and then click the Tables button on the Objects bar.
2. Import the Excel worksheet named PT Costume Hours. (Make sure you change the Files of type option to *Microsoft Excel*, and then double-click *PT Costume Hours* in the list box. Do not make any changes to the first Import Spreadsheet Wizard dialog box. At the second dialog box, make sure there is a check mark in the First Row Contains Column Headings option. Make sure the In a New Table option is selected at the third dialog box. Do make changes to the fourth dialog box, and click the No Primary key option at the fifth dialog box. At the sixth dialog box, key **Design Hours** in the Import to Table text box, and then click the Finish button.)
3. Open the new Design Hours table.
4. Print and then close the Design Hours table.
5. Close the PT Costumes database file.

Activity 5: LINKING DATA TO A NEW TABLE AND EDITING LINKED DATA

1. Open Excel and then open FCT Bookings.
2. Save the worksheet with Save As and name it Int E2-R2.
3. Make Access the active program, open the FCT Commissions database file (remove the read-only attribute), and then click the Tables button on the Objects bar.
4. Link the Excel worksheet Int E2-R2 with the FCT Commissions database file. (At the Link dialog box, make sure you change the Files of type option to *Microsoft Excel*. At the third Link Spreadsheet Wizard dialog box, key **Linked Commissions** in the Linked Table Name text box.)
5. Open, print, and then close the new Linked Commissions table.
6. Click the button on the Taskbar representing the Excel worksheet Int E2-R2.
7. Make cell C2 active, key the formula **=B2*0.03**, and then press Enter.
8. Make cell C2 active and then use the fill handle to copy the formula down to cell C13.
9. Save, print, and then close Int E2-R2.
10. Click the button on the Taskbar representing the FCT Commissions Access database file and then open the Linked Commissions table.
11. Save, print, and then close the Linked Commissions table.
12. Close the FCT Commissions database file.
13. Exit Access and then exit Excel.

INDEX

ACCESS

Access. *See* Microsoft Access
Access data
  backing up/restoring, 17
  exporting to Excel, 142
  exporting to Word, 142
Access report: exporting to Word, 142
Access table
  features, 28
  importing data to new, 136-137
  linking data to new, 138-140
Action queries, 69
Append query, 69
Apply Filter button: on Table Datasheet toolbar, 115
Ask a Question box, 24
AutoForm, 80
  forms created using, 52-53
AutoForm Wizard, 76
AVERAGE, 140

Backgrounds: in forms, 76

Calculated controls
  adding to forms, 104-105
  creating, 106-109, 124
Calculated fields: creating, 73, 92
Calculated forms, 125
Calculations: performing in queries, 72-73
Close button: on Field Properties title bar, 73
Close button: on Main Switchboard Title bar, 57
Close button: on Microsoft Access Help Title bar, 25
Colors: in forms, 76
Column headers: changing in datasheet, 22
Column widths: adjusting, 8-9, 29, 30
Columns: freezing, 23
Compact and repair
  automatic, 27
  using, 32
Control objects: deleting and moving, 81
Control properties: modifying, 109
Controls
  adding to form, 82-83
  modifying in forms, 80-81
  and report sections, 89
  resizing, 88-89, 93
Criteria: adding, 94
Criteria statements
  adding, 66, 92
  examples of, 71
  records extracted using, 70-71
Customer lists, 3

Data
  adding in new field, 101
  backing up/restoring, 17
  converting to uppercase, 103
  features for, 122
  importing to new table, 136-137, 143
  in deleted fields, 100
  linking to new table, 143
  maintaining in Access tables, 3-32
  saving, 9
Data access pages
  creating, 116-119
  Design view, 117
  using, 119
Data source: and merge, 135
Data types, 37
Database design: finding information on, 32
Database files: creating new, using wizard, 54
Database management system, 3
Database objects: exploring, 4-7
Database wizards, 54
Databases, 4
  compacting and repairing, 26-27
  creating new, 63
  elements of, 7
  planning and designing, 7
Datasheet Formatting dialog box, 22
Datasheet view, 84
  navigating in, 8-9
  records added in, 12-13
  records deleted in, 16-17
  records entered into table in, 34
  sorting by multiple columns in, 19
  sorting by single field in, 19
  tables opened in, 9
Datasheets
  formatting, 22-23, 31
  query results, 67
  and subdatasheets, 112
Default field size, 47
Default value: modifying, 46-47
Default Value property, 46
Defragmenting files, 26
Delete query, 69
Delete Record button: on Table Datasheet toolbar, 16
Delete Rows button: on Table Design toolbar, 49, 100
Deleting relationships: finding information on, 63-64

Design View
  queries created in, 66-67, 94
  reports created in, 87
  resizing control objects in, 89
  and table creation, 33
  tables created in, 34-37, 59, 61
  tables displayed in, 98
  tables edited in, 48

E-mail address hyperlinks, 121
Edit Relationships dialog box, 50
Enter Parameter Value dialog box, 75
Entries: validating, 62
Envelopes: creating, 135
Error-checking tools, 44
Excel: Access data exported to, 130-131, 142
Expand indicator, 112

Field entries: validating, 44-45
Field List Box, 87
Field properties: modifying, 102-103, 124
Field properties option message, 34
Field size
  changing, 59, 62
  modifying, 46-47
  property, 46
  setting, 47
Fields
  finding information on adding, to existing report, 128
  input masks created for, 43
  inserting and deleting, 100-101
  moving, 98-99
  moving and deleting, 124
  primary key, 13
Filter by Form, 114, 115
Filter by Form button: on Table Datasheet toolbar, 114
Filter by Selection, 114, 115
Filter By Selection button: on Table Datasheet toolbar, 114
Filtering: by multiple criteria, 115
Filters: applying and removing, 114-115, 127
Find and Replace dialog box
  Replace tab in, 11
  Title bar, 10
Find button: on Database toolbar, 10
Find command, 10
First Record button: on Record Navigation bar, 15
Fonts: changing, 23, 30
Form control objects: resizing, 81
Form view, 12
  records added in, 14-15
  scrolling in, using keyboard, 15
Form Wizard, 80
  forms created using, 76-79, 92
Format menu, 22
Formatting: datasheets, 22-23, 31
Forms, 65, 95
  calculated controls added to, 104-105
  calculated forms added to, 125
  controls added to, 82-83
  creating using AutoForm, 52-53
  creating using Form Wizard, 76-79, 92
  features for, 90
  information on adding pictures to, 96
  modifying, 93
  modifying controls in, 80-81
  vendor, 52
Forms button: on Objects bar, 6
Fragmented data, 26

Greater than symbol, 102
Gridlines: setting in datasheet, 22

Help resources, 24
Human resources information, 3
Hyperlink button: on Toolbox Palette, 120
Hyperlinks: inserting, 120-121, 125

Input mask, 40
  creating, 59, 62
  editing, 43
Input Mask Wizard, 40-43
Input Mask Wizard dialog box, 40, 41, 43
Insert Hyperlink dialog box, 120
Insert Rows button: on Table Design toolbar, 101
Insertion point, 10
Internet
  car shopping on, 64
  movie research on, 128
  travel destination research on, 96
Intranets, 97
Inventory articles, 3

Keyboard
  scrolling in Form view using, 15
  scrolling techniques with, 9

Label object button: in Toolbox, 82, 107
Label Wizard, 97, 110-111
Landscape orientation: changing to, 21
Last Record button: on Record Navigation bar, 9, 15
Layout: for fields, 76

Letters: creating, 135
Link to Objects bar: in Insert Hyperlink dialog box, 121
Link wizard, 138
Linked data: editing, 140-141, 143
Linked tables: deleting link to, 141
Long Integer field size, 47
Lookup field
  creating, 61
  creating using Lookup Wizard, 39
Lookup wizard: using, 38-39

Magnification, 20
Mail merge feature, 135
Mailing labels, 110
  creating, 127
  generating, 111
Main document: and merge, 135
Main Switchboard form, 54
Main Switchboard window, 56, 57
Make-table query, 69
Many-to-many relationships, 50
Margins: changing, 20, 21
Maximize button: on Database Title bar, 8, 57
Microsoft Access
  creating tables and relationships, 33-64
  data exported from, to Excel, 130-131
  data exported from, to Word, 132-133
  maintaining data in Access tables, 3-32
  merging data from with Word document, 135
  modifying tables and reports; performing calculations; viewing data, 97-128
  queries, forms, and reports, 65-96
  reports exported from, to Word, 134-135
  screen, 5
  starting, 7
Microsoft Office
  data exchanging with, 130
  Web site, 24
Microsoft Word
  Access data exported to, 132-133, 142
  Access reports exported to, 134-135, 142
Minus symbol (-): and subdatasheets, 112, 113
Movie research: on Internet, 128

New button: on Database toolbar, 54
New File Task Pane, 4
New Form dialog box, 53
New Record button: on Table Datasheet toolbar, 12, 112
Next Record button: on Record Navigation bar, 9

Objects: opening, 7
Office Assistant, 25
  using, 24-25
Office XP: Office Assistant in, 25
OfficeLinks button: on Database toolbar, 130. 132
One-to-many relationships, 50, 60
One-to-one relationships, 50, 51
Online help: using, 24-25

Page orientation: changing, 20, 30
Page Setup dialog box, 20
Page Wizard, 116
Parameter queries: creating, 74-75, 95
Pictures: information on addition of, to forms, 96
Plus symbol (+): and subdatasheets, 112, 113
Previewing: and printing, 20-21
Previous Record button: on Record Navigation bar, 9
Primary Key button: on Table Design toolbar, 35
Primary key field, 13, 18
Primary table, 50
Print button: on Microsoft Access Help toolbar, 24
Print button: on Print Preview toolbar, 21
Print button: on Table Datasheet toolbar, 20
Print Preview
  report page in, 86
  using, 30
Print Preview button: on Table Datasheet toolbar, 20
Printing
  and previewing, 20-21
  reports, 86-87
  tables, 30
Properties button: on Form Design toolbar, 104
Properties button: on Query Design toolbar, 73
Publish It, 134

Queries, 65
  action, 69
  calculations performed in, 72-73
  creating in Design view, 66-67, 94
  creating using Simple Query Wizard, 92
  criteria statements added to, 71
  features for, 90
  filters vs., 114
  parameter, 74-75
  sorting, 92
Queries button: on Objects bar, 66
Query results datasheet, 67

Records
  adding and deleting, 29, 31
  adding in datasheet view, 12-13

adding in Form view, 14-15
  deleting, 17
  deleting in Datasheet view, 16-17
  displaying in subdatasheets, 112-113
  entering, 92
  extracting using criteria statements, 70-71
  finding, 11
  finding and editing, 10-11, 29, 30-31, 32
  sorting, 18-19, 30
Redo button, 99
Related table, 50
Relational database management system, 50
Relationships
  creating, 33, 50, 51
  establishing, 62
  features, 58
  information on deletion of, 63-64
Relationships button: on Database toolbar, 50
Remove Filter button: on Table Datasheet toolbar, 114
Replace command: using, 11
Report sections: and controls, 89
Report Selector button, 109
Report Wizard, 84, 85, 87, 88, 106
Reports, 65
  controls resized in, 88-89
  creating, 93, 94
  creating and modifying, 124, 126
  creating, previewing, and printing, 84-87
  features for, 90, 122
  modifying, 106
  property sheets for, 109
Required entries: finding information on, 64
Restore button: on Database Title bar, 57
Rich-text format (rtf) file, 132
Row heights: increasing, 24
Run button: on Query Design toolbar, 67

Save button: on Database toolbar, 9
Sections of report: property sheets for, 109
Show Table dialog box, 50
Simple Query Wizard
  queries created using, 92
  using, 68-69
Sort Ascending button: on Table Datasheet toolbar, 18
Sort Descending button: on Table Datasheet toolbar, 18
Square brackets: field names encased in, 72
Structure: table, 34
Subdatasheets, 97
  displaying, 124, 125
  records displayed in, 112-113
Supplier lists, 3

Table AutoFit feature, 133
Table Design view, 38
Table Wizard, 33
  table creation with, 48-49, 60, 62
Tables, 4
  adjusting, 133
  creating, 33
  creating in Design view, 34-37, 59, 61
  creating using Table Wizard, 48-49, 60, 62
  entries, 35
  features, 58
  features for modifying, 122
  importing or linking, 137
  modifying, 125
  opening in datasheet view, 9
  printing, 30
  sorting in, 19
Tables button: on Objects bar, 141
Tabular AutoForm, 53
Text box control, 80, 81
Text Box object button: in Toolbox, 104, 108
Toolbox button: on Form Design toolbar, 82
Toolbox button: on Page Design toolbar, 120
Travel: researching on Internet, 96

Undo button: using, 99
Uniform Resource Locators, 120
Update query, 69
Uppercase: data converted to, 103
URLs. *See* Uniform Resource Locators

Validation rule, 59
  creating, 45
  examples of, 45
Validation Rule property, 44
Validation Text property, 44
Vendors form, 52
View button: on Query Datasheet toolbar, 69
View button: on Table Design toolbar, 35

Web browser window: employee benefits data access page in, 119
Web Page Preview: using, 125
Web pages
  creating, 125
  creating and modifying, 127
Wizard: new databases created using, 54-57
Word document: merging Access data with, 135

INTEGRATED 2
144
INDEX